The Danish Directors 2

For David Bordwell

The Danish Directors 2

Mette Hjort, Eva Jørholt, Eva Novrup Redvall

intellect Bristol, UK / Chicago, USA

First published in the UK in 2010 by
Intellect, The Mill, Parnall Road, Fishponds, Bristol, BS16 3JG, UK

First published in the USA in 2010 by
Intellect, The University of Chicago Press, 1427 E. 60th Street,
Chicago, IL 60637, USA

A catalogue record for this book is available from the British Library.

Cover designer: Holly Rose
Copy-editor: Rebecca Vaughan-Williams
Typesetting: Mac Style, Beverley, E. Yorkshire

Cover Image: Paprika Steen as Thea in Martin Pieter Zandvliet's *Applaus* (*Applause*, 2009), produced by Mikael Rieks, Koncern Film.

ISBN 978-1-84150-271-7

Printed and bound by Gutenberg Press, Malta.

Contents

Contents

Acknowledgements

We are grateful to all the directors included in this volume for having been willing to contribute to *The Danish Directors 2*, and for generously making time for us, in the midst of busy schedules. Each edited and translated interview has been vetted and approved by the relevant director, and for this too, we are grateful.

We would also like to thank the producers and producers' assistants who have helped us with our work, and who have granted us permission to print stills from their films. The list is long and includes Julie Lind-Holm and Anders Morgenthaler from Copenhagen Bombay; Thomas Gammeltoft and Tine Engelbrecht from Fine & Mellow Productions; Mikael Christian Rieks from Koncern Film; Claus Thobo-Carlsen from Nimbus Film; Thomas Heinesen from Nordisk Film Production; Ib Tardini, Anne Juul, Sisse Graum Jørgensen, Sidsel Hybschmann, Meta Foldager, Stine Meldgaard and Anders Wøldike from Zentropa; Anne Katrine Andersen and Jonas Frederiksen from XX Film; and Christian Potalivo from M&M Productions.

Our sincere thanks also go to the many photographers and cinematographers who have allowed us to publish portraits of the directors interviewed in *The Danish Directors 2*, and production stills. The names of these individuals can be found in the list of figures and also accompany the relevant images.

Christian Juhl Lemche from the Danish Film Institute has helped us by making films available along the way, and we are also grateful to the Danish Film Institute for a publication subsidy.

The work described in this book was partially supported by a grant from the Research Grants Council of the Hong Kong Special Administrative Region, China (Project No. LU340407). Mette Hjort is grateful for this support.

Sam King and May Yao at Intellect have been supportive commissioning editors throughout. An anonymous peer reviewer for Intellect provided inspiring and constructive comments that helped us to sharpen the focus of our Introduction.

This book is dedicated to David Bordwell, in recognition of his pioneering work on all aspects of film practice, and with gratitude for his staunch support for Danish cinema and those who think it important.

Acknowledgements

Introduction

Mette Hjort, Eva Jørholt, Eva Novrup Redvall

The Danish Directors 2 picks up the practitioners-based discussion of Danish cinema where *The Danish Directors: Dialogues on a Contemporary National Cinema* left off.[1] The interviews for *The Danish Directors* were conducted at a time when the 'New Danish Cinema' was only just beginning to emerge. While *The Danish Directors* includes interviews with Lars von Trier, Thomas Vinterberg, Ole Bornedal and Susanne Bier, filmmakers whose contributions to the New Danish Cinema have been significant, the first Danish directors book was very much weighted towards filmmakers who had been working in the industry for a long time, and whose directorial credits were lengthy. While the interviews saw filmmakers responding to a variety of questions, some of them contextual, others more focused on style, issues having to do with small nationhood and national cinema provided a common thread throughout.

The intention with *The Danish Directors 2* is very different from that motivating *The Danish Directors*, for the guiding aim here is to focus intensely on the New Danish Cinema, and, more specifically, on the various factors that allowed it to emerge. We are interested, that is, in the filmmakers' subjective understanding of the processes that contributed to the emergence of the New Danish Cinema. Scholarly accounts aimed at explaining what is sometimes referred to as the second 'golden age' of Danish cinema exist. Mette Hjort points to a mix of cultural policy (associated with the Danish Film Institute), training (afforded by the National Film School of Denmark) and artistic leadership (provided by Lars von Trier), and to the dynamics of a cinematic 'gift culture' in which various forms of generosity and collectivism become the means of enhancing the opportunities available to filmmakers, their efficacy as filmmakers and their visibility, both nationally and globally.[2] What a scholarly account cannot provide, however, is that direct encounter with the practitioners' subjective understanding of the conditions shaping their practices and aspirations as filmmakers. *The Danish Directors 2* is an attempt to get the filmmakers themselves to reflect on the personal, social and especially institutional factors that provide the enabling conditions for their work, as filmmakers whose films are very much part of the New Danish Cinema phenomenon.

The Danish Directors 2 is shaped by decisions regarding inclusion and exclusion, as well as conversational focus. One key decision is clearly reflected in the table of contents, where every name is new, relative to the first interview book. While Susanne Bier and Lars von Trier, both included in *The Danish Directors*, remain significant figures, and while both have been very productive since 2001, the work of these two filmmakers is well known at this point to international audiences, and thus far less in need of profiling than are the films and practices of a number of internationally less prominent, or still emerging, but highly promising, filmmakers. Given our interest in the institutional underpinnings of the New Danish Cinema, we were committed to interviewing graduates from the National Film School of Denmark, as well as filmmakers who had made their way into the Danish film industry by following other paths. We were also interested in interviewing actresses who had managed to negotiate a new role for themselves as directors. We were intent on making sure that so-called 'new Danes', Danes of mixed ethnicity, were given the opportunity to talk frankly about the challenges and opportunities that arise in Denmark as a result of race and ethnicity. And, finally, we wanted *The Danish Directors 2* to reflect the extent to which the New Danish Cinema can be legitimately associated with the intelligent hard work of a number of very thoughtful women. Internationally, the term 'New Danish Cinema' immediately brings to mind Lars von Trier and his brethren. Yet, some of the New Danish Cinema's biggest successes, in both critical and box-office terms, are the results of women's efforts as directors, a fact that is well worth noting and trying to understand, given just how rare it is to find women participating in a film industry, in significant numbers, as directors and producers. The seventeen filmmakers included in *The Danish Directors 2* are all accomplished figures in their own right. When brought together as a group they allow for the kind of diversity we have just identified as desirable.

Each of the interviews is an edited and approved transcript of an exchange that was far longer than the published text suggests. In each case the decision as to what to include in the text for publication was to a significant extent determined by the focus on which we, as interviewers, had agreed. Lengthy discussions of a given film's plot, for example, were thus sacrificed, at times reluctantly, in order to make room for exchanges having to do with the following research questions:

1. What are the established paths leading to a filmmaking career in Denmark? And to what extent are those paths accessible to all Danes, including aspiring filmmakers from the provinces, and from immigrant backgrounds?
2. What do filmmakers see as the strengths and weaknesses of the various institutions that exist in Denmark for the purpose of training filmmakers? More specifically, how do filmmakers see the European Film College, the National Film School and the Film Workshop?
3. To what extent can the robust networks and the collaborative or collectivist ethos that define the practices of filmmaking in Denmark be traced to the National Film School of Denmark?

4. To what extent are filmmakers who did not graduate from the National Film School of Denmark outsiders in relation to the more robust filmmakers' networks?
5. To what extent do Danish filmmakers see themselves as participating in Nordic networks, or other transnational networks?
6. What are some of the salient forms of collaborative practice being pursued by Danish film practitioners?
7. How successful have key policy decisions been in fostering collaborative practices that are deemed to raise the level of Danish filmmaking?
8. Is the strong acting that is widely regarded as a feature of the New Danish Cinema a result of curricular emphases at the National Film School?
9. Dogma 95 helped to define the New Danish Cinema. Which aspects of the Dogma programme persist in Danish cinema today? Are filmmakers articulating responses to the question 'What comes after Dogma?' Are filmmakers' views on what comes after Dogma convergent, or are they relatively diverse?
10. New Danish Screen was introduced as a means of stimulating innovation and renewal in the Danish filmmaking milieu. What has this initiative meant to directors?
11. The New Danish Cinema includes films by a significant number of women directors. What is it about the Danish film milieu that makes it unusually hospitable to film practitioners who are women?
12. Two of these women established successful acting careers before becoming directors. How difficult is it in a Danish context to make the shift from acting to directing?
13. A conception of filmmaking as involving research, and as itself a basis for learning, has emerged in the Danish context. How widespread is this conception and what, more specifically, does it entail?
14. The New Danish Cinema is intimately associated with two key production companies, Zentropa and Nimbus Film. What does it mean to work for these companies, as a director?
15. Zentropa was established in a spirit of defiance, particularly in relation to Nordisk (with which it nonetheless merged in 2008). What has Zentropa meant to filmmakers? What role does Zentropa play today?
16. Several of the directors who have contributed to the New Danish Cinema phenomenon have established their own production companies. What were their reasons for doing so?
17. The New Danish Cinema was in many ways defined by the concept of doing more with less, and by the idea that limited resources, usually viewed as a prohibitive constraint, might become a basis for creativity. How, at this point, do Danish directors reason about the issue of money in relation to creativity?
18. Several of the directors associated with the New Danish Cinema have had the opportunity to pursue their filmmaking careers outside Denmark. What, in the light of relevant comparisons, do they see as the advantages of the Danish filmmaking milieu?
19. Several of the directors have also worked for Danish television. What has television meant for their personal careers and for the New Danish Cinema in general?

20. The New Danish Cinema emerged at a time when the political will to sustain, and further develop film as art in Denmark was strong. With the Social Democrats no longer in power, and with the new Film Accords emphasizing a far more commercial direction for Danish film, how do Danish directors see the future of Danish film?

In order to make *The Danish Directors 2* as useful as possible for the purposes of research and cross-border inspiration, we have included a subject index that identifies core topics and issues, and that thus allows the reader to bring together a series of related reflections, for the purposes of developing a fuller perspective. A second index provides a list of proper names, and the titles of all the films discussed in the interviews. In the glossary readers will find brief profiles of people who are frequently mentioned in the interviews, and of key institutions, as well as definitions of central terms.

The Danish Directors was the result of collaboration between two scholars, Mette Hjort and Ib Bondebjerg (the latter having also served as Chairman of the Board of the Danish Film Institute for several years). *The Danish Directors 2* involves three, rather than two interviewers, and the aim has been to pursue the work of interviewing as a team, with each interviewer liaising with the two others about foci for the individual interviews. Our interview team brings together three scholars with a long-standing interest in Danish cinema, each of them with well-established links to the film milieu and to the Danish Film Institute. The Chair Professor of Visual Studies at Lingnan University in China, Mette Hjort has been publishing on Danish cinema since the mid-1990s, and has helped to develop an analytic and conceptual framework for the analysis of small national cinemas. She is series editor, with Peter Schepelern, for the Nordic Film Classics Series, which the Danish Film Institute helps to fund. As an Affiliate Professor of Scandinavian Studies at the University of Washington, Seattle, Hjort contributes to a ScanDesign-funded 'Copenhagen Classroom' each summer, providing students with diverse disciplinary backgrounds from the University of Washington with opportunities to visit the Film Town in Avedøre, the Film School and the Film House, and to talk at length with filmmakers, producers, policy makers, scriptwriters and actors. In addition to teaching at the University of Copenhagen, Eva Jørholt is the editor of *Kosmorama* (published by the Danish Film Institute), and a member of the Council for Feature Films, a body that advises the Danish Film Institute regarding feature film production, and helps to appoint the DFI's consultants in the area. She was for many years a film critic for *Information*, one of Denmark's most rigorous dailies. A PhD student at the University of Copenhagen, Eva Novrup Redvall has worked as a film critic for *Information* since 1999, and as a programmer for the DFI's Cinematheque. Her PhD dissertation is a case-based exploration of collaborative processes involving scriptwriters and directors, with particular emphasis on the work of directors Annette K. Olesen and Per Fly.

Why interview?

What motivates us, as film scholars, to undertake an interview book with filmmakers? Interview books, after all, are an enormous amount of work, especially if they are to be published in a language (English) other than that (Danish) in which the interviews were conducted. The commitment of time that is involved in producing a high quality interview book is unlikely to be duly recognized by the various committees and panels charged with assessing the performance of researchers, measured in terms of various categories of 'outputs'. Unlike the monograph, article or book chapter, which all have their own assessment category, the interview book shares a home with all 'Other' outputs, a category that catches not everything, but what is left once the institutionally valued outputs have been duly reported. For academics working within the context of ambitious universities that hold their employees to what currently counts as high research standards, to engage in the production of an interview book is, necessarily, to commit to a very significant amount of *additional* work. An annual research report, after all, that includes only entries in the 'Other' category can only be deficient. Whereas peer-reviewed articles and monographs satisfy the researcher's contractual obligations, interview books, quite clearly, do not. With the globalization of models of university governance emphasizing performance indicators, accountability and strategically planned research, the interview book begins to look like a rather naïve labour of love.[3]

The Danish Directors 2 is certainly an expression of considerable affection and admiration. To pursue filmmaking as something more than the production of an industrial, commercial product is necessarily, even in a welfare state context with considerable social safety nets, to embrace a life that is fraught with risks and involves consciously taking risks, again and again.[4] To draw attention to the films that are produced as a result of this willingness to embrace a wide range of uncertainties, and to do so through the genre of the practitioner's interview, is to foreground worthy choices and pursuits, life paths that are shaped by what philosopher Charles Taylor calls 'moral sources'.[5] Consisting of moral intuitions about what makes for a life worth living, these sources provide the frameworks that allow us, as agents, to assess actions, modes of life and modes of feeling in qualitative terms, to see some as more worthy than others. The filmmakers interviewed in *The Danish Directors 2* are all agents who have thought deeply and honestly about what makes for a meaningful life, and who are unusually articulate about their commitments to such quintessentially modern sources as creativity and its expression. To achieve clarity about what counts as creativity, about why it matters, and how it is best fostered is by no means an easy task. Just as difficult, if not more so, is the task of acting in a consequential way once some level of clarity about these issues has been achieved. Collaborative by nature, and far more costly than most creative media, filmmaking can easily become a struggle to remain true to certain core self-understandings. The filmmakers whom we have chosen to engage in dialogue have all, to varying degrees, had to struggle in these different ways in order to make the kinds of contributions to film's history that would warrant their inclusion in an interview book in the first place. Our book, let there be no doubt about it, finds a starting point in admiration: admiration for the quality of the filmmakers' work, for the lucidity of their reflections about their practices and for the courage and tenacity that define their lives as practitioners.

In its own way *The Danish Directors 2* mounts a modest challenge to the categorial framework that currently underpins research outputs and their assessment. It is our firm conviction that practitioners' interviews, if properly executed, constitute a form of research, and, what is more, facilitate research of a more theoretical or conceptual nature. Indeed, we are willing to defend the claim that progress on some of the thorny issues with which film theorists are concerned can only be made if practitioner's agency, defined as including the perspectives of *actual* practitioners, is brought into play. Before providing an example that supports this claim, let us pause to consider the nature of so-called anecdotal evidence, for it is misconceptions about the interview format's anecdotal nature that prevents the practitioner's interview from being recognized as research-relevant.

Definitions of the term 'anecdotal evidence' point to some of the reasons why the research value of interview books has been insufficiently acknowledged in the context of Film Studies. The online *Dictionary.com* defines 'anecdotal evidence' as follows: 'based on personal observation, case study reports, or *random* investigations rather than systematic scientific evaluation' (emphasis added).[6] It is our contention that interview books, especially those comprising a *series* of practitioner's interviews with different filmmakers and those conducted by a well-integrated *team* of researchers, can be systematic, and thus much more than merely random investigations. The research relevance of an interview book depends, then, not only on the quality of the stories that the practitioners tell in response to the film scholar's questions, but on the film scholar's ability, through brief statements and conversationally appropriate questions, to encourage the practitioners to talk about issues that are central to ongoing research debates. Whether the film scholar succeeds in so engaging the practitioner will depend, in turn, on the scholar's capacity to ask research-driven questions without in any way bringing the off-putting and conversation-stopping apparatus of scholarship, with its insular jargon and other forms of stuffiness, into the conversational space. If the interview team comprises scholars who are conversationally versatile, if the interviewees are selected with clearly defined criteria in mind and if the film scholars' questions arise out of an ongoing research programme, and are motivated by a desire to take ongoing scholarly debates forward, it would seem more prejudicial than scientific to dismiss the practitioner's interview as mere storytelling.

Having gestured towards a methodological defence of the practitioner's interview, as a response to the charge or, more mildly, suspicion of scholarly irrelevance, let us return now to the question of practitioner's agency. To embrace the concept of practitioner's agency is to acknowledge that films are made by persons, or, as philosophers put it, by agents. Films, that is, are the result, to a very considerable extent, although not exclusively (chance and institutional circumstances being an inevitable factor) of agents' articulation of plans and sub-plans, and of their deliberations and decision-making with reference to such plans. By foregrounding the idea of filmmaking as an activity undertaken by agents, we give explanatory priority to the self-understandings, to the subjective rationality, of those who are involved in the making of films. We acknowledge that films are made in a social context, and that there are larger social forces that impinge on the filmmaking process. We further recognize that agents are not always lucid about their intentions, and that their self-understandings may be distorted to various degrees. It should be noted, however, that the term 'subjective rationality' by no means encourages a probing of a narrowly inward psychological space, for agents reason, not only about how they see themselves, about their preferred self-concepts and about how a given film project might be related to such concepts, but also about the viability of their cinematic undertakings, given various external, and properly social, constraints. In this sense the subjective rationality of filmmakers necessarily includes these agents' thoughts about the institutional dimensions of filmmaking, about cultural policy, for example, about specific funding schemes and the priorities of those who devise and implement them.

With regard to the issue of distorted self-understandings, the qualifier 'subjective' signals a recognition of the various opacities by which human agency is shaped. It would be wrongheaded, however, to see the inevitability of such opacities as an obstacle to an agency-oriented approach to the understanding of film. To commit to practitioner's agency, as an analytic approach, is to welcome the full spectrum of practitioners' reasoning, from distorted to lucid, into the context of analysis. Distortion, while no doubt an inevitable feature of human agency, is, in our view, more likely to arise in connection with self-concepts, concepts that define an agent's sense of self, and less likely to arise in connection with what might be called 'craft-based decision-making'. A filmmaker who finds herself embroiled in conflict with her producer may have a wrongheaded understanding of the nature of that conflict on account of less than lucid self-conceptions. Yet that same filmmaker may reason very lucidly indeed about why she has a strong preference for a given visual style, and about how that visual style is best achieved. As interviewers with the firm conviction that the practitioner's interview has a legitimate role to play in film scholarship, we are interested in practitioner's agency as a phenomenon encompassing reflexive reasoning about the practitioner as a self, as well as more punctual, craft-related deliberations.

Practitioner's agency can be explored in a largely theoretical manner, with the film theorist postulating craft-related reasoning, and an *implicit* film author, on the basis of textual properties in a cinematic work or oeuvre.[7] In our case, the interest in practitioner's agency is at once theoretical and practical, our sense being that a purely theoretical and inferential approach is ultimately inadequate. Put differently, any theoretical account of practitioner's agency is likely to be better, and more robust, if it is developed on the basis of empirical data that goes beyond what can be inferred from, or speculatively proposed on the basis of, an analysis of particular cinematic works. Not all film scholars or film theorists can be expected to have easy, direct access to film practitioners, but if this is a problem (as we believe it is), it can be resolved in large measure by ensuring that those who do are given the opportunity to share the conversations that access to the film milieu over a significant period of time makes possible. Film scholars with a strong interest in small cinemas have a central role to play in this regard, for there are typically fewer obstacles to access in the kind of small-nation contexts in which such cinemas are produced.[8]

We neglect the practitioner's interview book at our own scholarly peril, for in some instances understanding practitioner's agency, defined as encompassing actual and not merely inferred or theoretically postulated practitioner's reasoning, is what makes progress on thorny issues in film scholarship possible. A brief example suffices to make this point. In the wake of the manifesto-based, rule-governed film initiative known as Dogma 95, a number of film scholars became interested in the theoretical literature on creativity under constraint.[9] Dogma 95's 'Vow of Chastity', which identified ten rules to which any Dogma director would have to submit, was seen as illustrating perfectly, both in theory and practice, the related ideas that creativity can be stimulated through constraints and that constraints, far from being an obstacle to creativity, in fact are a condition of its possibility. Hjort, whose early work on Dogma helped to foreground the relevance of the theoretical literature on creativity under constraint for understanding the film initiative in question, has been able, in more recent work, to refine the theoretical framework, but only as a result of a series of in-depth practitioners' interviews. In *Lone Scherfig's 'Italian for Beginners'*,[10] Hjort draws on practitioners' interviews with the director of the award-winning Dogma film, and with her editor, cinematographer, and sound designer, and with actors Peter Gantzler and Anders W. Berthelsen. As Hjort probes the creativity under constraint idea, through a range of research questions addressed to the practitioners, it becomes clear that further conceptual differentiation is needed. While the Dogma rules appear to fit the creativity under constraint idea, the practitioners' interviews reveal the extent to which the impact of the ten rules differs as a function of the practitioners' professional roles within the collaborative process of filmmaking. For an editor, for example, the creative gains to be derived from the Dogma set-up are very limited indeed. Actors, on the other hand, and directors too, stand to lose very little from the same set-up, and to profit from considerable creative gains. Once the empirical work of actually talking to practitioners has been carried out, the need to take the differentiated impact of the rules into account seems self-evident, and, thus theoretically imaginable within the context of a purely inferential and text-based account of cinematic agency. Yet, the likelihood of fully grasping the need for further conceptual refinement on account of the actual, differentiated impact of the rules in the context of practice is surely far greater if the film scholar is willing to engage with the practitioners about their craft. Dialogue is also what allows the film scholar to determine the extent and nature of the required conceptual refinements. In this sense the practitioner's interview provides the impetus for theory formation, and the data that thus softens the heavy-handedness of theory.

We have been proposing a conception of the practitioner's interview that sees it as both a form of research and as a genre with clear research relevance. And it is time now to say a few words about what we understand by the term 'research relevance'. 'Relevance', as used here, signals a position that sees the practitioner's interview as providing relatively 'raw' data that have the potential to become bona fide research findings, but only through a process of scholarly interpretation and argumentation. To publish a series of practitioners' interviews is not, then, to make available a set of *research findings*, but to provide film scholars and critics with the kind of *research-motivated empirical data* that will allow some of them, all depending on the nature of their research questions, to take their research programmes forward.

In response to the question 'Why Interview?' we have more than a defence of the practitioner's interview as research-relevant to propose. We can begin to get at the additional reasons for undertaking practitioner's interviews by taking up the question, increasingly urgent as universities (are required to) review their priorities, of the film scholar's job description. What is it that film scholars do, as colleagues working in the Business Faculty or the Faculty of Social Sciences might put it? And what kinds of contributions do the activities engaged in by film scholars typically make? The discussion of the practitioner's interview as research-relevant is linked to one possible justification of the film scholar's existence: film is a complex, significant, persistent (although changing) and salient phenomenon, the systematic investigation of which promises cognitive gains in various areas. There is, of course, much more to be said along these lines. What we would like to do here, however, is shift the discussion away from the idea of the film scholar as variously engaged in theoretical and analytical research, in order to bring some more 'applied' forms of research into focus. With universities increasingly being asked to demonstrate their relevance to society, and with scholars in some parts of the world being encouraged to engage in what is known as 'knowledge transfer', it is worth asking what film scholars have to offer in the context of these tendencies. We acknowledge that film scholars have produced a large body of work that is essentially critical (of realities shaped negatively by race, class and gender, for example), and in this sense practically oriented. At the same time it seems fair to say that the impact of much of what film scholars publish is limited to the context of academe itself, and perhaps even to a limited readership within academe, one consisting mostly of fellow travellers. If film scholars are interested in having a greater impact through their work, they will need to think more imaginatively, and expansively, about the kinds of tasks that they are able to take up. What is more, they will need to ensure that these tasks are explicitly defined, and in ways that will make sense to a far broader audience, one comprising policy makers, film practitioners, university administrators, film school administrators and teachers, secondary school teachers and festival organizers, to mention but some of the kinds of readers to whom we see *The Danish Directors 2* as being addressed.

In the context of *The Danish Directors 2* we have essentially three 'applied' tasks to propose, each of them highly worthwhile as far as we are concerned, and entirely consistent with the values of the research we undertake with more traditional, limited-impact 'outputs' in view. These tasks have to do with meta-culture, knowledge transfer and the identification, through an analytic and interpretive process, of *implicit* best practices. Let us explore these in turn:

1. Meta-culture: Taking up the task of audience- and institution-building

As anthropologist Greg Urban points out, meta-culture, culture about culture, 'imparts an accelerative force to culture'. Meta-culture 'aids culture in its motion through space and time. It gives a boost to the culture that it is about, helping to propel it on its journey.'[11] Film reviews are an example of meta-culture, as are scholarly articles and books about stardom, national cinemas (whether small or large), screen acting, film movements and any number of other well-established research topics in Film Studies. While film scholars have produced a very significant amount of meta-culture since the emergence of Film Studies as an academic discipline many decades ago, the institutionally validated forms of meta-culture – peer-reviewed articles and books – have generally had the weakest accelerative force to offer. Speaking programmatically, and thus very succinctly, it is time for film scholars to pursue the production of a much wider range of types of meta-culture, and for them to defend their new pursuits vigorously, in terms of enhanced impact and social relevance, if necessary. Appealing as they ideally do to a readership that extends well beyond the academy, interview books have considerable 'accelerative force' to offer. As Meaghan Morris, a staunch defender of the anecdote, points out, anecdotes have a capacity to '*touch* (address) a mixed audience; as any journalist knows, anecdotes *work* to make contact and catch people's attention, although they can fail in their nudging, insinuating mission'.[12] In the context of culture that originates in small nations, and in contexts of various forms of marginality, degrees of accelerative force are hardly a matter of indifference. If they choose their meta-culture carefully, film scholars can create platforms for the culture that their meta-culture is about. The interview book is thus best motivated by well-reasoned affection and considered admiration, for in dialoguing with the relevant practitioners the interviewers potentially strengthen existing platforms for the filmmakers' work, and help forge new paths for its circulation.

As indicated, *The Danish Directors 2* follows on an original *Danish Directors* (published in 2000) and is itself to be followed by a *Danish Directors 3* (focusing on documentary filmmaking). What is more, both *The Danish Directors 2* and *Danish Directors 3* will have a web presence after their print release, on the official Danish Film Institute website. As a result of the series concept, the digital and print formats and the practitioner's interview *qua* meta-cultural type, the *Danish Directors* books become, not just a means of achieving cognitive gains related to knowledge and understanding, but an attempt at audience-building. The existence of in-depth, accessible interviews in English makes it possible for some of the relevant films to make their way into film courses around the world, and into schools where films, among other things, might be used illustratively to explore such phenomena as bullying, racism, social exclusion and moral deliberation. It is hoped that the existence of the interview books might encourage scholars looking for data relevant to certain research programmes to turn their attention to the small national cinema in question, instead of looking to some of the traditionally more established cinemas. There are reasons, in addition to the intrinsic merit of the films, for turning to small national cinemas: in the Danish case, the limited scale that is a feature of small national cinemas makes a significant degree of coverage possible in just three interview books, the result being research-relevant data that are fairly comprehensive in certain respects. Lest the term 'significant' be overlooked here, we hasten to add that we have not been able to include *all* deserving directors in our books, and hope that other scholars might take up the still remaining, and no doubt rewarding task of interviewing such figures as Martin Zandvliet, Charlotte Sachs Bostrup, Tomas Villum Jensen and Nicolas Winding Refn, among others.

2. Knowledge transfer

A second task for film scholars is that of knowledge transfer. Knowledge transfer was evoked as early as the 1980s in the United Kingdom, and has since been taken up by policy makers in Scandinavia, the Netherlands, France and Italy, typically in connection with the need to make universities more responsive to the requirements of industry and the knowledge economy.[13] University/industry linkages have been a preferred means of facilitating knowledge transfer, and such linkages have often been a matter of technology transfer, an area in which Arts and Humanities scholars have had little to offer. Yet there are, as Aldo Geuna and Alessandro Muscio remark, 'soft'[14] forms of knowledge transfer, and there is every reason to believe that film scholars can be key players in this area. Indeed, there are examples of efforts along these lines, with the Department of Film Studies at the University of St Andrews playing a pioneering role, also in this regard. The department's collaboration with the New Picture House Cinema involves highly trained film scholars putting their expertise to work as programmers, the aim being to bring art-house film to the St Andrews community, inclusively (town and gown) construed. The Dynamics of World Cinema project, led by Dina Iordanova, involves elements of outreach and knowledge transfer, as a result of the framework it provides for productive dialogue among scholars, festival organizers, policy makers and members of various funding bodies.

Knowledge transfer is often discussed in terms of networks of exchange *within* a given national space, with knowledge flowing from one sector of society to another. In the case of Film Studies, some of the more interesting opportunities for knowledge transfer are transnational in scope, with knowledge crossing national borders, in response, for example, to incipient or established partnerships, based on a recognition of shared problems, or shared values.[15] The Danish context presents film scholars with clear opportunities in this regard. Film scholars can take up the challenge of articulating the conditions that have allowed Danish cinema to thrive, against all odds, from the late 1990s onwards.[16] These conditions are to a significant extent institutional, arising as they do from a political will to support the art of film, and from a plethora of cultural and educational policies, all overseen by specific, state-funded institutions, and developed and refined over time. This institutional basis for the success of what is sometimes called the New Danish Cinema interacts productively with the informal, private-sector institution-building that has been pursued by especially producers and directors, Lars von Trier's Zentropa, with its Film Town and collectivist ethos, being the most obvious example. The point is that embedded within the institutional conditions that allow this small-nation cinema to thrive is a wide range of models – educational models, communicative models, policy models and production models, among many others. While there has been considerable synergy among these various models, many of them are to some extent mutually detachable and individually transferable to other contexts where the desire for cinema is systematically thwarted by the many constraints of small nationhood. In this sense these models are all potential cultural resources, and the film scholar can make it his or her task to facilitate their wider circulation, through publications and especially talks in such geographically distant small-nation contexts as Scotland, Hong Kong and Qatar. By choosing to prioritize audiences in what some would consider 'peripheral' places, the film scholar can encourage film scholars, practitioners and policy makers to look, not to some putative centre, but to the periphery, for workable concepts and practices. In 2001, for example, there were no discernible links between Hong Kong and Denmark in the area of film. The situation in 2010 is a very different one, with leading Hong Kong scholars and public intellectuals such as Ping-kwan Leung encouraging an awareness of Danish models of film education, broadly construed.

Knowledge transfer, in the case of the interview book, is focused on what the *practitioners* know, and on what the scholar-interviewer deems these practitioners to know. In this sense the scholar-interviewer is the instigator and facilitator of a transfer of practitioner's knowledge. The practitioner's interview, we noted, requires the scholar's interpretive and analytic efforts to become more than simply research-relevant, and a comparable point can be made with regard to the issue of knowledge transfer. The practitioners *point* us in the direction of institutional set-ups and types of practice that are workable, but their reflections are, and quite rightly so, deeply personal, rather than abstractive, as models ultimately must be. Through the practitioners' accounts of what does and does not facilitate their practice, and of how they have met the challenges of small-nation filmmaking, we achieve clarity about the various contextual realities that warrant further analysis and discussion, with an eye to transforming the achievements of the New Danish Cinema into cultural resources of far more than mere national significance.

3. The identification of *implicit* best practices

A third task that film scholars can take up is the somewhat difficult one of trying to have an impact on filmmakers' priorities, through talks and publications that aim to encourage public debate about film. It can be a matter here of analysing the practices that are brought into focus through the interview process, and of proposing a way of understanding those practices that helps to bring out their implicit and thus insufficiently acknowledged promise, when considered in terms of precise criteria. Hjort, for example, has argued that in the context of growing concerns about the environmental costs associated with the production of films, film scholars should look to small national cinemas for incipient models of environmentally sustainable filmmaking, and help to promote these models in any context, small or large. In an article entitled 'Film and the Environment: Risk Off-Screen', Richard Maxwell and Toby Miller evoke the extent of the problems accompanying big-budget filmmaking, Hollywood-style:

> A study of Hollywood's environmental impact has disclosed massive use of electricity and petroleum and the release of hundreds of thousands of tons of deadly emissions each year. In fact, the motion-picture industry is *the biggest producer of conventional pollutants* in the Los Angeles area.[17]

By contrast, having worked hard to turn the constraints of small-nation filmmaking into productive, creative opportunities, the many practitioners who have contributed to the New Danish Cinema have also helped to chart what could become a model for much 'greener' filmmaking practices. The success of the New Danish Cinema is attributable in large measure to the way in which its practitioners embraced the concept of 'less is more', forging a broad consensus about necessarily limited budgets as a potentially creativity-enhancing constraint. In 2008 the average production budget for a Danish feature film was a mere 2.9 million Euros, and many films were produced with far less money. While the use of digital video, by no means a 'green' technology, played a role in limiting production costs, it is important to note that costs were also kept in check, among many, many other reasons, because film practitioners consciously and systematically chose to work with film locations that would reduce transportation costs.[18] In this sense the small-nation cinema that not only survives, but thrives, on less provides a positive contrast to the environmental reality of that über-big cinema, Hollywood: '*MSNBC.com* admonishes that although "the Prius reigns supreme as the current status symbol" in Hollywood, "trucks that carry equipment from studios to locations and back continue to emit exhaust from diesel engines," as do generators on-set.'[19]

Whereas knowledge transfer brings into play the models, concepts and practices that film practitioners are very much aware of, the articulation of *implicit* best practices involves drawing out the positive *entailments* of certain approaches to filmmaking. The term 'implicit' underscores the extent to which these entailments remain largely unacknowledged, even in the very contexts of practice where they actually arise. Thus, for example, it is fair to assert that while Danish filmmakers have a well-developed discourse about the positive links between creativity and fiscal restraint, they have yet to articulate, and embrace, the links between fiscal restraint and a second possible 'virtue term': sustainability. Should film scholars not see it as their task to encourage filmmakers to embrace those links? Should film scholars not see it as their task to encourage audiences to reflect on those links, and to choose films, not just on the basis of the narrative or visual pleasures they might afford, but on the basis of whether those films meet certain ethical standards? These questions are, of course, merely rhetorical, for the answer given here is a resounding 'yes'.

Contexts

Given our interest in introducing readers to the institutional conditions that made the New Danish Cinema possible, the final pages of this Introduction are devoted to the task of providing an account of two of the contexts that emerge as decisive from our series of practitioners' interviews: the contexts of training and cultural policy.

Learning to become a filmmaker in Denmark: The National Film School of Denmark, Super16 and the Film Workshop in Copenhagen

The National Film School of Denmark (NFSD) was established in 1966. Its current status as one of the world's most successful film schools is very much the result of strong, visionary leadership, especially on the part of former Head Henning Camre and current Head, Poul Nesgaard.[20] One of the features of the New Danish Cinema, as compared with Danish cinema in the 1970s and 1980s, for example, is that most of the directors associated with Denmark's 'second golden age' were trained at the NFSD. Indeed, the NFSD has trained not only the vast majority of directors currently making feature films in Denmark, but also most of the cinematographers, editors, sound engineers, producers and scriptwriters with whom they collaborate.

The NFSD is a state school that falls under the auspices of the Danish Ministry of Cultural Affairs. As the interview with Lone Scherfig indicates, those associated with the school believe that there is much at stake in its affiliation with the Ministry of Cultural Affairs, as opposed to the Ministry of Education. In an interview with Hjort, Poul Nesgaard indicated that the school's status as an elite, conservatoire-style institution focused on film as art would likely be undermined, were the school to become part of the Ministry of Education's portfolio, and thus subject to some of the dictates arising from the basic parameters of mass education at the tertiary level.[21] As indicated on its website, the NFSD sees itself as an art school that aims to develop and support the unique talents and expressive capacities of each and every individual student.[22] At the same time, the school is committed to teaching students filmmaking as a collaborative craft, the idea being that such an approach not only enhances graduates' opportunities within the film industry, but also the quality of their work. The dual focus on film as both an art and a craft is a defining feature of the NFSD's vision, and a key to its success.

As the one official film school in the small country of Denmark, the NFSD has played a decisive role in shaping the outlook of the film practitioners working in the Danish film industry today, as well as the tendencies by which the New Danish Cinema is defined. One of the intentions motivating *The Danish Directors 2* is to chart the significance of the NFSD's teachings, as seen from the perspective of the practitioners themselves.

Of the seventeen directors interviewed for *The Danish Directors 2*, twelve were trained by the NFSD (ten of them as feature film directors, one as an editor and yet another as an animation filmmaker). Of the remaining five directors, two made their way into filmmaking via the Odense Theatre Drama School, and on the basis of their careers as well-known performers. Finally, three of the directors interviewed were able to break into filmmaking as a result of a number of other institutions capable of offering equipment and modest forms of financial support to aspiring filmmakers. Let us, in the first instance, look at the NFSD.

Many of the directors foreground the role of the NFSD's Scriptwriting Department, and this comes as no surprise. Mogens Rukov, by now an internationally known figure on account of his scriptwriting contributions to a long list of contemporary Danish film classics, was for many years the founding Head of the Scriptwriting Department. During his years as Head, Rukov, himself a university graduate with a background in Nordic philology, literature and film, helped to replace a traditional auteur concept (based on the idea of the director as writer), with a more collaborative conception of cinematic authorship. Rukov argued convincingly for the value of having directors collaborate with scriptwriters, and this commitment to collaboration continues to inform the pedagogical practices of the Scriptwriting Department under its new Head, Lars Detlefsen.[23]

Several of the directors refer to creativity under constraint as one of the specificities of the NFSD's curricular set-up. They make reference, more specifically, to the NFSD's so-called 'penneprøver' – clearly defined assignments requiring the students to work with a strict set of externally imposed rules. The key figure in this regard is the filmmaker Jørgen Leth, well known to international audiences at this point on account of *De fem benspænd* (*The Five Obstructions*, 2003; dirs Leth and Lars von Trier). Leth taught Lars von Trier when the latter was a student at the NFSD, and he was teaching full time at the NFSD when the 'golden cohort', consisting of Thomas Vinterberg, Per Fly and Ole Christian Madsen, among others, was at the school. Leth's entire filmmaking oeuvre, and indeed his artistic oeuvre more generally, find a starting point in the idea that various constraints, such as externally or self-imposed rules, are the very basis for creativity, a source of inspiration and thus also a means of stimulating or heightening the creativity of artists, including filmmakers. It is by no means a stretch to see Dogma 95 as a flamboyant and publicity-savvy attempt to make some of the NFSD's well-instituted pedagogical practices the very basis for a global filmmaking movement with capacity-generating implications for the originating small-nation context. Nor is it a stretch to see *The Five Obstructions* as an extended philosophical meditation, through the medium of film, on the very philosophy of creativity under constraint that has long been a central feature of the NFSD's teachings.[24]

Another recurring theme in the various interviews has to do with interaction between professional actors and students at the NFSD. Whereas some of the directors recall a time when the NFSD failed to acknowledge the importance of teaching directors how to work with actors, others regard themselves as fortunate because they attended the school after steps had been taken to give student directors as much experience as possible with professional actors. The filmmaker and occasional film school teacher Lone Scherfig is mentioned in this connection, and in her interview Scherfig discusses her reasons for having worked hard to establish the institutional alliances that would enable directors to overcome their perfectly natural fear of actors. The idea, she clearly suggests, is to overcome such fears before graduating, so as to avoid being hamstrung by them during the already sufficiently complicated process of making a first feature film as a newly minted film school graduate.

Interestingly, the impact of the NFSD extends well beyond the actual practices of filmmaking, reaching into the institutional dimensions of the film industry. The school has long provided a context for the initial development of a variety of productive creative alliances, and this as a result of its pedagogical emphasis on teamwork and collaboration. In some instances the alliances have continued well beyond the relevant practitioners' film school years. Nimbus and Zentropa, the two production companies most closely associated with the emergence of the New Danish Cinema, both found a starting point at the NFSD. What is more, the NFSD has helped to shape cultural policy, inasmuch as the success of its pedagogical emphases has motivated the development of schemes reflecting a similar commitment to rule-governed frameworks and teamwork. The school's insistence on the importance of nurturing closely knit teams consisting of a producer, director and scriptwriter, has, for example, been taken up in various ways by the policy makers at the Danish Film Institute (DFI). The DFI has helped to further institutionalize this 'holy trinity' through such initiatives as New Danish Screen, which is clearly a matter of cultural policy taking a cue from an important artistic initiative – Dogma 95 – and thus from the pedagogical priorities of the NFSD.

While all of the NFSD graduates acknowledge the school's strengths, they are also aware of the growing sense in recent years that the institution may have become dominant to the point of contributing to a certain mainstreaming of Danish film. In the late 1990s and first few years of the new millennium, the NFSD was explicitly linked to Dogma, and to a series of popular small-nation blockbusters that helped to give Danish films market shares well above the European norm. In more recent times, however, the school has had to contend with various criticisms, and some of these emerge as recurring themes in *The Danish Directors 2*. Some would have it that the school is now too oriented towards the industry, whereas others contend that Danish cinema needs to explore a much wider range of cinematic expressions, a range that the school could be doing more to make salient.

With the emergence of the New Danish Cinema, the NFSD became a magnet for talented young people, the result being that the admissions process became even more competitive. The eye-of-the-needle phenomenon to which several of the interviewees refer has itself spawned alternative arrangements that could become part of the solution to the kind of mainstreaming of Danish film production with which the NFSD is now being charged from time to time. Super16, a student-driven film school established in 1999, by applicants to the NFSD who failed to gain admission to the elite school, is a fascinating example of an official, state-funded cultural institution generating its opposite, an unofficial, private sector initiative where budget lines are replaced by various forms of gift culture, by voluntary gifts of time, equipment and expertise. Super16 accepts eight producers and eight directors every three years, and these students then put together an eclectic curriculum, in close collaboration with the established film industry, and especially, at least during the early years, with Nordisk. While *The Danish Directors 2* does not include interviews with any of the Super16 graduates, the interview with Paprika Steen does make reference to the feature film debut of one of the relevant filmmakers, to Martin Zandvliet's award-winning *Applaus* (*Applause*, 2009). Predictions are always dangerous, but we are willing to hazard one here: the diversity that is needed to sustain the vitality of Danish cinema will hinge on the emergence of a less monolithic institutional landscape. In this sense the kind of 'unofficial' film school phenomenon to which Super16 contributes, and in fascinating ways, could well be crucial.

In addition to the official film school, the Danish state funds a number of workshops, the idea being to nurture new talent, and to democratize access to filmmaking. *The Danish Directors 2* clearly suggests that these various spaces, one of them in the capital, others in the provinces, play an important role, particularly with regard to the issue of access. In his interview with Redvall, Omar Shargawi tells the fascinating story of how his award-winning feature film *Gå med fred Jamil* (*Ma Salama Jamil*, 2008) started out as a short film supported by the Film Workshop in Copenhagen. And both Pernille Fischer Christensen and Nikolaj Arcel recount how their workshop films became their means of gaining access to the NFSD. The role of the Film Workshop in Copenhagen, and of others like it in the provinces, cannot, however, be reduced to the issue of access, for these spaces also provide a warrant to experiment with images, and thus the conditions under which talented filmmakers with the capacity to innovate within a norm-governed system can emerge.

Many of the directors in this book express gratitude for the opportunities and mentoring relationships they have encountered on their path to feature filmmaking. Motivated by gratitude and a desire to give back, a number of these directors are now trying to pass on their current knowledge to upcoming filmmakers, as teachers and guest lecturers at the NFSD and for Super16, as participants in Film Workshop seminars, or as professional mentors on Dvoted.net. Dvoted.net provides yet another example of the institutional landscape being diversified through various departures from the model of the traditional conservatoire-style film school. In this case, unlike that of Super16, the institutional arrangement is the result of a top-down, rather than grassroots, initiative. Established in 2006, and with the support of all of the Nordic film institutes, Dvoted.net is a web-based mentoring arrangement designed to create a sense of community among aspiring young filmmakers, to establish a platform where these filmmakers' early efforts at filmmaking can be shown and to foster a network of partnerships that links experienced filmmakers with novices. The willingness to share knowledge is a theme that runs through several of the interviews, and one of the Danish film milieu's most important assets.

Dialogue, sharing, generosity and collaboration, these are all attitudes, practices or traits that are seen as being traceable to the institutional culture that the NFSD has fostered, at least insofar as they concern the Danish film milieu. What is more, the institutional culture of some of the key production companies is also held by some to mirror that of the NFSD. The interviews in *The Danish Directors 2* do draw attention to the issue of competition in a small film industry where resources are necessarily limited, but they also underscore the extent to which collaboration and sharing are valued, and practised. Many of the directors clearly have the sense that working together, and helping each other out, are approaches that ultimately benefit everyone. The Danish film milieu is not one where zero-sum reasoning predominates, in the sense that one person's gain is by no means seen as somebody else's loss. As Lone Scherfig puts it: 'People really do wish each other well, if only for selfish reasons. Every time a Danish film succeeds, things become that much easier for everyone else.'

The Danish Film Institute

A key to understanding Danish cinema and the success it has enjoyed in recent years is the publicly funded film subsidy system administered by the Danish Film Institute (DFI). The DFI was established in 1972 through a Film Act that was proudly described by all relevant parties as, quite simply, 'the best in the world'. Besides establishing the framework for a publicly subsidized national film production, the 1972 Film Act also envisaged a structure aimed at supporting art cinemas in Denmark, cultural magazines devoted to film, the promotion of Danish films abroad, the national film archive, the distribution in Denmark of artistically valuable foreign films, among many other things.

In 1997, a new Film Act called for the merging of three previously separate institutions: The National Film Board (Statens Filmcentral), which was a state-run distribution company specializing in documentary films, The Danish Film Museum (Det Danske Filmmuseum) and the Danish Film Institute (Det Danske Filminstitut). Referred to as the Danish Film Institute, the new institutional entity was housed in a specially renovated Film House in Gothersgade, with Henning Camre, a cinematographer and former Head of the National Film School of Denmark and of the National Film and Television School in the United Kingdom, as its first CEO.

The success of the first Dogma films – Thomas Vinterberg's *Festen* (*The Celebration*) and Lars von Trier's *Idioterne* (*The Idiots*) – in 1998 put Danish cinema in the international limelight, and helped to secure a significant increase in government support for film. During the ten-year period from 1999 to 2009, the average annual production volume increased from 14–16 to 25–27 feature films, and the average production budget for a Danish feature film increased from 1.6 million Euro in 2001 to 2.9 million Euro in 2008.

Today most Danish films are subsidized through the DFI, and although the subsidy system that was introduced in 1972 was modified in subsequent Film Acts, some of its core elements remain in force. One such core element is the so-called 'consultant scheme'. The point of the relevant institutional arrangement, which involves the appointment of DFI consultants or film commissioners, is to ensure the production of artistically valuable films. Whereas the 'old' DFI often drew on academics with literary degrees when selecting consultants, the 'new' DFI has tended to appoint practitioners – writers, editors and dramaturgists – as its consultants. The DFI commissioners play a decisive role, inasmuch as they assess the various film projects for which DFI support is being sought, and thus determine which films merit funding. The consultant scheme has a number of strengths, the most important being that each film project is handled by just one consultant, whose task it is to follow a given film through all of its phases, that is, from the stage of an initial pitch to the final product. During this entire process the consultant is expected to function as a competent sparring partner, in relation to the scriptwriter, the director and/or the producer. The decision ultimately to grant a production subsidy, or to refrain from doing so, is thus based on the consultant's intimate knowledge of the project as it has evolved, rather than on a more or less informed decision by committee. The emphasis on a single expert's competence and judgement is a defining feature of the consultant scheme, and clearly one of the main reasons why unconventional films stand a chance, in the context of Danish cinema, of securing funding. Although the consultant scheme has been criticized on account of the enormous power that it effectively places in the hands of a very small number of individuals, most Danish directors see the consultant scheme as valuable, as well worth retaining and, indeed, as well worth defending. Most of the films discussed in *The Danish Directors 2* were subsidized through the consultant scheme.

In 1989 another subsidy scheme, the so-called 50/50 scheme was introduced. The aim was not to replace the consultant scheme, but rather to tackle some of the problems associated with it. With its emphasis on art films, and with its track record of funding a large number of films that failed to attract a reasonably sized audience, the consultant scheme was seen as needing to be complemented by a quite different approach. The 50/50 scheme was thus an attempt, on the part of the government and the DFI administration, to facilitate the production of films with popular appeal, and to provide a more capacious approach to the allocation of DFI funding. The 50/50 scheme, which was re-named the 60/40 scheme in 1997, made it possible for producers to obtain funding from the DFI, without having to secure the support of a particular individual with, inevitably, a number of personal likes and dislikes.[25] The 50/50 scheme enabled the DFI to support the production of a commercially oriented film, through a straightforward matching policy. A production company that was able to raise 50 per cent of a commercial film's budget could expect to see the DFI match the amount. The current 60/40 scheme only requires the production company to come up with 40 per cent of the required budget, and to present a financially and technically sound project. Although films produced through the 60/40 scheme usually fare better domestically, there are cases of 60/40 films having secured international distribution. Examples of internationally distributed 60/40 films include *De grønne slagtere* (*The Green Butchers*; dir. Anders Thomas Jensen, 2003), *Oh Happy Day* (Hella Joof, 2004), and *De fortabte sjæles ø* (*Island of Lost Souls*; dir. Nikolaj Arcel, 2007), all films discussed in *The Danish Directors 2*.

From 1999 onwards the financial framework and political objectives for Danish cinema have been laid down by the Danish parliament in four-year Film Policy Accords. The accord for 2003–2006 introduced a new talent development scheme called New Danish Screen. Emphasizing risk-taking, teamwork and low-budget film production, the mandate of New Danish Screen is to foster innovative cinematic works, to provide filmmakers with the opportunity to experiment with film (both formally and at the level of narrative) and to enable filmmakers to focus on filmmaking as a genuinely creative process.[26] New Danish Screen is a clear example of policy being inspired by practice, in this instance the rule-governed Dogma 95 initiative, which, among other things, demonstrated that the budgetary constraints of small-nation filmmaking can become the basis for creativity. New Danish Screen is also a clear case of policy makers attempting to sustain the successes of the New Danish Cinema. Practitioners and policy makers are well acquainted with the pattern of small-nation cinemas enjoying international favour for only a limited period of time. New Danish Screen was created in anticipation of the moment when Danish cinema would once again recede into the background, and as a concerted institutional effort to challenge the inevitability of that very process. Pernille Fischer Christensen's *En Soap* (*A Soap*, 2006), Christoffer Boe's *Offscreen* (2006), Anders Morgenthaler's *Princess* (2006) and *Ekko* (*Echo*, 2007), as well as Omar Shargawi's *Ma Salama Jamil* (2008), are all films that have received support through New Danish Screen. Their status as ground-breaking works has helped to legitimate the existence of New Danish Screen, and suggests that the DFI's efforts to foster innovation and renewal are far from misguided.

Producers and directors may draw on one of the three subsidy schemes described above, but they may also seek funding through the two Danish public service television stations. The most recent Film Policy Accord, which runs from 2007 to 2010, requires the Danish Broadcasting Corporation (Danmarks Radio) and TV 2 to co-produce a number of feature films as part of their public service obligation. During the specified period, these TV stations are to allocate a total of 145 million DKK (19.5 million Euros), on an annual basis, to such co-productions. Currently most Danish feature film projects require a co-production agreement with one of the television stations in order to be financially viable. The 2007–2010 Film Accord further specifies that at least 40 per cent of the DFI's allocation should be spent on the 60/40 scheme, and at least 40 per cent on the consultant scheme. This envisaged distribution of funds has been difficult to implement, given that the consultant system receives far more applications than the 60/40 scheme. The prioritizing of the commercially oriented 60/40 scheme has been highly controversial, inasmuch as it is seen as an expression of the current government's preferences for populist films that are commercially viable. There is less and less space, it is widely agreed, in the landscape of Danish film, for the practices that support film as art, and this as a result of the last two Film Accords, both of them the work of right-of-center governments.

In the case of both the consultant scheme and the 60/40 scheme, government funding is released in phases, through the DFI. Thus, the first phase of the subsidy process typically involves an application for a so-called script subsidy, the granting of which enables the scriptwriter to develop the script in a situation of relative financial tranquility. The next step is usually an application for a so-called development subsidy, which, if granted, allows the production company to refine its project. Finally, the production company can apply for an actual production subsidy. Each phase of the process is autonomous, in the sense that the granting of a production subsidy by no means is entailed or guaranteed by the earlier granting of script and development subsidies.

In recent years, there have been several cases of filmmakers having been granted script and development subsidies, and even conditional DFI production subsidies, only to fail to secure the support of the TV stations, the very condition on which the DFI production subsidies are hinged. It is a matter here of film practitioners having worked on projects for more than a year, even longer, and then having failed to convince the TV programmers of the prime time appeal of their projects. The lack of enthusiasm on the part of the TV stations undermined the budgetary planning in question, to the point of making it impossible to produce the films. This kind of situation is most unfortunate, and, interestingly, it is one that is considered regrettable by TV programmers and filmmakers alike, as some of the filmmakers included in *The Danish Directors 2* make clear.

The two national public service TV stations' involvement in the Danish film industry has not, however, been purely negative, for they have contributed significantly to the professionalization of Danish cinema, and this by hiring scriptwriters and directors from the industry to write and direct many of their new, award-winning Danish television series (e.g. *Rejseholdet* [*Unit One*, 2000–2003] and *Taxa* [*Taxi*, 1997–1999]). The tough production conditions that prevail in the context of TV production have simply functioned as a kind of boot camp for many young directors, affording emerging directors invaluable training, particularly with regard to such matters as effective decision-making, and the management of large numbers of people.

At the time of writing, a new four-year accord (spanning 2011 to 2014) is being negotiated; and anticipated, not without trepidation, by the film industry, the DFI and the film school community. Time will tell whether the government's new accord will provide the necessary framework for the continued success of Danish cinema, whether the political will is there to sustain the legacy of Denmark's second 'golden age'. The complex convergence of factors underwriting that second 'golden age', the synergies among cultural policies, curricula and various forms of talent, clearly demonstrate, and inspiringly so, that scale matters, that big is not always better and that much can be achieved on a small scale. Let us hope that the politicians understand just how significant a contribution the New Danish Cinema has made, and not just as a corpus of interesting films. The New Danish Cinema provides a model, parts of which are transferable, for sustainable film production in small-nation contexts, and points to an approach to environmentally responsible filmmaking that has relevance in all contexts. It is not hyperbolic to say that the New Danish Cinema has been a source of inspiration and hope beyond the borders of Denmark, in contexts where filmmakers and policy makers have long been grappling with politicians who favour market forces and populism. As we send *The Danish Directors 2* to the press, we find ourselves sincerely hoping that in the years to come Danish cinema will continue to provide a hopeful alternative to some of the more gloomy scenarios faced by filmmakers in many places around the globe.

Notes

1. Mette Hjort and Ib Bondebjerg, *The Danish Directors: Dialogues on a Contemporary National Cinema* (Bristol: Intellect, 2001).
2. Mette Hjort, 'Denmark', in *The Cinema of Small Nations*, eds Mette Hjort and Duncan Petrie (Edinburgh: Edinburgh University Press, 2007).
3. For a discussion of these models, see Mette Hjort, 'The Assessment Game: On Institutions that Punch above Their Weight, and Why the Quality of the Work Environment Also Matters', in *Instituting Cultural Studies*, eds Meaghan Morris and Mette Hjort (forthcoming).
4. See Mette Hjort, ed., *Film and Risk* (forthcoming) for in-depth explorations of the various types of risk that filmmaking entails.
5. Charles Taylor, *Sources of the Self: The Making of the Modern Identity* (Cambridge, Mass.: Harvard University Press, 1989).
6. http://dictionary.reference.com/browse/anecdotal (accessed 1 January 2010).
7. Scholars who come to mind in this connection are Jerrold Levinson and Noël Carroll.
8. For a detailed discussion of the various possible meanings of 'small', see the 'Introduction' to *The Cinema of Small Nations*, eds Mette Hjort and Duncan Petrie (Edinburgh: Edinburgh University Press, 2007).
9. See Jon Elster, 'Conventions, Creativity, Originality', in *Rules and Conventions: Literature, Philosophy, Social Theory*, ed. Mette Hjort (Baltimore: The Johns Hopkins University Press, 1992); Jon Elster, *Ulysses Unbound: Studies in Rationality, Precommitment, and Constraints* (Cambridge: Cambridge University Press, 2000). See also *Purity and Provocation*, eds Mette Hjort and Scott MacKenzie (London: BFI Publishing, 2003).
10. Seattle: University of Washington Press, 2010.
11. Greg Urban, *Metaculture: How Culture Moves through the World* (Minneapolis: University of Minnesota Press, 2001), p. 135. Cited in Mette Hjort, 'The Globalisation of Dogma', in *Purity and Provocation*, pp. 133–157 (135).
12. Meaghan Morris, *Identity Anecdotes: Translation and Media Culture* (London: Sage Publications, 2006), p. 5.
13. Aldo Geuna and Alessandro Muscio, 'The Governance of University Knowledge Transfer', *SEWPS* 173 (2008).
14. Ibid., 5.
15. See Mette Hjort on affinitive transnationalism, 'On the Plurality of Cinematic Transnationalism', in *World Cinemas, Transnational Perspectives*, eds Natasa Durovicova and Kathleen E. Newman (London: Routledge/American Film Institute Reader, 2009); 'Affinitive and Milieu-Building Transnationalism: The *Advance Party* Project', in *Cinema at the Periphery*, eds Dina Iordanova, David Martin-Jones and Belén Vidal (Detroit: Wayne State University Press, 2010).
16. Danish films had a 33 per cent share of the national market in 2008. DFI, *Facts & Figures 2009*, http://www.dfi.dk/English/Statistics/Facts-and-Figures.aspx (accessed 4 January 2010).
17. Richard Maxwell and Toby Miller, 'Film and the Environment: Risk Off-Screen', in *Film and Risk*, ed. Mette Hjort (forthcoming).
18. See Mette Hjort, *Lone Scherfig's Italian for Beginners* (Seattle: University of Washington Press, 2010).
19. Maxwell and Miller, note 5, which cites *MSNBC.com* (23 April 2008), msnbc.msn.com/id/24256817/ns/business-going_green.
20. For a comprehensive analysis of the National Film School of Denmark, see the PhD dissertation by Heidi Philipsen, entitled 'Dansk films nye bølge: Afsæt og aftryk fra Den Danske Filmskole', The University of Southern Denmark, 2004.

21. Mette Hjort, 'Interview with Poul Nesgaard', National Film School of Denmark, 14 January 2009.
22. http://filmskolen.dk/index.php?id=24.
23. For more on the Scriptwriting Department, see Eva Novrup Redvall, 'Teaching Screenwriting in a Time of Storytelling Blindness: The Meeting of the Auteur and the Screenwriting Tradition in Danish Film-Making', *Journal of Screenwriting* 1 (2010), 59–81.
24. See Mette Hjort, ed., *Dekalog 01: On The Five Obstructions* (London: Wallflower Press, 2008).
25. For a fuller, and more theoretically oriented discussion of 50/50, and also of New Danish Screen, see Mette Hjort, *Small Nation, Global Cinema: The New Danish Cinema* (Minneapolis: University of Minnesota Press, 2005).
26. For a discussion of New Danish Screen and the issue of risk, see Eva Novrup Redvall, 'Encouraging Artistic Risk-Taking through Film Policy: The Case of New Danish Screen', in *Film and Risk*, ed. Mette Hjort (forthcoming).

Chapter 1

Nikolaj Arcel

Born 1972. In 2001 Nikolaj Arcel graduated from the National Film School of Denmark as a director, and three years later he firmly established himself on the Danish film scene with the feature film debut *Kongekabale* (*King's Game*). At the time, Danish film was dominated by Dogma 95 and everyday dramas, and, with its political thriller plot and stylish look, *King's Game* was a welcome departure from the norm. The story is about a young political journalist who uncovers a conspiracy that could well involve the country's future Prime Minister. He gradually discovers that he is up against powerful forces, should he wish to print the truth, rather than simply doing as he is told by charismatic party leaders and spin doctors. The tightly constructed drama was a box-office hit, with over half a million tickets sold, and it won both a Robert and a Bodil award as best film of the year. The film established Arcel's profile, not only as a director, but also as a scriptwriter (along with his co-author Rasmus Heisterberg). Arcel wrote the script for Hans Fabian Wullenweber's bank heist children's film, *Klatretøsen* (*Catch that Girl*, 2002; remade as *Catch that Kid*, 2004) while still at the Film School, and in the wake of *King's Game* he has co-authored scripts with Heisterberg, for both his own films and those of others. Arcel's second feature film, as a director, was the large-scale adventure film, *De fortabte sjæles ø* (*Island of Lost Souls*, 2007), which is about a fourteen-year-old girl, who has to fight occult forces when her little brother is possessed by a spirit. The film set new standards for CGI in Danish film and was hailed as an impressive national take on a Spielberg-inspired family film. In 2009 Arcel started working on an American remake of *Island of Lost Souls*.

Left: Nikolaj Arcel. Photography: Jan Buus.

Feature films

2007 *De fortabte sjæles ø* (*Island of Lost Souls*)
2004 *Kongekabale* (*King's Game*)

Short films

2001 *Woyzecks sidste symfoni* (*Woyzeck's Last Symphony*, graduation film)

Scripts for feature films

2009 *Män som hatar kvinnor* (*The Girl with the Dragon Tattoo*, with Rasmus Heisterberg; dir. Niels Arden Oplev)
2008 *Rejsen til Saturn* (*Journey to Saturn*, with Rasmus Heisterberg; dirs Kresten Vestbjerg, Thorbjørn Christoffersen, Craig Frank)
2007 *De fortabte sjæles ø* (*Island of Lost Souls*, with Rasmus Heisterberg; dir. Nikolaj Arcel)
2007 *Fighter* (with Rasmus Heisterberg and Natasha Arthy; dir. Natasha Arthy)
2007 *Cecilie* (with Rasmus Heisterberg; dir. Hans Fabian Wullenweber)
2004 *King's Game* (with Rasmus Heisterberg; dir. Nikolaj Arcel)
2004 *Catch that Kid* (co-author of the script for the remake of *Catch that Girl*; dir. Bart Freundlich)
2002 *Klatretøsen* (*Catch that Girl*; dir. Hans Fabian Wullenweber)

Redvall: Many of the collaborative working relationships in Danish film are established at the National Film School of Denmark, where students often work in teams. You've worked with the cinematographer Rasmus Videbæk, the editor Mikkel E.G. Nielsen and the scriptwriter Rasmus Heisterberg, on a recurring basis. You met Heisterberg during an eight-month stay at the European Film College in Ebeltoft, before your time at the National Film School. What made you apply to the Film College?

Arcel: Most young people who dream about making films don't really dare to believe in their own dreams. The dream seems diffuse and directed at something that might be fun at some point in the future. When the Film College was established in the mid-1990s, I saw it as an opportunity to find out whether filmmaking was for me. Back then I didn't know that I'd want to become a director. I thought I wanted to be a writer. I'd written and written for five or six years, but decided I wanted to have a go at film. I knew that I was too young to apply to the Film School, and a stay at the Film College was perfect preparation for a subsequent application.

When you're young it's important to meet people who are likeminded. Before the Film College I didn't know anyone who wanted to make films. My friends wanted to create rock bands or do something entirely different. There was no context where I could express all my nerdy film interests, and the sense of community at the Film College was decisive in terms of my decision to pursue film. At the Film College, I started to believe that becoming a filmmaker might be possible, and I made some friends who also wanted to get into film. After the Film College we simply stayed together. Rasmus Videbæk got into the Film School straight away, and I worked as a runner and production assistant in different places and ended up at Nimbus Film. When the Film Workshop gave me financing for the short film *De vendte aldrig hjem* (*They Never Returned Home*), I was able to draw on Rasmus, who'd learnt a bit about shooting film, and together we made the film that I ended up applying to the Film School with.

Redvall: What does it mean to you as a director to have steady collaborators?

Arcel: It's extremely important to me. It's a comfort thing. Lately I've thought a lot about how my collaborators have the capacity to work with many different people. My cameraman and co-writer both work with other directors. I work with the same people every time, because as a director you only make one film every other year or so. I started thinking that I have to make sure I don't just automatically work with the same people, but my natural inclination is to go back to those same people. If you've produced something good together, you'll want to work together again. There's a sense of security there, but there's also the rapidity with which you can work. Because of the mutual understanding you don't have to get to know people from scratch. Everybody knows who I am and what I want from them. I know what their abilities are, and I also know their limitations. So we're able to make good use of each other. The more you work together, the more you're able to make creative use of each other, provided you keep challenging each other and yourself.

Redvall: You went to the film school in 1998–2001 when Dogma films like *Festen* (*The Celebration*; dir. Thomas Vinterberg, 1998), *Idioterne* (*The Idiots*; dir. Lars von Trier, 1998) and *Italiensk for begyndere* (*Italian for Beginners*; dir. Lone Scherfig, 2000) were opening the world's eyes to Danish film. Did the success of the Dogma films influence your time at the Film School, and what was your perception of Dogma 95 as a student?

Arcel: At first I thought Dogma 95 sounded like a really bad idea. I'd grown up watching films based on classical Hollywood storytelling and style, and that's what I dreamed of producing myself. I wanted to challenge the cinematic language of Danish film, because I felt Danes were hopelessly behind when it came not only to narrative technique, but also to visual and sound imagery. Then the Dogma films came along and made it fashionable to trash everything, and to film cheaply and simply; to concentrate on the story rather than the visuals. In spite of myself

I started to become quite fascinated by this. I think it was my salvation, in a way, that the Dogma films came along, because I became intrigued by that emphasis on the story, and I moved away from this idea that everything should be about the visuals, and about film form.

Redvall: While you were at the school the Scriptwriting Department really took off. Mogens Rukov entered the spotlight, as co-writer on *The Celebration*, and his thoughts about the 'natural story', which were at the core of his dramaturgy classes, became well known in the industry. What's your take on the role of scriptwriting at the school?

Arcel: The Scriptwriting Department is the secret to the Film School's success. At film school festivals around the world people are surprised, again and again, by how good the Danish films are. You don't even need to look at the films with nationalist glasses to see this, because there's this strong focus on the story. I think that many other film schools focus on the element of personal expression, and some form of artistic ambition aimed at producing something different. It may be true that the National Film School of Denmark streamlines the students a bit, but the school's emphasis on telling basic, classic stories is also what makes the films worth seeing. The Scriptwriting Department emphasizes this, but it also attaches a lot of importance to the director's ability to tell stories. There are times when this creates a certain amount of conflict with the Scriptwriting Department, but I do think it's important. You can't be a director if you can't write a story. If you can't come up with a story then why are you a filmmaker? In that case you might as well produce music videos. The Film School is more in the business of training storytellers than visual artists.

Redvall: The auteur concept has been a central feature of European film. What are your thoughts on the auteur concept, and how did that thinking fit with dominant trends at the Film School?

Arcel: The Film School is very much dominated by directors. I think that the Film School swears by the auteur concept, because they've always put the director in the high seat. In the end the director always decides which film will get made, but personally I don't believe in the auteur theory. And that's in spite of my dual role as both scriptwriter and director. Making a film is such an amazingly slow and complex process, and there are so many people involved. If you don't have the right cameraman, or the right consultant, who says the right thing at the right time, then what do you have? Then you have nothing. There are very few genuine auteurs. You'd have to write, direct, shoot and edit the film. And you'd almost have to play all the parts. Then you'd be an auteur! Everything else is based on collaboration. I suppose you could say that, from an artistic point of view, I don't believe in the auteur process. But I do believe in the idea of the director as the commander in chief, as the boss who requires an answer to every possible question. There has to be someone in charge, and that person has to lay down what needs to be done every single day. But this is no different from what the boss of a large corporation does, and you'd never call that person an auteur. You'd just say that he or she is a good leader.

Redvall: In relation to collaboration, there's talk in the Danish film milieu of a fertile openness, with film practitioners drawing on each other in the process of making their films. How much do you draw on other Danish directors in your work?

Arcel: In my case there are essentially three people – Thomas Vinterberg, Lars von Trier and Per Fly – whom I've drawn on off and on, and who might also draw on me. I think you have to be careful not to go too far with this. You don't necessarily respect everybody, and not everyone understands the ideas you're working with. Depending on the nature of the project, I draw on different people. At the moment I'm working on a historical film about Queen Caroline Mathilde [1751–1775], and in this case von Trier is perfect because the film is a melodrama about a princess who sacrifices herself! But we're incredibly tough with each other. Absolutely ruthless. And there aren't a lot of people who dare to be ruthless with you once you've reached a certain level of achievement. Suddenly there's almost too much respect, and this sense that you probably have all the answers yourself. That's when you need to draw on someone else, preferably someone who's better than you are, so that there's no beating around the bush.

Redvall: You won a series of prizes for your graduation film *Woyzeck's Last Symphony*, and graduated from the Film School at a time when Danish film was doing well. How did you experience the transition from being a student to working in the industry?

Arcel: My graduation film was well received, but I had a really bad time making it and was personally very disappointed and insecure about it all. Making it was incredibly stressful, far worse than my first feature film actually. I so wanted to make a really good film, and to prove how amazing I was. Today I can't stand to watch my graduation film. It is a mishmash of all sorts of genres and the acting is all over the place. I can see what I was trying to prove to the world; namely, that I could do anything. And that's just not possible. You might be able to do everything, but not in one film. After that experience I promised myself that the first thing I'd do after film school would be to make a film that was properly unified. A straight-up genre film. It took me ages to figure out what kind of genre film I wanted to make. I spent an entire year just sitting there, sweating, and starting up projects, none of which ever went anywhere. Not until *King's Game*...

Redvall: Before writing *King's Game* with Rasmus Heisterberg you wrote the script for *Catch that Girl* on your own, and Hans Fabian Wullenweber directed this as his first feature film. It's a straight-up genre film, with a bank heist plot involving children. Why didn't you direct it yourself?

Arcel: *Catch that Girl* was commissioned work that came my way while I was at the Film School. I was contacted by Nimbus Film. As I said, I used to work for them as a runner, and so on. They asked me whether I'd be interested in writing a script for a new director. The story was supposed to be about some children who pulled off a bank robbery. That's all they'd come up with, so I was basically given a free hand. And I felt I was exactly the right person for this, because here I was thinking about making really good genre films and action movies in Danish. I put a lot of energy into trying to think the plot through, and into making all the strands come together in a subtle and amusing way. I don't think there's been a lot of that in Danish film. *Catch that Girl* is still my favourite script today because it has it all: emotions, humour, thrills and funny little ideas and surprises. And I think Hans Fabian did a wonderful job of directing the film, and the children in it. That was lucky for me. The film was a success, which meant that I'd written the script for a really well-received film by the time I got out of film school. That made it a lot easier for me to move on after film school, as compared with the rest of my cohort. When I showed up at the Danish Film Institute with an idea, I was the guy who'd written *Catch that Girl*.

Redvall: There's a more or less established sequence in Danish film, where you start out by going to film school, then you make shorter films or do some TV work, before making a first feature film. The script for *Catch that Girl* clearly helped you, but was it also your intention to go straight from film school to feature filmmaking?

Arcel: Yes, I refused to make a short film, even though a lot of people said 'Make a short film, make a short film.' I said 'No, because I don't want to.' I'd written this script that had been produced as a feature film, so why should I make a short film? I didn't grow up with short films. I don't know how to make short films. I've grown up with 90-minute stories, and so I'm better at making films that length. I'm really glad I stuck to my guns back then. I'm glad I waited until I found the right feature film, even though it was a frustrating time. I know a lot of people who have directed a short film, or some episodes of a TV series, because they think that's the way forward. But it hasn't helped them in any way. They haven't spent any time figuring out ideas for feature films, and people see them as short film directors or TV directors. You're quickly given a label. It pays to wait for the right thing. It might sound like a cliché, but you have to listen to yourself, and you have to think about what *you* like, instead of thinking in terms of steps towards the real goal, or in terms of what other people might think you should do. Right now the refrain is: 'First you make a film that costs 2 million DKK, then you make one that costs 7 million, and then you…' No, no. If you're really good at making films that cost 18 million DKK, if you really have what it takes, then that's what you should be doing, instead of a bunch of things you can't be proud of.

Redvall: The film you waited for was, of course, *King's Game*, which would become one of the most important first features in recent Danish film history, not least because it was a political thriller and thus drew on genre conventions for which there is no real tradition in Danish film. How did you end up settling on precisely this story for your first feature film?

Søren Pilmark as the top politician Erik Dreier in the centre of the ruthless power struggle in *Kongekabale* (*King's Game*). Photography: Per Arnesen.

Arcel: My co-writer, Rasmus Heisterberg, and I had long talked about how much fun it would be to make a political thriller, precisely because there weren't any such films in Danish. We really wanted to do something different. I wanted my first feature film as a director to be something genuinely new. The idea, of course, was to create ripples throughout the entire Danish film industry! We tried to come up with some ideas, but we weren't able to think of anything that worked because we didn't actually know much about what was going on in Danish politics. Then my producer, Meta Foldager, gave us the book *King's Game* (*Kongekabale*, 2000) by former parliamentary Press Officer Niels Krause Kjær. It was about a disputed chairmanship, and that then became the framework for the film we ended up writing. At first the material seemed a bit boring for a film, but the plot was solid enough, and then we started talking: 'What if we make him young? What if the chairman is a woman? What if we introduce a new character, who's a crazy, rebellious journalist?' We liked the basic idea of a journalist re-connecting with his idealism, on account of a very unscrupulous man who's about to become Prime Minister. And then we added all kinds of things. When we started doing our research, we became absolutely fascinated by it all. We had enough material for five feature films, and that was really wonderful because then it's just a matter of extracting what's essential, while including as many details as possible.

Redvall: You wrote the scripts for both of your feature films together with Rasmus Heisterberg. But you and Rasmus have also written scripts together for other directors. How do you experience that mix of being a director and part of a scriptwriting team for others?

Arcel: I love writing scripts. Rasmus and I are really enjoying our collaborative work these days. We recently wrote the story for the animated film *Rejsen til Saturn* (*Journey to Saturn*), and we just had so much fun. At the same time it's incredibly liberating to be involved in writing something you don't actually have to realize yourself. You're able to release a lot of creative energy without having to think: 'Oh no, how am I going to do all this?' And seen from a purely practical angle, I don't have to make commercials, which is something I'd hate to have to do. Between films I'm able to support myself by writing scripts for others. Collaboration in connection with the writing process is somewhat rare in Denmark. I think it's important to collaborate in this way only if you really want to, and then you have to work out some really clear agreements regarding how the royalties and so on are to be shared. Nobody is forcing Rasmus and me to work together. We work together because we want to, and we've come up with this super socialistic agreement to the effect that we share everything absolutely equally, regardless of who does the most work. You have to respect each other and acknowledge each other properly. I just had a weird experience with an American project, where I'd pitched an idea and an American writer was hired to do the writing. We emailed back and forth about the story, which I came up with. In fact, I wrote ten pages' worth of very precise notes detailing my understanding of the story. Then he wrote it up in a way that could be read by others, and just put his own name on it. I phoned him and said: 'I'm sorry, shouldn't my name be on there too?' And the answer was: 'No, I'm the writer.' That hit home.

Redvall: The carefully composed visual style of *King's Game* was a clear departure from what was current at the time, namely Dogma films and everyday realism. On the DVD edition of the film you talk about how some of the images in the film are directly inspired by the American film director Michael Mann, among others. How did you approach the issue of visual style in your first feature?

Arcel: Our starting point was to see the story as an adventure. In a sense the milieu is actually quite realistic, but we didn't want Christiansborg [the site of the Danish parliament] to look like the real Christiansborg. We wanted to create a mythological Christiansborg, full of small, dark corners, in contrast to reality's large, light and attractive offices with Arne Jacobsen furniture. We wanted to show the workings of old-style power politics, and the production design unit was decisive in terms of the film's visual style. They steered us towards a look that was dark, blueish and cool. And apart from that we just wanted to make a beautiful film. The film really didn't match a hand-held camera style. Because there's so much talking in the film, it really needed to have a certain beauty for it even to be interesting to watch. In many ways the film signalled the emergence of a new generation, not that I want to blow my own horn. That my film came first is a mere coincidence, but at this point it's clear that it was the beginning of a trend. There's a new generation now that's interested in thinking about film in very visual terms.

Redvall: *King's Game* got good reviews and also did well at the box office. You recently commented on how you feel about film reviews as a director, and you gave critics ten pieces of advice. The starting point was how you experienced the expectations of both the audience and the critics after the success of *King's Game*. As a director, how much do you think about what others expect from you?

Arcel: I think it's all a bit of a weird game, the reviews and the cultural criticism. After *King's Game* I was very preoccupied with how I'd won awards and received good reviews. Things were going rather well, and now I had to find a way of maintaining that as the status quo. You can become very focused on this idea that you're the 'bright new light in Danish film', and that's the most suffocating thing that can happen to an artist. It happened to Thomas Vinterberg after *The Celebration*, and it happened to me a little bit too. Making my second film was an amazing experience, but I was ultimately disappointed with the story, as compared with the first film. The contrast is between making a film with your head and your heart, and with enormous motivation, and then just making a popcorn film mostly just for fun. I knew I'd taken that rollercoaster ride, and that I'd made a film that was more or less trivial, but I still wanted the reviewers to think I was brilliant. Suddenly the coin dropped and I thought 'The road to happiness is to make good films and to cut the crap.' I decided to write an article about the joys and disappointments that come with filmmaking as a way of freeing up my own energy, and as a way of marking my decision from then on to make films because I think filmmaking is the most important thing in the world, and not because I want success, and not because I want to please other people. I have this persistent dream about making a film in every genre before I die, and I intend to hold onto it! Sometimes people will like what you come up with, sometimes they won't.

Redvall: *Island of Lost Souls* is a large-scale adventure film with visual and narrative elements that are reminiscent of Hollywood films. As a result the film was compared to American films, and ended up competing on their terms, instead of being discussed on its merits as a Danish film. What's your view on making a very American film in Danish?

Arcel: I don't think I thought about that issue. Thinking about this in retrospect, I think that it's true that *Island of Lost Souls* competes more with American films than with Danish ones, and I'd probably have made it differently had I known what I know now after having made the film. It would have been really fun to make an adventure film with an incredibly strong Danish identity. That was actually what the script for *Catch that Girl* was like, whereas *Island of Lost Souls* is really an American film.

Redvall: How could the film have been given a clearer Danish identity? The language and milieu point clearly to Denmark.

Arcel: It's strange what makes the difference. It's got something to do with the nature of the risks you're willing to take, and with the film's style. It's got something to do with taking things just a little bit further. *Island of Lost Souls* is very neat and harmless in terms of its characterization. *Catch that Girl*, on the other hand, is about a girl whose father is dying, and *that*'s why she robs a bank. At the same time she also has to struggle with being in love, with a mother who's completely overworked, and with a whole slew of everyday problems. In Denmark, and Europe more generally, we're good at anchoring the story in strong, nuanced characters, and in a mix of everyday drama and genre conventions.

Redvall: Steven Spielberg was mentioned a fair bit in connection with *Island of Lost Souls*, and you've talked about how much you like his films. Would you say the film is influenced by Spielberg?

Arcel: I see nothing but Spielberg in that film. Again, that's part of the lesson from making that film. I've never tried to hide the fact that I'm a huge Spielberg fan. He's the reason why I'm making films in the first place, and his films always hit home with me, visually as well as on a sort of primal, emotional level. The storytelling is almost always sublime. Whether or not the film is good, there's just always something to his way of telling the story, to his way of doing things. With a film like *Island of Lost Souls* I couldn't help but look to the master. That entire film is a sort of declaration of love that acknowledges my childhood fascination with

Lars Mikkelsen as the evil Necromancer in *De fortabte sjæles ø* (*Island of Lost Souls*). Photography: Rasmus Videbæk.

Spielberg. So the film took me back to my childhood, but it also took me away from my Danish identity. After that film I could feel that I was a bit tired of being compared to Spielberg, and so I'm not quite so vocal about my admiration for him. But I've always liked to insist on the value of films like *E.T.* (1982), because in Denmark those films are seen as not particularly refined. When I was asked what kind of films I wanted to make, during the final interview for the Film School, I said: '*Jaws* (1975), *Raiders of the Lost Ark* (1981)'. What they mostly heard back then was 'films like Godard's'. Daring to defend those films became my brand, in a way, but I'm not so interested in that any more.

Redvall: After *Island of Lost Souls* you went to Hollywood for three months, to look into the possibility of making films there. You subsequently reported on your 60 meetings over there, and recounted how you left the place disillusioned. How would you sum up your experiences in Hollywood?

Arcel: My trip to Hollywood was really an eye opener, because I've always dreamed about making films there, and I've had all these ideas about what it was like. But I came back with a sense of really liking Denmark. It wasn't that I was disappointed, because I actually took three interesting projects home with me, which I'm still working on, and I also met some very nice people. But the attitude towards making films, and the entire game that's involved, made me feel that it's really hard to make good films in that context. What you have is this system, with thousands of people, all of whom have a say, and you end up waiting and waiting. It's all so unbearably slow, because everything's done through committees. If you have an idea, it's ground through the system until it comes out as a pre-packaged McDonald's project. So the cliché is true. There are plenty of people with good intentions, but boy, it's difficult to get anything done. My Hollywood dream used to be big and shiny, but now it's more like 'Yes, maybe, perhaps someday.' By being over there I learnt just how wonderful it is to make films in Europe.

Redvall: What is it that's particularly favourable about the European context?

Arcel: In the States they're constantly talking about target groups. I went to 60 meetings and there was not one meeting where they didn't talk about having to remember the thirteen year olds, because the thirteen year olds are important. When you pitched an idea, the first question was 'Is it PG or PG13?' It's not about the story. And things have to be labelled right away. If you say something, people react the way the characters in *The Player* (dir. Robert Altman, 1992) do; 'Oh, I see, it's *American Pie* meets *Bad*.' People also start to talk about actors very quickly. Before you're half way through your presentation, someone has already said 'That's Tobey Maguire, that one!' Because this is how they think. They've been forced to think this way, because it's virtually impossible to make a film, and so everyone has to be really good at selling their idea. People are good at selling shit like it was the best project in the world, and everyone's used to it. The producers have ten meetings every day where people scream and shout and pitch and sell. I couldn't handle it. I showed up and behaved in a typically Danish way. I was quite reserved and would say things like 'Maybe; that might be a good idea.' People became suspicious when I didn't immediately leap out of my chair and scream about how fantastic everything was. They're just not used to discussing things. They think that if you're not busy selling your project then you must be having doubts about it, and I just couldn't stand that at all. I was happy to get back to Denmark, and to be able to talk about film on a sensible level, because you also have to be able to be critical of yourself, otherwise you're courting disaster. I actually don't understand how they manage to make any films over there. For every inch of progress that's made on my projects over there, there are five months when nothing happens, because we just need to hear from someone or other. It takes ten times longer than it does here. But I have nonetheless agreed to do a remake of *Island of Lost Souls*, and I am still looking forward to that.

Chapter 2

Christoffer Boe

Christoffer Boe. Photography: Jan Buus.

Born 1974. After studying film at the University of Copenhagen, Boe was admitted to the director's stream at the National Film School of Denmark, graduating in 2001. With a group of his fellow students – cinematographer Manuel Alberto Claro, editor Mikkel E.G. Nielsen, sound designer Morten Green and producer Tine Grew Pfeiffer – he created the production team Mr Boe & Co. Mr Boe & Co. made an experimental trilogy of short films on love, obsession and jealousy – *Obsession* (1999), *Virginity* (2000) and the award-winning graduation film *Anxiety* (2001). With the same team, Boe took the love theme further in his aesthetically refined, meta-filmic first feature film, *Reconstruction* (2003), which gave him an international breakthrough and was awarded a number of prizes, among them the Caméra d'or prize at the Cannes film festival in 2003.

In the romantic science fiction film *Allegro* (2005) – about a world famous pianist whose memories about the woman he loved have been contained in a physical space, the so-called 'Zone' in the centre of Copenhagen – Boe continued his cinematic investigation of love, identity, fiction, time and space, once again expressed in a visual language both almost supernaturally beautiful and sensuously concrete. *Offscreen* (2006) – about an actor obsessed with the desire to film himself and his surroundings – explored the relationship between fiction and reality in a radically new way. More specifically, the actors played fictive versions of themselves, and the camera was placed consistently in the hands of the main actor, Nicolas Bro. *Offscreen* was awarded a number of both national and international prizes.

Alongside some of the contemporary international film scene's most significant directors, Boe also contributed to the two omnibus films *Visions of Europe* (2004) – Boe's contribution, *Europe Does Not Exist*, is about a man who cannot or will not come to terms with the English pronunciation of 'Europe' – and *Paris, je t'aime* (*Paris, I Love You*, 2006). As the latter ended up too long, Boe's contribution about the 15th arrondissement was not included in the final film, however.

For television he has made both the philosophical crazy comedy series *Kissmeyer Basic* (2001), about a man who loses his identity, and a documentary portrait of the controversial Danish financial tycoon Klaus Riskær Pedersen, who had just been sentenced to seven years in prison for fraud. Using a strongly self-reflexive approach, *Riskær – Avantgardekapitalisten* ('Riskær – The Avant Garde Capitalist', 2008) examines the relationship between creative business methods and art.

In 2003, Boe and Tine Grew Pfeiffer created the production company Alphaville Pictures Copenhagen.

Feature films

2010 *Alting bliver godt igen* (*Everything Will Be Fine*)
2006 *Offscreen*
2005 *Allegro*
2003 *Reconstruction*

Short films

2004 *Europe Does Not Exist* (contribution to the omnibus film *Visions of Europe*)
2001 *Hr. Boe & Co.'s Anxiety* (graduation film)
2000 *Virginity*
1999 *Obsession*

Television

2008 *Riskær – Avantgardekapitalisten* (documentary) ('Riskær – The Avant Garde Capitalist')
2001 *Kissmeyer Basic* (comedy series, six episodes)

Jørholt: Looking back, what was the most important aspect of your four years in film school?

Boe: After Film Studies at the University of Copenhagen, where studying meant studying on your own, I didn't expect the Film School to teach me anything. What mattered more than anything was that I was given access to this huge toy box with equipment. In that sense, my time at the Film School was very happy. I entered the world of film without any technical experience. I knew nothing, but of course I'd seen a lot of films and I generally liked film. The school gave me four years of freedom to play with the equipment, four years to discover my own mode of expression, all without the pressure of having to sell my stuff or please anybody else.

Film school was a place both for learning and for playing, and I still insist on the play dimension of filmmaking. To me, all good films – even the serious ones – have this playful attitude towards the medium. A playful attitude is a precondition for personal films. Besides, I learnt the danger of over-planning. I love to make precise films, but in film school we were sometimes given two months to make just one minute of film, and the result was usually brooding, contrived and rigid. You have to make room for spontaneity in your hopefully grand visions.

But filmmaking is also a collective process, and meeting kindred spirits was fantastic. I met some people with whom I still work. From the outset, we called ourselves Mr Boe & Co., and today I run a production company with Tine Pfeiffer: Alphaville Pictures Copenhagen. The small community we established then is still of tremendous importance to me today. We are like a small guerrilla army on our own secret mission – sometimes, unfortunately, secret even to ourselves. But that too is an important dimension of filmmaking. Filmmaking should be entertaining but also a journey of discovery.

It was, of course, also of vital importance to have a teacher as inspiring as Mogens Rukov. He has an amazing eye for what makes a film good. Mogens is a good man to have as the ideal spectator – it's all about making Mogens happy!

So, a lot of things happened to me during my four years in that state-funded institution. When I started at the school I had some film interests and some methods, and these changed radically during my time there. By the time I graduated, I was making films that were very different from the films I thought I'd be making when I first entered the school.

Jørholt: And yet, there seems to be a high degree of continuity from your film school productions to *Reconstruction*.

Boe: I'd ended up in a very contrived Godard/Tarkovsky universe, but then we made a film in just one weekend. We got hold of a camera, a couple of tapes, some sound equipment and found ourselves an editing room. With Morten [Green] as sound designer and Manuel [Claro] as cinematographer, we made *Obsession*, which Mikkel E.G. [Nielsen] edited. That process was immensely liberating, because I realized that if you have the right idea you can make a twenty-minute film with just two days of shooting. And because of that realization, I embarked on a somewhat new path that resulted in my mid-programme film, *Virginity*, and my graduation film, *Anxiety*. Halfway through film school I found something that could be my own cinematic language, a way of expressing myself that I could believe in.

Jørholt: But at the same time you continued to let yourself be inspired by the great masters. *Reconstruction*, for instance, seems to be quite indebted to Alain Resnais' *L'année dernière à Marienbad* (*Last Year in Marienbad*, 1961).

Boe: Given that *Last Year in Marienbad* is *the* modern film that everybody who's trying to be modernist somehow refers to, that's perhaps not so surprising. The overall meta-fictional aspect is very much inspired by Resnais, but the physical approach to life and the film's scenes were more inspired by Godard and his both loving and disrespectful, rock'n'roll-like approach to filmmaking. We were trying very hard to get at a certain youthful pulse, while we were still young.

Jørholt: Film scholars have discussed especially *Reconstruction* in terms of the theories of French intellectuals such as Gilles Deleuze, Michel de Certeau and Marc Augé. Do you consider yourself an intellectual director?

Boe: I think of the audience as consisting of mature interlocutors, and I do my best not to talk down to the people who see my films. But I consider myself to be a very emotional director. I'm interested in emotional mechanisms, and I may approach the depiction of emotions in an intellectual way, through the mechanical medium of film. But it's my hope that my detached approach will strengthen the emotional aspects of my films. Emotions tend to get stronger if you distance yourself a bit from them.

Reconstruction wasn't made with Deleuze and Guattari's *Mille plateaux* (*A Thousand Plateaus*) in mind. I guess my view of the world is inspired to a significant extent by literary theorists like Stanley Fish, and by his thoughts about what constitutes social reality. How do we create an identity? Who are we? How did we become what we are? And who do we ourselves think we are? My films address how we get lost in our own almost labyrinthine projections. To me those questions identify a subject matter that is basically very emotional. What or whom do we fall in love with? And how do we try to possess that person or thing?

Jørholt: All your films seem to be about the relationship between chaos and control, aesthetically as well as thematically. In *Reconstruction* this is quite graphically expressed through the contrast between the well-ordered, Google map-like views of the city and the emotional chaos on street level.

Boe: Actually, Google maps hadn't yet been invented at the time, but basically, the film plays with the idea that fiction is an attempt to create order or meaning out of chaos. The point is quite banal, really: there are no meanings other than the ones we ourselves create by means of various kinds of fictions. My characters try to create a story for themselves, a story in which they feel comfortable, but the story encounters resistance from reality.

Jørholt: Your films are very focused on the urban, on cityscapes. Never before had Copenhagen been represented the way you represent the city in both *Reconstruction* and *Allegro*.

Boe: I think my interest in the city is closely related to my general interest in human relations. To me, the city is a significant player in modern life. On a very tangible level, the city is full of memories of life that's been lived. The city is the place where we create our stories, and it contributes actively to the experience we have of our own lives. There are also some specific economic considerations: we make low-budget films, and we try to make them look more significant by using the city as a player who participates at no cost. The city provides an easy way of enhancing the production value of our films. Besides, I think Copenhagen is a very beautiful city. So, the answer to your question involves a combination of subject matter, practical issues and personal tastes.

Jørholt: Prior to *Reconstruction*, in 2002, you made the film *Prediction*, which is set in no fewer than four European cities: Copenhagen, Stockholm, Paris and Warsaw. Why was *Prediction* never released?

Boe: We'd received funding for writing a script but instead of writing we simply shot the film. Afterwards, we ran into some trouble with rights that needed clearing,

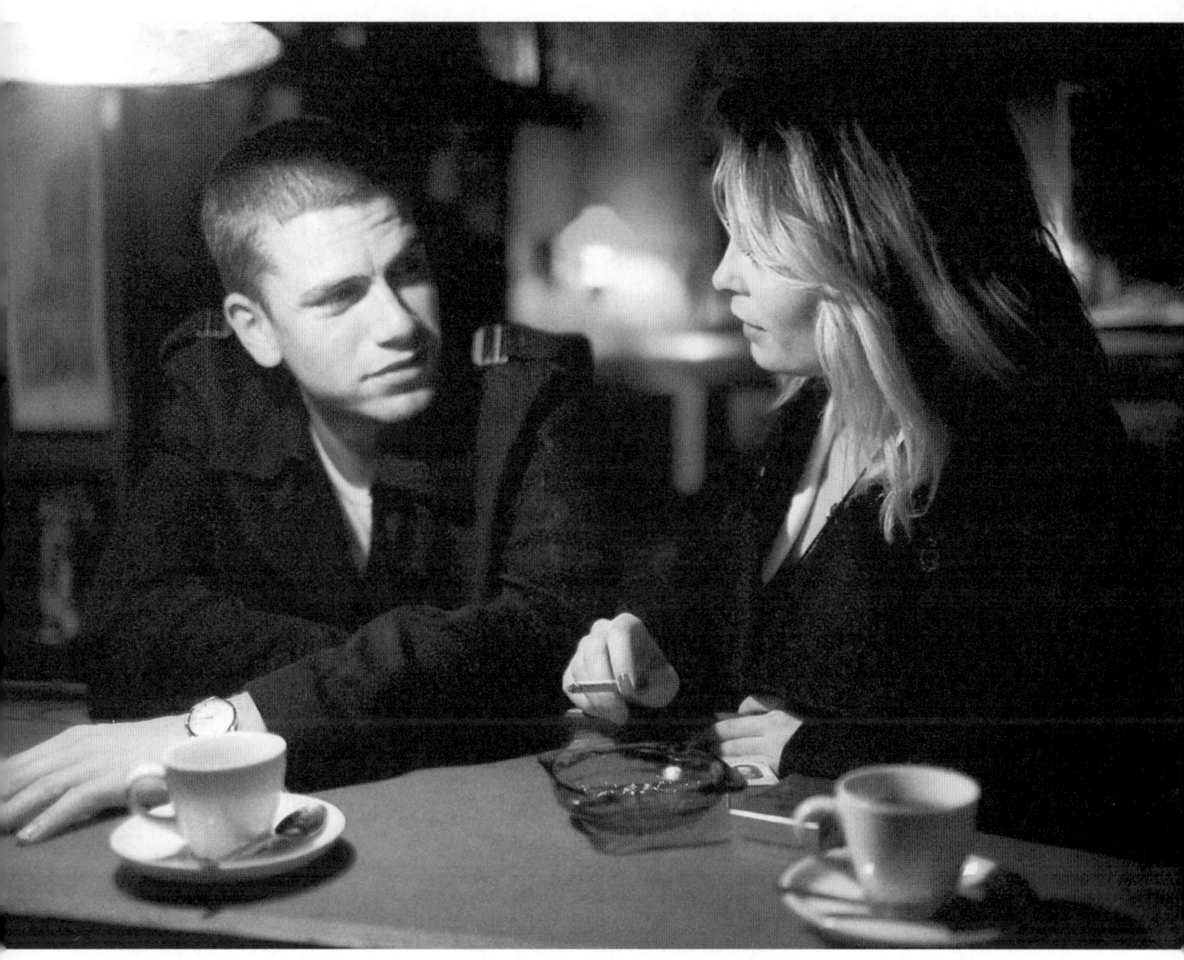

Nikolaj Lie Kaas and Maria Bonnevie in *Reconstruction*. Photography: Linn Sandholm.

and all of a sudden huge resources were needed to finish the film. At this point the market had changed radically, which made things very difficult for a small film like *Prediction*. I still hope to see it released one day, though. I think of it as a beautiful handicapped child that I'm very fond of. It's a film in which Denmark's greatest young actor, Nicolas Bro, who is also the largest, keeps running from beginning to end. When he finally sits down, it's because he's dead.

Jørholt: Prior to *Reconstruction*, you also made the comedy series *Kissmeyer Basic* with some of Denmark's most cherished standup comedians like Mikael Wulff, Frank Hvam and Casper Christensen, and with Anders Morgenthaler as your graphic artist. The comedy format may seem far removed from your feature films, but the story about a man who loses everything and has to create his own story, is very much you.

Boe: I've always cherished comedy, especially Woody Allen, the Marx Brothers and traditional Jewish humour. And yes, even though *Kissmeyer Basic* is comedy, it does explore some of my recurring themes: if everything is taken from you, who are you? How will you become somebody again? Or who will you become from here on in? I'm working with the romantic concept of ruins, the beauty of decay, but also with the idea that disaster holds its own productivity. Personal disaster is, of course, a kind of loss of identity, but it can be used constructively, in that it invites you to make new choices in life, to write some new life scripts now that the old one has come to an end. Personal disaster entails a kind of liberation, although this might not be immediately evident when you're in the midst of it all. You can imagine that I'm of little use to my friends when they're going through difficult times! I tend to marvel at all the possibilities that are suddenly available to them!

Jørholt: Mikael Wulff also worked on the script for *Allegro*.

Boe: Yes, I thought it might be fun to make use of his sparkling and transgressive wit, as well as his oblique way with words. Besides, we both have a soft spot for the old Danish comedies. So *Allegro* actually started out as much more of a traditional comedy, but then it gradually moved closer and closer to my own universe.

Jørholt: In *Allegro* one notices references or *homages* to Tarkovsky, Cocteau, Kubrick, Greenaway and Murnau, among others.

Boe: Yes, but I hope the audience will not see the film simply as a sort of catalogue of references. Leos Carax, who is one of the great heroes of my youth, once said that he didn't mind people paying attention to all the references, as long as they understood that if he let his characters eat a croissant, it wasn't necessarily meant as an homage to his baker. You're simply immersed in a world from which you draw inspiration. In my world there are lots and lots of films, but hopefully this context is not itself a precondition for engaging with *Allegro*. When I set out to make *Allegro*, I saw it as an encounter between Tarkovsky's *Stalker* (1979) and Minnelli's *Gigi* (1958). Would I be able to make the joyfulness of *Gigi* and the melancholy sci-fi tristesse of *Stalker* meet? That was the question.

Jørholt: *Offscreen* presents yet another character who tries to create order in his life, or to control his surroundings, this time by means of a camera. Do you see filmmaking as a way of staging yourself and your surroundings?

Boe: In a way, it's always a matter of staging your own life when you make films. The universe of the film can suddenly become as present as your everyday universe. You may, for instance, bring characters, gadgets and things from your own reality into the film, but the reverse may also occur. You take something from the set, and suddenly it's sitting there in your own apartment.

In real life, we organize the coincidences of our lives into a larger narrative, in order to give ourselves a direction and so as to confer meaning on chaos. I wish to draw attention to these real-life narrational processes and to incorporate them into the universe of my films.

All good fiction is engaged in a constant redefining of the borders between fiction and reality. To me it's essential to play with these borders in my film work. That's of course also the reason why Nicolas Bro and the rest of the actors in *Offscreen* are playing fictive versions of themselves.

Jørholt: Filmmaking is also about finding funding, meeting budgets, production schedules, etc. How do you feel about this aspect of filmmaking?

Boe: To me, the production aspect is very much part of the creative process. That's the only way of seeing it. Filmmaking involves a huge apparatus; it's not something you can do at home at your desk. Inasmuch as film is part of a mass culture, there are various requirements that have to be met. If you do not see that part of it as a challenge, a wall against which you can play ball, then it becomes daunting, and you turn into a person nurturing a hopeless vision of grand art that can't be realized. Godard once said, 'Show me a budget, and I will give you a script.' The money defines how we play the game. In the case of *Offscreen*, it was simply conceived with the very limited means that were at our disposal in mind. One of the things we could play around with was the shooting itself. Instead of shooting a film in six weeks we chose another production form and shot the film over an entire year. In that way, time became a player in its own right, a marker of the seasons, for example. And we could show changes in the protagonist's weight and in the length of his hair.

Playing with the possibilities and constraints inherent in the requirements that come with the money is an absolutely essential part of filmmaking. Big budgets do not necessarily make for better films. I see limited funding as a reality check, a particular kind of productive rule of the game. Almost all art is based on some sort of rules. In some cases rules that you define yourself, as in Dogma, and in other cases rules that have been forced on you from the outside. It's all about what you can achieve in a very specific field of operation, with a set of very specific rules. A bit like football: if you could just run away with the ball and decide that the goal was wherever you'd like it to be, it would no longer be football.

Jørholt: *Reconstruction* was produced within the framework of Nordisk Film's Director's Cut programme which, among other things, tried to simplify the road from idea to finished film. Do you find the way through the ordinary Danish support system long?

Boe: It takes many sources of funding to make a film, and the conditions change all the time. The most recent four year Media Policy Accord with the film sector increased the influence that the television stations have on Danish film. The result is that we're now in a situation where, in my experience, you can get a go ahead from the Danish Film Institute fairly quickly, but still find yourself looking for two-thirds of the funding. And you're supposed to get the rest from the television stations, and others. In the last few years, we've watched the National Broadcasting Corporation run out of money. For instance, when I presented the script for my new film to them, they'd spent every penny they had four weeks earlier: there was simply no more money left. And I had to wait nine months until there was money again. I don't see this kind of constraint as being in any way creative. But I spent the time polishing the script which, hopefully, improved as a result of the delay. But right now the funding system is a bit wobbly. I think everyone would agree with me on that point.

The National Broadcasting Corporation isn't even happy with the role it's been given, which is essentially that of a stop mechanism that controls the fate of Danish feature films. Indeed, it's not unusual for projects that received funding from the DFI to die when they reach the television stations, where the primary concern is ratings.

Jørholt: What does it mean to you to have your own production company?

Boe: A lot of extra work but of course also the freedom to decide. I'm very much in favour of making the 'whole package' a form of personal expression, from the theme and look of the film itself to the poster and commentary track on the DVD. Everything connected to the film should express that we've done our best. People may not like the final product but at least they should recognize that we've really done our utmost to create some kind of expressive whole. Having my own company gives me more control over the entire process.

Jørholt: It's been a number of years since *Offscreen*. What have you been doing in the meantime, other than working on the script for your next film?

Boe: All the time and energy I'd put into placing the camera in my earlier films, and all the ethical considerations that went into that process, well I let go of all that with *Offscreen*. In *Offscreen* I took the camera into the fiction by giving it to the actors, and by doing so I removed a burden from my own shoulders. So I've spent time redefining my role, or defining where I'd like to go now. I've writtten about 50 scripts, more or less based on the same story but in many different shadings, in order to clarify for myself what I'm trying to achieve. In addition to that, I've made a documentary, *The Avant Garde Capitalist*, about the financial wizard Klaus

Nicolas Bro playing Nicolas Bro obsessed with a video camera borrowed from Christoffer Boe in *Offscreen*. Photography: Nicolas Bro.

Riskær Pedersen. I've taken up some consultancy work, and our small company has produced some films by others. All in all, I've been able to make a living, but from a financial point of view it's also about time I made another feature film.

Jørholt: *The Avant Garde Capitalist* is a portrait of Klaus Riskær Pedersen who has been sentenced to prison for his creative business methods, but you portray him as a kind of artist. Can business be art?

Boe: Riskær plays with other people's money, which raises some moral issues, but I disagree with the divide people from my world often establish between artists on the one hand and business people on the other. Business people are not always mere merchants who are only in it for the buck. To me, there are many similarities between art and business, and it interested me to investigate what we have in common when it comes to creativity, getting ideas and bringing them to life. A new film is just like a new product. It's impossible to tell beforehand whether someone will need it.

Jørholt: Even though it's a documentary, *The Avant Garde Capitalist* is very much a Boe film: Riskær is on his way to jail and about to lose his identity as he has come to know it.

Boe: To me it was interesting to see whether I could make something that would meet TV's prime time requirements while also exploring some of the 'fine art' meta-themes that interest me. It was exciting to merge some of my desires and personal tastes with a more mainstream narrative form.

Jørholt: But unlike many of your colleagues, you've never made any television series – besides *Kissmeyer Basic*, I mean, which could hardly be called an ordinary television series.

Boe: No, to me that would be just a job, and in that case, I'm better off spending my time doing something else. Simply executing an episode that somebody else has conceived is not my idea of filmmaking. One of the teachers at the Film School once called me into his office and said, 'You can do it, Christoffer, but the way you go about things, nobody will ever offer you an episode of *Taxa* (*Taxi*).' No, probably not. I've made a few commercials, but it's very difficult for me to operate on a set where I'm to set aside my own desires in order to satisfy those of some undefined consumer who has some undefined need of something.

Jørholt: Do you think about the audience at all when you're making a film? Danish cinema has been criticized for having become far too spectator-oriented, but I suppose that doesn't apply to you.

Boe: Judging from my box-office results, you would not think so! However, as a filmmaker you always have some ideal spectator in mind. But I have to believe that my own taste and my own desires will take the film to a place where it will become fun and exciting for others, if possible, even a large audience. That hasn't actually happened yet, though.

Jørholt: You've said that the 'cultivation of the off-mainstream is having a hard time in Danish cinema'. Would you care to elaborate on that?

Boe: If you make a film that's only seen by 3,000 people, it's not a success. Those are the realities of the market, no matter how important the film may be. Film is a mass medium and thus requires a certain economic base, and viewers simply don't want to see off-mainstream films. But without naming anyone in particular, I have to say that many Danish films simply aren't interesting. The vast majority of the films involve a thoughtless repetition of archaic formulae and styles. Whereas I firmly believe that it's possible to redefine the formal aspects of cinematic expression and still maintain a popular dimension.

Now and then there are small pockets of time when viewers are looking for something new and different. Dogma coincided with this kind of time pocket when viewers were hungry for new modes of expression and narration. And Danish cinema was able to deliver something new, thanks to new technology and the concept of the 'natural story', a concept Mogens Rukov had banged into the heads of an entire generation of Danish directors. Unfortunately, the international market for foreign films has been in decline for the last five years. It has become more difficult to sell a Danish-language film abroad. There used to be an international market for European art films. Although they only had a small share of the market, in the larger game that share wasn't negligible. But those days are gone. Maybe the new digital modes of distribution will eventually open up new possibilities for films that are not conceived in popular or mainstream ways.

Jørholt: You've contributed to a couple of international omnibus films. Have you received other international offers?

Boe: I believe all Danish directors who have achieved a certain level of success, commercially or on the festival circuit, have been invited to Hollywood where they're constantly on the lookout for fresh young blood to make some odd film that everybody else has turned down. That's not serious though. But I do cooperate quite a lot with French companies. They're co-producing my new film, for example.

Jørholt: Is your new film also off-mainstream?

Boe: I use a basic structure related to the thriller genre, and through this strong generic motor I hope to be able to create a mode of expression that will appeal to a larger audience. But we've just started editing, so it's hard to tell.

Jørholt: Do you ever draw on your colleagues, on other Danish directors, for help when you're facing some kind of problem in your work?

Boe: I started out in the business as a kind of outsider. When I was admitted to the Film School, I knew nothing about the Danish film production environment, whereas many of the other students had worked at Nimbus or Zentropa. After having made films for more than ten years, I still feel that holding a certain outsider position is basically a good thing. There must be a standard to play against, and I like to use Danish cinema as a standard that defines what I should *not* do. But having said that, yes, there are a few other directors with whom I discuss things, and who read my scripts. Anders Morgenthaler, for instance, often sees early versions of my films. And since Alphaville is producing films by other directors, I also see and comment on films by some of my Danish colleagues. The Danish film environment is very small, but basically open and friendly.

Jørholt: What does the national dimension mean to you?

Boe: Nothing at all. Of course we've all been coded and contextualized through-and-through by our upbringing in Denmark, and I do operate within a national production environment, but I don't think any of us think about the national dimension when we make our films. Actually, I hope some of us are more or less successfully making things that are 'out of context'.

Jørholt: What, in your view, are the primary reasons for the Danish film boom in the 1990s?

Boe: There are three reasons: a good support system, Mogens Rukov and Lars von Trier. Lars von Trier paved the way and brought international attention to Danish cinema. And he created a production environment where he himself has functioned as an engaged consultant on lots of productions. Also, he created the Dogma rules which harmonize perfectly with the concept of the 'natural story' that Mogens has been advocating. The point was to make films that are original, important and personal but using basic dramaturgical and narrative forms.

Jørholt: Where will Danish cinema be in ten years?

Boe: I have absolutely no idea. In the last ten to fifteen years, there's been a pronounced professionalization of our industry. Before that, we simply weren't skilled enough from a purely technical point of view. But now we've achieved a professional technical standard that is currently used mainly for the purposes of a somewhat thoughtless reproduction of international genres. But I hope to see more personal forms of expression with a high professional technical standard in a few years.

Chapter 3

Pernille Fischer Christensen

Pernille Fischer Christensen. Photography: Erik Molberg.

Born 1969. Pernille Fischer Christensen graduated from the National Film School of Denmark in 1999. Before, and during, her film school years she made a series of short films with support from the Film Workshop in Copenhagen. With Super 8 images transferred to video, the so-called 'Hypnogram Films' are visually intriguing explorations of states of mind between full consciousness and sleep. Structured in terms of a young girl's diary, *Poesie Album* (1994) used 16 mm images, Super 8 images, black and white images, colour images and animation to engage the spectator in a series of quietly suggested reflections. Christensen's graduation film, *Indien* (*India*, 1999), focused on a woman on the verge of a nervous breakdown, and grew out of *Ramone*, a short film made in response to one of a series of film school assignments. With *Habibti min elskede* (*Habibti My Love*, 2002), Christensen set aside her interest in the materiality of the visual image, in favour of a straightforward narrative about the crisis that arises when a young immigrant woman of Islamic faith becomes pregnant as a result of her relationship with a young Danish man. Christensen's first feature film, the low-budget *En Soap* (*A Soap*, 2006), was one of the first films to be produced through the Danish Film Institute's New Danish Screen scheme. With a script written in collaboration with the prolific Kim Fupz Aakeson, this film about the relationship between the brutish Charlotte (Trine Dyrholm) and the sensitive transvestite Veronica (David Dencik) won both the Silver Bear and the best first feature awards at the Berlin International Film Festival. Christensen continued her collaboration with both Aakeson and Dyrholm with her second feature film, *Dansen* (*Dancers*, 2008), which has Dyrholm, as Annika, discovering the violent past of her lover Lasse, played by Anders W. Berthelsen. Pernille Fischer Christensen's films reveal a thoughtful commitment to film as art, and to the idea of filmmaking as itself a means of probing the realities that shape human existence. She is one of a number of contemporary Danish filmmakers for whom research, in the form of an actual engagement with real world contexts, is an integral part of the process of story and script development.

Feature films

2010	*En familie* (*A Family*)
2008	*Dansen* (*Dancers*)
2006	*En Soap* (*A Soap*)

Short films

2002	*Habibti min elskede* (*Habibti My Love*)
1999	*Indien* (*India*, graduation film)
1994–1996	*Hypnogramfilm* (*Honda, Honda; Sandsagn; Rimhinde; Pigen som var søster*) (*Hypnogram Films* [*Honda, Honda; Sandsagn; Rimhinde; The Girl Named Sister*])
1994	*Poesie Album*

Hjort: How would you describe the path that led you to filmmaking?

Christensen: I don't come from an artistic family, not at all. My grandfather and father were both radiologists, and my mother was a teacher. I actually started working in an X-ray department at the age of ten. I helped develop the images. With X-rays the whole point is to study the image really carefully. I've spent hours with my father and grandfather looking at images, and at the details of images. My father loved to study the world, and this is something he passed on to me. When he looked at things he'd see more than most people, or something different. When he looked at clouds, he never just saw clouds. He taught me to take an extra look at things. As a child I was often told that I was staring at someone or something. And I still do this. I'm capable of losing myself completely in the act of looking.

My mother was quite a special person. She was a twin and an extremely shy person, but she loved to go to the cinema. I was watching films by Kurosawa at the Posthus Theatre by the time I was eight. I remember seeing Bertolucci's *1900* (1976) at a really early age. My mother was a socialist so I saw a lot of films with those values. I saw Polish films with my mother, and all the Russian films that were available. Every Friday she'd check to see whether there was a new film that was worth seeing, and if there was, we'd see it together.

The principal of my school happened to be a film critic. And his son, Jakob Stegelmann, worked in the film industry and was studying film at Copenhagen University. Jakob knew all about animation, and his father simply hired him to teach us about film. So by the time I was twelve or thirteen, I found myself watching Pasolini's *Il Vangelo secondo Matteo* (*The Gospel According to Saint*

Matthew, 1964) together with a professional film practitioner. Krebs wasn't a particularly artistic school otherwise; it's probably the most academically oriented school in Denmark. But I was friends with a boy whose parents were artists. His mother is an actress and his father a painter. That family opened up a door to the art world.

But it took me a while to figure out that I wanted to be a director. I wrote poems, and explored dance and music. And then I started studying Art History. I spent time in Italy in connection with my studies, and I travelled a lot, in order to look at art. I went to Mexico, for example, because I wanted to see the work of the Mexican muralists. But what I quickly discovered was that I'm really not a scholar at heart. I felt like a complete misfit in the academic milieu. The very analytic approach to things that was emphasized there made me really unhappy. It just so happened that my cousin had a boyfriend who was at the National Film School. And it suddenly occurred to me that maybe I could pursue my fascination with images through film somehow. Maybe I could become an editor. That way I'd be able to work with images and with music, with all those things that meant so much to me. My cousin's boyfriend got me involved in the student productions. He said, 'Look, I'll get you in as a scripter. That way you'll have a chance to work closely with the directors.' And that's what happened. I volunteered to help out on I don't know how many different student productions.

Also, my mother came home one day and said she'd met someone called Jesper Jargil, who was a filmmaker. And she'd told him that her daughter was crazy about film, and he'd been very sweet and had said that I could give him a call. And so I did. When we met I think he thought 'cool kid'. He said, 'Look, one of my best friends is an editor and I'll give him a call.' About a day later Jesper called me and said, 'Just give Tómas Gislason a call. He's done this and this and this.' I had no idea who Gislason was, and it never occurred to me that he might be Denmark's star editor. Tómas was dealing with a huge personal crisis at the time, a divorce, and I think he really needed somebody to just sort of sit there with him. So I was allowed to watch him work. He expected me to be quiet, but if he asked me a question he also expected my response to show that I'd been paying attention to what he was doing. That encounter with Tómas was really important. Tómas had been working with von Trier for years, and had helped him to develop his visual style. He'd helped to pioneer this idea that one's starting point as a filmmaker should be, not a script, but a strong desire to explore the formal potential of film as a medium, to examine film as film.

I'd also started spending time at the Film Workshop in Copenhagen. And one day I met an old school friend there, and she'd just returned from New York, where she'd studied film at NYU. And she'd come back to Denmark with a small black and white Super 8 film in her suitcase. That was a huge eye opener for me, this idea that you could produce something with real aesthetic qualities on a tiny camera and without spending a whole lot of money. Super 8 cameras allow you to produce images that have some real potency, unlike digital video which has never interested me. So while I was assisting Tómas I started to write a number of small scripts. Actually, these scripts were more like shot lists, and they were all very Tarkovsky-like; more suggestive than narrative, and very inspired by the cinematic universe that Tómas and Lars had created. I started showing these things to the people at the Film Workshop, and was then given the opportunity to make *Honda, Honda*, *Poesie Album*, and *The Girl Named Sister*.

Hjort: The Film Workshop allowed you to make *Poesie Album* and the four *Hypnogram* films, and that's essentially how you got through the eye of the needle and into the National Film School. How do you remember your days at the Film Workshop?

Christensen: I was there in the early 90s, and what was wonderful about the place back then was that it was so anarchic. In a way it was also a very nepotistic place, because it was all about somebody knowing somebody who was doing something interesting. But this way of operating did mean that people who weren't particularly articulate about their projects, myself included, nonetheless were given the opportunity to use the workshop. We were allowed to produce the strangest things and were given enormous freedom. It was genuinely a workshop, in the sense that we were constantly experimenting with film as an art form, and if things didn't work out, we'd just try something else instead. I virtually lived there, and we'd often sleep there. That was also true of the Film School, actually. We simply worked day and night.

Hjort: You got into the National Film School of Denmark in 1995. This is supposed to be one of the world's best film schools. What was important about the four years you spent there?

Christensen: I'm really very lucky because I was at both the 'old' film school and the 'new' one. I was part of the cohort that moved from Christianshavn to Holmen. The school that I got into was actually very much like the Film Workshop. It was an anarchic and somewhat muddled place, and in the beginning it was difficult to figure out what the point of it all was and what the hell was going on. And it was full of people who took up a lot of space and whose teaching – and here I'm thinking especially of Mogens Rukov – made sense some of the time, but by no means all of the time. Some of the teaching was extremely abstract and deeply philosophical, and it was pitched at a level that made it impossible to follow. My problem was that I was incredibly interested in images, while the teaching emphasized stories and how to structure them. I found it all really alienating and troubling, and there were times during the dramaturgy classes when I felt that I was back in a mathematics class. I felt like an outsider a lot of the time, and that people were trying to make me do things that didn't make any sense to me. I didn't actually understand the idea of plot points and those basic dramaturgical principles until years later. The scriptwriter Kim Leona helped me understand these things when we worked on a script together. Although the script never went anywhere, I did learn the things I'd never understood while I was at the Film School as a result of that collaborative process.

But the Film School was also wonderful. I was allowed to experiment with all kinds of things. I made 3D films, and I worked with slow motion, all sorts of slow motion. I was one of the first people in Denmark to work with ENR, a particular chemical process used in the development of film.

Lone Scherfig was also a really crucial part of my film school experience. Lone had had a baby and needed a less gruelling schedule for a while, so she'd accepted a teaching position at the Film School. And she was with us for about two years, and was also on the panel that admitted me to the school. And she was an absolute dynamo. She'd ask herself really basic questions like 'What does a director need to know?', 'What should the graduating directors know how to do?' And then she'd figure out how to provide the kind of teaching that was needed. She felt that we really needed to learn how to work with actors, so she approached the Danish Actors Association and managed to broker a deal that enabled us to work with professional actors on our student productions. So after something like three weeks at the Film School I found myself clutching a couple of scenes from Ingmar Bergman's *Scenes from a Marriage* (*Scener ur ett äktenskap*, 1973) and opposite Søren Pilmark and Ann Eleonora Jørgensen, whom I was supposed to direct. Søren Pilmark just directed himself, because I simply didn't have a clue about directing. Learning how to work with actors is actually really hard. You have these people in front of you and you're supposed to tell them what to do. And at the same time you don't want it to look like they were told what to do. Everyone is looking to you for guidance and answers. Everyone in my cohort had a melt down about all this, at some point or another. I remember an incident with Ole Lemmeke who ended up telling the directors what to do rather than the other way around. And there was so much tension about this that he finally had to leave.

Gert Fredholm was another director who worked really hard to give us the opportunities he felt we needed. He'd organized a trip to New York where we were to work with actors at the Actors Studio. And that was also quite a traumatic experience. I couldn't handle it and ended up simply abandoning the actors and walking down 44th Street in a state of hurt and fury.

Another important thing that happened during my film school years was that I met Trine Dyrholm. At that point she had a role in the popular Danish TV series *Taxa* (*Taxi*). She hadn't yet really done any of the things that she's known for today, and was still very much the Trine we all knew from her Eurovision Song Contest entry as a fourteen year old. I wasn't following *Taxi*, but at one point the TV was on when I was visiting my mother and there was this image of Trine emerging from the sea, without make-up and with her hair all slicked back. And I just thought 'Wow'. So I called her the next day, because I had to do what they called a 'penneprøve' for the Film School. That was how we first started working together.

Hjort: There's been a lot of talk about these 'penneprøver', because they're seen as having inspired Dogma 95. What exactly is a 'penneprøve'?

Christensen: It's a small cinematic assignment, with basic parameters – basic rules and constraints – defined in advance by the teacher. You might, for example, be told that you have one day for shooting, three rolls of film, two days to do the sound and eight hours to do the actual shooting. You're required to do six or seven of these assignments in the course of the entire programme.

Hjort: And the film you did with Trine Dyrholm was *Ramone*?

Christensen: Yes. And that encounter with Trine was an incredibly important one. When I first started working with her I once again had this feeling that I was supposed to crack some system, and then I'd know how to direct her properly. But Trine really helped me to feel confident about my own way of doing things, and about my approach to the cinematic medium, which was about seeing film as a kind of expressive language. She simply accepted that my cinematic language wouldn't necessarily be the same as some other director's. And she was very supportive of my desire to use the cinematic medium in a genuinely visual way. I think Trine would probably say that she also learnt something from me. My tendency to want to look at things more closely, to examine things, to look at them with a sense of wonder, I think all of that had an impact on Trine as an actress. Trine is an extraordinary actress, and I think her performances in both *A Soap* and *Dancers* are really strong.

Hjort: What has New Danish Screen meant to you, as a subsidy scheme aimed at supporting emerging talent, risk-taking and innovation?

Christensen: My graduation film, *India*, was quite unlike the other films made by members of my cohort. It was anything but a mainstream production. These days the National Film School talks a lot about how it's an art school, but when I was there, that wasn't the discourse at all. It was very industry-oriented. And I think I received the worst assessment of anyone in my cohort for *India*. There were two teachers who defended what I'd done, but the rest of them thought the film was weird and really not very good. So I left the Film School depressed and in a real state of crisis. I spent a lot of time thinking about

Annika (Trine Dyrholm) with her lover Lasse (Anders W. Berthelsen) in *Dansen* (*Dancers*). Photography: Christian Geisnæs.

how I simply didn't fit in, in Denmark. But then I got lucky, because *India* got accepted by Cannes, and from there it went to all kinds of other festivals and ended up winning a lot of prizes. So Cannes was really important, because it restored my faith in myself and showed me that there was a completely different way of talking about film out there.

I started to think about my future in Denmark in a much more strategic way. I decided I needed to make a short film with a clear story. So I made *Habibti My Love*, and I got lucky with that film too, because it won a Robert prize. At that point I started to think that I might actually have a chance at a filmmaking career in Denmark, and that I didn't need to think so hard about fleeing the country. So I started working on a script together with Kim Leona, and Vinca Wiedemann was the DFI consultant on that project. It was an incredibly exciting process for me. Kim Leona had written the script for *Bænken* (*The Bench*; dir. Per Fly, 2000). But our project didn't go anywhere. Vinca moved from her consultant position to the directorship of New Danish Screen, and the new consultant didn't like our project. And Kim Leona was suddenly diagnosed with cancer. It was all very difficult, but the idea of just abandoning the project was also hard. Finally Vinca came up with the idea of making the film with support from New Danish Screen. At that point in time New Danish Screen was able to provide support of up to 3.8 million DKK, something like that. And the film we'd been working on was this road movie that would have cost much, much more to make. In the meantime I'd received an email from Kim Fupz Aakeson and he wanted to explore the idea of doing something together. My first reaction was that this was of absolutely no interest to me. I'd seen *Den eneste ene* (*The One and Only*; dir. Susanne Bier, 1999) while I was at the Film School, and I thought Fupz was much too mainstream. But Vinca was asking me to come up with a new idea, and there was that email from Fupz, and so I finally decided that what I needed to do was simply produce a concept for a film that could be made for the 3.8 million I hoped to get from New Danish Screen if I could line up a producer. I'd simply try to extract the good material from the first project and integrate it into the new one. So I wrote to Fupz and told him that if he was willing to make the cheapest film imaginable, I'd like to collaborate with him. We thought in terms of two characters and their respective apartments, and this idea that they'd move in and out of these two spaces. Fupz then suggested that we structure it all like a TV soap, and that was very helpful, because suddenly we had an entire tradition we could dialogue with. We also decided that if Veronica was a woman in a man's body, then Charlotte was a man in a woman's body. We didn't give Trine [Dyrholm] and David [Dencik] the script to start with. Instead we did improvisation work with them for about two weeks, and then Fupz and I finalized the script and gave it to them. The

Charlotte (Trine Dyrholm) with Veronica (David Dencik) in *En soap* (*A Soap*). Photography: Lars Wahl.

story was there, but the improvisation work helped us to test it and to explore it. I'm very, very thorough when it comes to my scripts.

Hjort: *A Soap* was one of the very first New Danish Screen films. How did Nimbus Film end up producing it?

Christensen: That was complicated. I talked to any number of producers, and nobody wanted to have anything to do with the film. I mean I was proposing a film that was a love story between a woman and a transvestite who is hoping for a sex change operation. And I have to say that the response at a place like Nordisk was 'Pernille, come up with something else. Please!' My experience was also that the producers were generally very sceptical about New Danish Screen. And the scheme was later revised, because the Danish Film Institute realized that the ceiling for support had simply been set too low. Anyway, I went back to Vinca and told her about the long list of no's I'd received. Vinca told me that her mother had once had a lover who was a transsexual, and that she really liked my idea. So she decided to give Henning Camre, then CEO of the Danish Film Institute, a quick call. I didn't hear their conversation, but after having spoken to Camre, Vinca gave me a letter of intent promising me 200,000 DKK to support the development of my film. I then went back to Nimbus, with that letter in my hand, and said that I'd really like it if they'd sign on as my producer. I also made a point of saying that if companies like Nimbus don't help recent graduates from the Film School, then none of us stand a chance of making our first feature. The Film School sends six new directors out into the world every second year. And when you consider how many talented directors there are in Denmark, and then factor in the talented actors who also want to direct, you quickly realize that it's not easy. But I'd come up with an idea for a really, really cheap film, and I had my letter of intent from Vinca, and Nimbus finally signed on.

Hjort: New Danish Screen is supposed to provide directors with a sparring partner, through the scheme's director. It sounds like Vinca was in fact very involved in the development of *A Soap*.

Christensen: Yes, she was. And she's producing my next film, together with Sisse Graum Jørgensen at Zentropa. So she's stuck with me, or, rather, we've stayed together! I just really value the conversations we have, and all the questions that somehow come up when we talk. In my case Vinca has really functioned as a creative producer. She read the script very, very carefully, and we discussed it from all kinds of angles, including visual style and form.

Hjort: Nimbus produced your first feature film, and Zentropa produced *Dancers*. What's the difference between working for the one, as compared with the other?

Christensen: I loved working with Nimbus, and I especially enjoyed Lars Bredo Rahbek. But Nimbus is a small company, and things haven't been easy for them in recent times. So it's not that easy for them to provide you with any real support, above and beyond what you've been able to generate yourself, to put it diplomatically. The advantage of working for a much larger operation is that you get a lot more support. They can provide you with assistants, they can help you sort out your personal finances and so on and so forth. And because things weren't going that well at Nimbus, there was a pervasive sense of anxiety there. And it's really unpleasant to work in that kind of milieu. At Zentropa there's a completely different tone, and every now and again it does take your breath away, because sometimes there's a loudness and a bluntness to it all. But there's also an incredible devil-may-care attitude that I really like. Nothing is taken for granted. And there's that sense of anarchy that I thrive on. You do have to fight for your ideas, but if you do you're given a chance to prove their worth. I have never been met with a 'no' at Zentropa. Meta Louise Foldager, who produced *Dancers* for Zentropa, was wonderful to work with. She's very much the director's friend, and she's stubborn and forceful and a really good reader. I'm working on another project with her, a collaborative project that pairs up artists and directors, five pairs in total. We're doing this through New Danish Screen, and the participating directors are Lone Scherfig, Martin de Thurah, Dagur Kári, Christoffer Boe and myself.

Hjort: Your film credits suggest that research is an important element in your filmmaking practice. What form does your research take?

Christensen: I do an enormous amount of research. I'm doing a lot of research for my next film, even though it's based on autobiographical material. The story plays out in a baker's family, and I'm not from a baker's family. I now know absolutely everything about bread, yeast and dough. I've done a lot of research, not only on bread, but on various theological issues. I start with a basic idea, and then I read as much as I possibly can. Once I feel I have a very basic grasp of the material, I start to contact people and to set up meetings with them. In the case of *A Soap* I met with a lot of transsexuals. I spent a lot of time with a man who was preparing for his operation, and we became very good friends. My method is to define my material, learn about it and then take what I've learnt out into the world, so that I'm forced to test what I think I know against reality. And as that testing begins to occur, I inevitably find myself asking new questions, and looking at my material from a new angle. It's important to me that the films I make be connected to, rooted in, an actual physically existing reality, that things really *are* as they are in the films. It means a lot to me to know that things *are* that way, that what I show on the screen isn't all just a product of my own mind. This approach extends to my actors, because they're also involved in the research process. David (Dencik) did a lot of research for his role as Veronica. Viewers may think that a film like *A Soap* is very poetic, and has little to do with reality, but that's just not the case.

Hjort: Another core element in your philosophy of filmmaking is the idea of doing a lot with very little. Could you comment on this idea?

Christensen: One of the really sad things about being a filmmaker is that it costs so much to make films. The issue of money is always there, and it's a huge constraint. People will sometimes tell me that I'm lucky because I'm doing exactly what I want to do. And I'll say, 'No I'm not.' And the reason I'm not is that financial considerations always get in the way. But the fact is that the cheaper your film is the greater your chances are of being able to do what you want. So reducing cost is a very high priority for me, always. There's also an ascetic dimension to my practice. I really dislike wastefulness. Not that I'm opposed to anything expensive as such, but the expense has to have been properly thought through, so that it can really be justified.

Hjort: The idea of choosing to make 'mistakes' in the course of filmmaking has also been a guiding principle for you. *India* was discussed in these terms, as a series of intended departures from accepted practice, in much the same way, I suppose, that Dogma 95 imposed rules that thwarted the conventions of mainstream film practice.

Christensen: I'm in many ways a perfectionist, but I don't like things that look too perfect. And that's generally true, not just in relation to film. I value a sense of balance, but there's a rigidity and sterility to perfection. Perfection, of course, can be many things. But I'm always searching for that tiny sign of vitality. I love things that are drawn by hand, and that thereby reveal their human provenance. That's why I have such a soft spot for Super 8 cameras. They produce images that have the qualities that I look for. Those images don't reek of money, but suggest instead a human presence. I want my films to have those elements of materiality and vitality. Yes, *India* was my little revolt against the Film School. The idea was really to make as many 'mistakes' as possible, in a confronting way.

Hjort: You've developed a real partnership with the editor Åsa Mossberg, who edited *Habibti*, *A Soap* and *Dancers*.

Christensen: Yes, she's an incredibly important part of my work. We weren't at the Film School at the same time, but I got to know her through the Film School network. She's originally Swedish, but then decided to stay on in Denmark once she'd completed her training at the Film School. She co-edited Lars von Trier's *Antichrist* (2009), and it's easy to understand why he chose her. She has an extraordinary sense of rhythm, but her talent also has to do with her personal qualities. She's very capacious as a person, and she's also got this incredible sense of solidarity in relation to the actors. She's simply always trying to optimize their performances through the editing. And she never gives up. She's unbelievably stubborn, and also very wise.

Hjort: You've worked with a lot of Swedish musicians, with Adam Nordén on *Dancers*, with Magnus Jarlbo and Sebastian Öberg on *A Soap* and with Sebastian on *Habibti*. Why the preference for Swedish musicians?

Christensen: Denmark is a very small country, and the art world is thus also very small. In a small context the talent pool is necessarily limited. And in my experience what tends to happen is that a few people will distinguish themselves as particularly talented, and then everyone will simply converge on them. And the next thing you know all Danish films sound alike, because the same two or three musicians are responsible for most of the music. Sweden is just on the other side of the Sound, and there are a lot of talented people there, so why not tap into that talent pool? My sense is that there are others who are also beginning to do this.

The music is incredibly important to me. I played various instruments as a child, I collect music and I spend a lot of time listening to music. And I love the collaborative process with the musicians, shaping the music, recording it and editing it. In *A Soap* we basically worked with one theme. The music that you hear within the context of the TV soap is the opposite of the theme that connects the distinct parts of the film, its chapters if you will. The music in the TV soap is saccharine, whereas the music used in connection with the transitions from one part to the next is more sober, more restrained. And throughout the film we also worked with the same theme, but in a more fleeting way and just to suggest a certain mood. And then those three variations on a theme come together in the final scene, where they merge into an integrated composition.

Hjort: Nan Goldin's photographs were an important visual source for *A Soap*. What is it that you like about her photographs?

Christensen: I'm always drawing on paintings, on photographs, and I could name so many different people who have been important at various stages of my work with film. But Nan Goldin's *I'll Be Your Mirror* has been especially important. I've come back to that book again and again. She's simply a genius when it comes to getting something out of nothing. I like the way she frames things, and the way her carefully composed pictures end up having a snapshot-like quality. I'm fascinated by the way she uses space, and how she situates people within a given space. They're often placed against a wall, and then there'll be some tiny detail that gives the image extraordinary narrative force. Another thing that fascinates me about her work is the sense of immediacy that pervades it, the sense of her having been there and having witnessed something. And when I talk to my cinematographers I often say that I want us to feel that we're witnessing something that was already happening. In other words, we shouldn't feel as though we first staged something and then filmed it. There should be this sense of our filming something that was already in process, and that we've been allowed somehow to observe.

Hjort: You've been involved, as a mentor, with Dvoted.net, the pan-Nordic, web-based initiative supported by the Nordic Council and the Nordic film institutes. The aim was to give aspiring young Nordic filmmakers easy access to professional advice. Did you find that you received a lot of requests for advice when you were a Dvoted.net mentor?

Christensen: I was part of Dvoted.net for a year, and, yes, I received all kinds of requests and questions. Someone might ask you to share your experiences of working with actors, or to provide tips on how to help actors to perform really well on camera. Or someone might be having doubts about a story, whether it's really worth telling or whether it hangs together properly. I remember being asked about sound/image relations and about my approach to music in film. I'd also get messages of a more personal nature, things like 'I'm twenty years old and I really want to be a filmmaker, but I'm finding it really hard to make my way.'

Hjort: In terms of your current projects, could you say a few final words about the film you mentioned about a baker's family?

Christensen: *En familie* (*A Family*) is very different from the other two feature films I've made. With *A Soap* and *Dancers*, but also with *Habibti*, the idea was to be deeply curious about a somewhat distant milieu. My third feature draws on autobiographical material. It's about a family and what happens when the father becomes very ill and is told that he'll die. It's about the impact of all of this on a divorce that happened a long time ago, and about what happens to various family dynamics as a result. It's also a father/daughter story.

Chapter 4

Per Fly

Per Fly. Photography: Morten Abrahamsen.

Born 1960. Per Fly graduated from the National Film School of Denmark in 1993 as part of the 'golden cohort' that also included the directors Thomas Vinterberg and Ole Christian Madsen. Along with Vinterberg and Madsen, and the producers Birgitte Hald and Bo Ehrhardt, Fly helped to establish the production company Nimbus Film, where he worked for a number of years. For Nimbus Film, he made the short children's film – *kalder Katrine!* (*Calling Katrine*, 1993), but after a series of failed projects he began collaborating with the Zentropa producer Ib Tardini, initially in connection with the puppet films *Den lille ridder* (*The Little Knight*, 1999) and *Prop og Berta* (*Prop and Berta*, 2000). It was with Tardini that Fly won both a Bodil and a Robert award for best film of the year in 2000. The award winning *Bænken* (*The Bench*) is about the alcoholic Kaj (Jesper Christensen), and was written in collaboration with the scriptwriter Kim Leona after considerable research in relevant real world environments and following improvisations with the actors. The first film in a trilogy about the three dominant social classes in Denmark, the film revitalized Danish social realism. The next two films in the trilogy garnered a whole host of awards for Fly and his actors. *Arven* (*The Inheritance*, 2003), which looks at the Danish upper class, tells the story of a man (Ulrich Thomsen) who reluctantly assumes responsibility for carrying on the family business, following his father's suicide. In *Drabet* (*Manslaughter*, 2005) Jesper Christensen returned to the trilogy, as the high-school teacher Carsten, whose middle-class life takes a dramatic turn when a young woman, with whom he's having an affair, is arrested as an accomplice to murder in connection with a political action. Consisting of *The Bench*, *The Inheritance* and *Manslaughter*, Fly's trilogy was a milestone in Danish film, and a considerable success, both critically and at the box office. Afterwards Fly made the narratively complex, six-episode TV series *Forestillinger* (*Performances*, 2007), which shows how six different people experience the same six-week rehearsal period at a Copenhagen theatre. Fly's most recent project is the feature film *Kvinden der drømte om en mand* (*The Woman Who Dreamt About a Man*, 2010).

Feature films

2010	*Kvinden der drømte om en mand* (*The Woman Who Dreamt About a Man*)
2005	*Drabet* (*Manslaughter*)
2003	*Arven* (*The Inheritance*)
2000	*Bænken* (*The Bench*)
2000	*Prop og Berta* (*Prop and Berta*)

Short films

1999	*Den lille ridder* (*The Little Knight*)
1993	*– kalder Katrine!* (*Calling Katrine*)
1993	*Værelse 17* (*Room 17*, graduation film)

TV

2007	*Forestillinger* (*Performances*, TV series, six episodes)
1997–1999	*Taxa* (*Taxi*, three episodes)
1997	*Chock 4 – Liftarflickan* (*The Hitchhiking Girl*, short fiction for TV)

Redvall: You entered the National Film School of Denmark at the age of twenty-nine, after having worked with music for a number of years. How did you discover you wanted to make films?

Fly: For many years I worked hard to become a musician. I'm a product of that 80s period, when the art world was based on there being unemployed people on social benefits around, and on the idea that artists should really pursue their dreams. My dream was to play music and I worked hard to get in to the Rhythmic Music Conservatory. I practised four hours every day, and I didn't get in. That was a hard blow, and it's taken me a long time to accept the conclusion that I simply wasn't talented enough. I had to practise twice as much to achieve the same result as my friends who had talent. When I didn't get in I didn't know what to do. But then I directed a play, *Liebeslied* (*Love Song*) at Gellerup Scenen. The play was quite elaborate, with six dancers, three musicians and a visual artist, and I was successful in mounting it. It was nothing special, but to me the mere fact of having pulled it off was a huge victory. Afterwards I stopped dead in my tracks because I didn't know what to do next. The show didn't open any doors, and I was twenty-eight and felt that it was time something happened. Then my girlfriend, who was studying to be an actor and was in a workshop at the Film School, brought me a brochure about the school. It turned out that the application deadline was two days later and I simply decided to try for it. My application included *Liebeslied* and an art video that I'd made with Niels Lomholt.

Redvall: The Film School only accepts six students every year and many apply several times before getting in. What's your recollection of the process, especially given that you didn't know much about film?

Fly: The application process lasted a few months and included a whole series of tests. It was a turning point for me. I could feel that what had happened to me, in terms of my commitment to music, was that I'd started lying more and more about my abilities. I was always pretending to be better than I was. And so I made the decision to be truthful throughout the application process. I simply decided I wasn't going to say that I could do something that I couldn't actually do. It was a good decision because it had a calming effect. When I got into the Film School, it became clear to me that film was much more my field. And that realization was very vitalizing. Being at the Film School was initially pretty weird because I knew nothing about film. I knew something about video but I'd never seen a cutting table. I was the one who'd stick up a hand and ask who Dolly was! But in my case this sense of ignorance provided a good starting point, because I didn't feel I had to defend anything. I had ambitions and desires, and the first two years at the school were incredibly happy ones. I'd sit in the cinema and watch three films per day, and I'd feel that everything was simply amazing.

Redvall: Then what happened? It takes four years to graduate from the Film School.

Fly: My girlfriend and I split up and that was very hard. At the same time my mid-programme film ended up becoming a negative turning point. I was given such a hard time about that film, and I just wasn't equipped to handle the criticisms. The third year at the school is also angst-provoking because you have to make your graduation film. What are you going to do? Who will end up with the right team? While I was at the school there was a team of very strong-willed producers, and they didn't make it any easier on the director. For example, they'd have a set-up whereby people from the outside also could contribute ideas to the filmmaking process. So there was actually a lot of competition. Only much later did I understand that you simply have to take a very public stance, and explicitly state things as you see them: 'This is where we're going to start. At this point, that's all I know. I'm not entirely sure how we're going to proceed, but this is the direction I'd like us to go in, and this is essentially what I want.' I couldn't find the energy for this at the school. My strategy was avoidance, and yet the very basis for doing anything at all with film is daring to occupy that space of uncertainty.

Redvall: As far as storytelling tools are concerned, your cohort seems to have been the first to show real interest in the Scriptwriting Department, and to have worked with both Mogens Rukov and the scriptwriting students. What did you take with you from the school with regard to storytelling and scriptwriting?

Fly: Several of the directors developed good collaborative working relations with the scriptwriters, but that didn't happen in my case, so I ended up working on the script for my graduation film on my own. When I teach at the school nowawadays I really try to dissuade the students from adopting that kind of approach, because it makes everything really hard. Since my film school days I've learnt to enjoy the process of collaborating on scripts. I especially enjoy the conversations. I invite those discussions, and I look for people who can help me move beyond the blank page. I have huge respect for first drafts. I've actually never written a first draft myself. It's the hardest thing to do!

Scriptwriting is very much about identifying partners who will help you to challenge yourself. I never really understood Mogens Rukov while I was at the Film School. I did feel there was something there, but I was probably too shy really to acknowledge it. I come from a small community in Jutland. You can be scared or crazy there, but you're also always just an ordinary person. Mogens is *never* an ordinary person, and that's why I didn't know how to relate to him, even though it was obvious that he had enormous affection for our class.

Since then I've benefited greatly from having him as a philosophical benchmark. It's possible to have the most incredible conversations with Mogens. He's also capable of confusing you a lot because he approaches things in a way that's different. He hasn't contributed a single line to any of our films, and yet's he's still been completely indispensable. In many ways he's an alchemist. Alchemists dreamt of creating gold, of creating the sublime; and yet it was the creative process itself that became the basis for their 'science', and never the results. Mogens has a similarly obsessive attitude when it comes to stories, and that's a source of enormous energy.

Redvall: You didn't start working with scriptwriters Kim Leona and Lars Kjeldgaard until much later, but your graduation film *Room 17* did give you the opportunity to collaborate with a number of people who've since become regular members of your team. I'm thinking of the editor Morten Giese, and the composer Halfdan E. How important is it to you to work with the same people from one project to the next?

Fly: It means a lot to me. I discovered Halfdan and Morten at the school. Birgitte Hald produced *Room 17* and she was part of establishing Nimbus Film after film school. In more recent times Ib Tardini has been an important anchor for me at Zentropa. So the team aspect means a lot to me, but I'm always aware that there are dangers associated with this approach. When I'd completed *Performances*, I got up and gave a speech, in which I fired everybody. The point was to make it clear that I needed to be able to act unencumbered by personal ties. It's nice working with people you know, for the banal reason that there are so many things that don't require discussion. But you can only continue to work together if the people involved retain their vitality. I always try to avoid hiring people for the

Jesper Christensen and Marius Sonne Janischefska on the bench in *Bænken* (*The Bench*). Photography: Ole Kragh-Jacobsen.

sake of feeling safe, and to focus instead on the story and how it can contribute something new to the collaborative teamwork.

Redvall: You finished film school in 1993 but didn't make your first feature film until 2000. What was it like establishing yourself in the industry?

Fly: Shortly after film school I made the short film *Calling Katrine*, and this film, along with Thomas Vinterberg's *Drengen der gik baglæns* (*The Boy Who Walked Backwards*, 1994) helped to start up Nimbus Film. I remember our first year out of film school as being a time when we sort of created a mafia. That was a really cool time. We threw lots of parties and thought of ourselves as royalty. First we had our own premises, but then we moved in with Zentropa in Ryesgade. It was a lot of fun initially, but after a while there was this sense of things perhaps not being that easy after all. There was no natural space for us, and we had to fight hard to create some space. I'd start up one project after another, only to see them get turned down. It was incredibly unpleasant, and exhausting. At the same time I didn't agree with some of the things that were happening at Nimbus, so I finally decided to leave the company. I did some satirical work for TV, and I made some music videos. I also went off to Sweden, where I directed a short horror film, *The Hitchhiking Girl*, but I couldn't make the transition to the feature format. Something happened, though, when I met Ib Tardini, with whom I first made the puppet film *The Little Knight*. That short film then led to the feature film *Prop and Berta*, also with puppets, and I lived off that while I was making *The Bench*.

Redvall: The story of the making of *The Bench* has become almost legendary in the Danish film milieu. The film was based on extensive research, it was made against all odds, for only 6.5 million DKK, and yet it ended up winning both a Bodil and a Robert award as best film of the year. How did *The Bench* come about?

Fly: I ended up at Zentropa after having spent seven years trying to get a green light to make a feature film, and I'd simply decided I'd make this film about people who spent their lives sitting on a bench, whether I could get the money or not. I shared my idea with Ib Tardini and told him I'd make the film without getting any salary, on the condition that he promised to make it with me. Ib was a left-wing schoolteacher in a former life, and at the time he'd just finished producing the Morten Korch series, and if you've got the background he has, you can't sink much lower than Korch. He's since told me that I approached him at just the right time. He agreed to make the film, money or no money, and we went into Peter Aalbæk Jensen's office, where Ib told Peter that we'd be using Zentropa's equipment for six weeks in a year's time. And that meant we had one year to do our research and scriptwriting. Ib also told Peter that if we didn't get any money for the film, then he'd serve as the film's production leader, something he hadn't done for years. He simply powered ahead at full speed. At the time it was important to me not to think in terms of the regular funding system. I didn't want the film to depend on whether the Danish Film Institute wanted to support it, because I'd tried that approach three or four times already, without any luck. My thought was simply: 'We're making this film no matter what!' And that was an invigorating decision. It turned me into a driving force, and then people who wanted to could simply jump on board. The idea for *The Bench* wasn't necessarily better than the ones that I'd had rejected, but the more forceful approach just made it possible to avoid all the nonsense. The question was very simple: 'We're making this film and want to know whether you're in or not?' That forcefulness was good, and it's exactly what you need if you're going to be a director. You simply have to throw yourself into the thick of it, instead of trying to avoid all the possible humiliations. But at the time I really had my back against the wall. I knew it was then or never.

Redvall: You've previously said that you couldn't have made *The Bench* with any company other than Zentropa. What's so different about Zentropa?

Fly: Zentropa is this amazingly creative environment that's been a magnet for a lot of skilled people. Zentropa has stood for innovative ways of thinking, and it's a place where initiative is rewarded with an enormous amount of support. It's also very anarchistic, because Peter Aalbæk is really good at anarchy. What that means is that things either don't move forward at all, or they move forward very quickly indeed. Every now and again there's a meltdown of some kind, but something's always happening. At the same time Zentropa has created a production machine based on the idea that geek films also merit a certain production volume. That's an idea that has worked really well. Lars has, of course, been a significant figure inasmuch as he's constantly established new milestones with regard to what a film could look like. And Ib has meant a lot to me on account of his experience, and because of his commitment to making films together, in spite of all possible obstacles. It's all been quite chaotic, but it's also been fun, and it's certainly been good for me. Filmmakers who are less able to handle a lot of chaos have been able to work at Nimbus instead, where the approach is more proper and generous. The tone at Zentropa is very direct and rough. Nobody works with kid gloves there, but I like that honesty.

Redvall: Where would you say Zentropa stands today, as compared with the year 2000, which is when you made *The Bench*?

Fly: Zentropa has been a real powerhouse, but it's definitely over. Zentropa has become very big and it's no longer fuelled by an oppositional mind-set. At this point my experience is that Peter Aalbæk spends a lot of time showing people around, and telling the same anecdotes for the 117th time. The question now is how Zentropa will develop, and whether anything new will come out of that process. At the moment Ole Christian Madsen and I are trying to do something different, by making two war films together. We'd like to try a different creative constellation, and to come up with a different way of thinking. We'll see how that goes.

Redvall: *The Bench* was made at Zentropa right after the popular Dogma films. It could perhaps even have been made following the rules from the Vow of Chastity. Why didn't you make a Dogma film?

Fly: While we were in the process of financing *The Bench*, Peter Aalbæk actually asked us if we wanted to make it as a Dogma film, but I wasn't interested in that. I couldn't imagine that film without music, and we were already deep into the process of making it. Afterwards it was sort of too late, because by then I had my own project, the trilogy. I was very proud of that. And so I had my own project, and Lars and the others had Dogma, and made a lot of good films using that framework. There's no doubt that if I'd made *The Bench* as a Dogma film it would have been more widely distributed than it was. There was a really powerful slipstream to Dogma, but I wasn't clever enough to see that!

Redvall: *The Bench* focused on characters situated on the fringes of Danish society, on people who'd fallen through the welfare state's various safety nets. This kind of milieu was very much absent from Danish cinema at the time. Where did the idea for the film come from?

Fly: The idea for the film came from reading a newspaper column about meeting people at their level. It touched me. I felt that Danish society was in a downward spiral, and I wanted to look at that. I'm also very fond of Ken Loach, and of many of Visconti's films and neorealism, so I wanted to make a film about people who weren't in a privileged social position. As far as I could tell, other Danish filmmakers weren't making films about that social milieu at the time, and I'd discovered, while making three episodes for the TV series *Taxi*, that I liked working-class characters. That's the environment I come from, so I felt very comfortable with the mode of expression that's needed. I also felt a sense of social indignation and was able to use that as a form of motivation. In that way directors are cannibals, because I could be working for the Salvation Army, but make films instead.

Another starting point for *The Bench* was that I wanted to engage with reality. When I was at the Film School there was this idea that although we shot our films in Copenhagen, there should be no evidence of this in the films themselves. The urban context had to be represented in such a way as to suggest any city in the world other than Copenhagen. We were really phobic about reality, and with *The Bench* I simply decided to adopt an approach that involved going out into reality, talking to people and constructing a story on that basis. Instead of trying to escape from reality I wanted to make use of it. For this reason the milieus I chose were far more important than the idea of making a sociological film about an underprivileged class. It's also why I was aware of needing to find a space where the film's reality had a necessity far greater than the necessity I felt to become a director. By prioritizing the film's necessity you nullify a lot of parameters, because you in the same instance focus entirely on the film itself. This was all very invigorating and motivating, and I guess I was able to think this way because Ib had really committed himself to making this film.

Redvall: The film is based on extensive research in Avedøre [close to Zentropa's Film Town]. More specifically, you followed the work of a social worker for four months and then used that material to construct a fictional story, in collaboration, among others, with Mogens Rukov and Kim Leona. How did this process of using reality as a basis for fiction work?

Fly: I'd decided I wanted to be an expert on every aspect of the film's story. That's why I accompanied the social worker Jytte Lemche as she did her work. The research helped to give the fiction a certain energy, and, to be frank, it's just much more fun to talk to people than it is to sit at home in front of a piece of paper, trying to figure out an answer to the question 'What should my film be about?' The idea was to make use of documentary methods to seek out real people, and then to go home and reshape the material into a story. This approach brought a lot to the story, and it was also very helpful for the actors to be able to meet the real people behind the characters. Instead of sitting there with our lovely reading glasses on, and discussing things, we were really in the middle of everything all the time.

I also adopted this same method in my subsequent films, which are similarly an attempt to use the real world as a basis for a fictional story. I put an insane amount of effort into the fictional aspect. Realism provides the starting point for these films, but they don't ultimately tell realistic stories. This is the case, among other things, because I have a certain fondness for melodrama. I like Visconti a lot, and melodrama is also an important feature of neorealism more generally. I like it when there's an attempt to make a story bigger, to pull it up to a higher level. We've always tried to take this as far as we possibly could. The question was always: 'How far can we go without undermining the viewer's sense of the story being part of the world in which we live?'

You could say that there's an attempt in my films to heighten things. There's a great desire there to move towards the operatic, towards something that's larger than life, because pure realism is boring. You have to move the realism to a different place, and this is a very interesting process because it's hard to know exactly where the boundary between the realistic and unrealistic lies, or when the audience might cease to be convinced by the story. My approach also emphasizes the idea of storytelling on a less apparent level. If viewers have somehow accepted the story that lies at the core of the film, then they'll cut you a lot of slack. And that acceptance happens during the first ten minutes of the film. The first ten minutes establish the rules governing what viewers will and won't be inclined to accept, and I find working with that whole process absolutely fascinating. For instance, it's impressive that Lars [von Trier] can make a film [*Dogville*, 2003] with just chalk lines on the floor, and yet as viewers we just slide into that universe.

Redvall: Why did you decide to make a trilogy?

Fly: While we were filming *The Bench* it occurred to us that it would be interesting to see what Denmark looked like from those three different social sites. At the same time, I was really happy with the method I'd come up with, because it was the first time my efforts had actually resulted in a film. So I simply wanted to pursue that method further, and to continue to do the research that it involved. My thought was also that since it had taken a long time to finance the first film, Ib might as well look for financing for two films at the same time! Ib almost died laughing when I ran this idea by him, but he was very sweet and pretended that he'd probably be able to do that, so I was delighted.

Redvall: In addition to the approach that underpins them, the three films all share a focus on men who have to assume some form of responsibility: personal responsibility, responsibility for the family business, and political or social responsibility. In each instance there's a lot at stake in the decision that the central male character must make. Interestingly, the male leads in each of the films all won the Bodil award as best actor of the year. How would you say the trilogy compares to other Danish films from the relevant years?

Fly: To me all three films are about men who have a hard time relating to their feelings. I only realized this after I'd made the films, but in a way they all tell virtually the same story. In each case it's a matter of looking at the power that's involved in being a proud and stubborn person, and the price you have to pay for those traits. I also think the films are about responsibility. Where does responsibility begin, where does it end? In that sense you could say that the films are an attempt to contest a way of seeing things that harks back to '68. I was trying to say something like: 'Now listen here, our actions have consequences and I can show you what they are.' In that sense the films take issue with the particular kind of humanism that characterized a lot of Danish films at the time. In many of the films actions were shown to have no consequences, because everything could be forgiven and there was always a safety net. There were, of course, exceptions. A film like *Pusher* (dir. Nicolas Winding Refn, 1996) had a very different tone and style.

The emphasis on the question of action and consequences is something that emerged from my collaboration with Mogens Rukov. During the process of working together he'd insist, for example, that we didn't want to develop a character who accidentally has an affair. We wanted, rather, to see someone who makes the *decision* to have an affair. All three main characters make choices, and in so doing they say; 'This is where I stand.' The films then explore their dilemmas, presenting and assessing their choices from different angles. I like the fact that the characters don't have a sentimental way of dealing with life. Here too Mogens had a lot to contribute. He has this ability to get you to develop a more cynical take on the story, his point being of course that humanism isn't something you can get at by simply putting characters with humanistic attitudes on the screen. Humanism is something you get at by showing someone who's pulling in the other direction, and then it's my job to work hard to find the human qualities in that character's story, or to tell the story with some kind of basic human understanding. I was once told an anecdote about something Orson Welles said when he was making *The Trial* (1962). Anthony Perkins came up to him and said 'I've read the story.

Ulrich Thomsen among the factory workers in *Arven* (*Inheritance*). Photography: Per Arnesen.

It's really good. It's about this innocent man…' And Orson Welles slammed his hand onto the table and said 'What do you mean innocent? He's guilty. He's not innocent!' I think that's incredibly beautiful, because that's exactly the point: Watching a story about an innocent man is boring.

Redvall: As a result of the trilogy you went from being an unknown director to being a famous Dane with a number of awards to his name. Some Danish directors have chosen to use that kind of success as a springboard to big, English-language films. You didn't do this, and instead you chose to direct the experimental TV series *Performances* for the Danish Broadcasting Corporation. What was the nature of your reasoning about your options following the success of your trilogy?

Fly: I was very tired by the time I completed the trilogy, although I was also very pleased that *Manslaughter* had been so well received. It was all a bit surreal, and it was a good thing that I'd already committed myself to doing *Performances*. The Danish Broadcasting Corporation had approached me about doing something for them, so I found myself in a very fortunate position. Since they'd approached me, I felt at liberty to explore some really crazy ideas, and then say 'Perhaps this is too much as far as you're concerned.' But they were game, and the whole process was a very happy one. The work on the script was good fun and there was no nervousness regarding financing, so it was possible to plan everything properly. It's clear that making a TV series wasn't a good career move. I thought it would be, because of what I knew about *Riget* (*The Kingdom*; dir. Lars von Trier, 1994) and *Dekalog* (dir. Krzysztof Kieslowski, 1989–1990). I also felt we'd come up with a very interesting idea, but the worlds of film and TV turned out to be very far apart. They have very little in common.

Redvall: Yet a lot of Danish directors do move back and forth between directing episodes for the National Broadcasting Corporation's big drama series and directing their own films. In what sense are these worlds different?

Fly: I got a lot out of directing some episodes of *Taxi* at one point, because it was just so great to go straight to the production phase. It was just a matter of getting into the swing of things and then shooting the episode, and this as compared with a process where you're writing something that could well get rejected. Film and TV are two different worlds in that none of my feature film contacts were of any use in our efforts to sell *Performances*. We got a lot out of making the series, and it's been shown twice at San Sebastian, where the festival organizers showed the entire series in the context of a special screening. From the point of view of my career, however, the smarter move would have been to make a feature film that could have been put into the distribution system. But I'm very happy with the series and see it as a thematic development of the way I'd been working, in that it really is an attempt to see the world from different perspectives. What does the world look like if you see it from the bench frequented by alcoholics? What does it look like from here? In the series we looked at the world from several different angles, in the very same scene and context, and that was really a lot of fun. I don't think psychological reality had been explored in quite this way before.

Redvall: Had the National Broadcasting Corporation given you a particular framework for the series? You once mentioned that you and Lars von Trier came up with the original idea for the structure of the series together. But did the National Broadcasting Corporation provide any guidelines regarding what they were looking for?

Fly: The original idea was that they'd produce a series with fourteen episodes, perhaps more. There was a complete mismatch between our idea and what they had in mind. Lars [von Trier] is very good at coming up with concepts, and we came up with this one when we were talking about telling a story from different angles, the way Kurosawa does in *Rashômon* (1950). Initially the framework was a funeral, with the camera following a series of people to that funeral. Everything about that basic idea, with the exception of the overall concept of changing perspectives, changed the minute I started working together with Lars Kjeldgaard and Kim Leona. We did try to see whether the funeral idea would work with fourteen characters, but the whole thing became unmanageable. The National Broadcasting Corporation then suddenly found itself with a programming gap of seven weeks in its schedule, and that gave us the opportunity to produce a TV series that would run over a period of seven weeks. We wrote seven episodes, but were then allowed to limit the series to six episodes because there just wasn't enough meat on one of the stories. What emerged through the process of development was really far removed from what Trier and I had discussed, and Lars Kjeldgaard and Kim really put an enormous amount of work into it all.

Redvall: *Performances* is, on many different levels, about love, but it's also a meta-story about a chaotic, creative process. Why did the basic framework become a rehearsal at a theatre in Copenhagen?

Fly: I wanted to work with a world I knew well. Lars [Kjeldgaard], Kim and I have all worked in the theatre, and we thought it would be fun to work with that particular context. The National Broadcasting Corporation didn't like this idea at all. They didn't think the world in question was interesting enough. They wanted us to opt for a more political context, but nonetheless ended up accepting the theatre environment. Originally it was a story about the life of a great man, a story about a man who starts a theatre group in Aarhus and goes on to become the Minister of Cultural Affairs. The story had to grow out of that trajectory, but we realized that the effect of seeing things from different angles diminishes when you increase the temporal range. So we had to come up with a different kind of process, and since a rehearsal period typically spans six to seven weeks, that worked perfectly. There's a lot of intense interaction when actors are in rehearsal, so there was a natural story to be told that had an inherent progression.

Of course the structure posed challenges, because we agreed to play by a rule that stipulated that we couldn't jump around temporally. That rule provided a very productive element of constraint. Apart from that it was just a lot of fun because we were all so familiar with the relevant milieu. It was easy to make things up, not least when the actors showed up, because they of course knew the milieu even better than we did. It was a really fun process, and funnily enough there was no anxiety about it. I just think that series turned out really well. In any event, because of the series' complexity, it's also my most detailed account of human beings. I still dream of turning it into a feature film, because there's just such a good story in that material.

Redvall: Lately you've involved yourself in debates about film politics in the daily press. Among other things you've criticized the significantly enhanced power of the TV stations, on account of the most recent Film Accord. Where do you think Danish film stands today?

Fly: There's been a revolution in Danish film since the end of the 90s, but that wave has now rolled its course. What's needed now is a new wave, and I do think there are signs of such a thing. I feel we're in a phase of great upheaval, and I suspect that the uncertainty will be with us for a while yet. But I also think that something good will come out of this process, because we're all getting sharper. We just have to get used to a much faster pace, and to a higher degree of uncertainty.

A big problem in Danish film right now is that we're in the midst of creating a TV business instead of a film business. I don't think that anyone has consciously decided to do this; it's simply the result of a series of factors that we need to relate to. The TV stations have far too much power. This means that they're in a position to sign up the best film practitioners ahead of any of the film production companies. At the moment they're absorbing all the very best cinematographers, scriptwriters and so on, into the TV-making business. The film business, on the other hand, faces such uncertainty with regard to financing that nobody dares to offer anybody a contract until a few weeks before filming starts, and the result is that you lose the good people. The TV stations have the money these days, and so the quality of the TV series is really being enhanced at the cost of feature films. At the same time we're seeing the film industry recruit more and more TV directors and scriptwriters, and this is beginning to be reflected in what the cinemas have to offer. The shift is linked to the way in which these products are made. Who's actually committed to these films, to the point of feeling a stubborn love for them? I've spent a year and a half working on my new film, and I'll fight for it until the bitter end. The new structure that's emerging is in danger of producing half-bad films that lack that element of love or commitment, films like the ones Germany was producing at a certain point, and which the Germans finally had to abandon. You can't blame the TV stations for riding on their success, but it's not good for the film industry.

In terms of considerations that are internal to the film industry, I'd say there's an important decision to be made, and it concerns the issue of whether we want

Danish films to be seen by European audiences. I belong to a generation of directors that includes Susanne Bier, Lone Scherfig, Ole Christian Madsen and Thomas Vinterberg, and we're all involved with Europe in some way. Yet the set-up and political backing that are needed to help us get our films beyond Denmark and into Europe are simply lacking. Should we or shouldn't we aspire to have a European presence? We can't be sure European audiences will support us to the extent that Danish viewers do, and then what do we do? Figuring this sort of thing out could lead to something new that we could all rally around, and that would be interesting.

Redvall: What kind of European film scene would you hope to move into? There's still a lot of talk about the auteur as being at the heart of European film, whereas the debate in Danish film in recent years has focused on a collaborative auteur theory. What does the situation in European film look like from a Danish perspective?

Fly: If the director didn't actually make the artistic decisions, but nonetheless has the final cut, then that's a bad situation. But in my view what needs to be challenged is the final cut concept itself. It's my impression that a number of European directors aren't sufficiently challenged, and this makes for old fashioned films where you think; 'Yes, the director has been given a free hand here, but it just isn't good enough.' Very few people have a lump of art inside them which they can just pull out. Art is created through interplay, and as tension and harmony. I don't believe in the idea of a sacred artist who thinks in entirely his own way and then suddenly meets reality. What's difficult is that we're up against a lot of market mechanisms all the time, and you have to find a sensible way of dealing with it. I don't think it's possible to make films without giving any thought at all to the market and sales, and I don't think anyone in Danish film operates that way, but market pressures are really increasing. It's going to be a struggle in the years to come, and knowing when you've overstepped your own boundaries and made unacceptable as opposed to artistically productive compromises is also a struggle. It's always an ongoing process. Films cost a lot of money to make, so as a filmmaker you're necessarily faced with those questions. If I want people to give me money then I have to get them to understand why I don't want to make the film the way they want it made.

Redvall: It is my impression that in recent years, you, like many other Danish directors, have been more open to including the audience as part of the process, through methods like test screenings. How do you see your relationship with the audience?

Fly: There are indeed several of us who have turned more towards the audience, and it's true that our generation has embraced test screenings 100 per cent. I'm a big fan of test screenings, but only if they're used the right way, that is, if they're used to determine whether the film's story has been told in the right way. The problem with test screenings arises when you start sucking up to the audience, when filmmakers start producing what they think the audience wants. It's very easy to end up in a grey area. At the moment I think the grey area is dominated by commercial interests.

Redvall: Do you think some kind of balance can be achieved?

Fly: I think you have to get used to combining artistic and commercial elements. Art and commerce are not two separate things, although this is in fact the premise underwriting the Danish support system. That system includes the film consultant scheme, which supports the artistic films, and the 60/40 scheme, which funds the commercial films. To me the idea behind 60/40 seems completely wrongheaded and anachronistic inasmuch as it's based on responses from anonymous readers, on a point system, and on the idea that certain human factors need to be removed from the process. I don't believe in that sort of thing at all. There has to be an identifiable human being who says yes or no. Someone has to take responsibility for the funding decision, and there has to be room for trust in the system.

As a director I need trust. With all my films there's been this process during which they've slowly but surely improved. The trust that this will in fact happen needs to be there, as far as I'm concerned, because it takes a long time before I know exactly what the film should look like. That trust is disappearing from the system. As a director you really depend on there being people in the system who are willing to take risks, and our system really doesn't work very well when the economy is sluggish. That Danish filmmaking has become more professional on many levels is good, but I'd actually rather see more trust, and be allowed to cheat a little. So much time is spent on meetings, and accountability, and paperwork. In terms of accountability, the results would actually be better if we were allowed to cheat just a little, because, after all, none of us are making films for the sake of the money. But I doubt there's much sympathy out there for this position.

Chapter 5

Peter Schønau Fog

Peter Schønau Fog. Photography: Sine Ingemann

Born 1971. Peter Schønau Fog graduated as a director from the National Film School of Denmark in 1999. His award-winning graduation film, *Lille Mænsk* (*Little Man*, 1999) – about a young man who tries to return to a small island community after having caused the death of the wreck master's son – is a finely executed, epic drama from the island of Fanø (a small island off the west coast of Southern Jutland) where the director grew up. His first feature film, *Kunsten at græde i kor* (*The Art of Crying*, 2007), is a free adaptation of the Danish writer Erling Jepsen's eponymous novel about incest and grotesque family relations in a small community in Southern Jutland in the 1970s, told with both humour and delicacy. The film was awarded more than 35 national and international prizes.

Feature films

2007 *Kunsten at græde i kor* (*The Art of Crying*)

Short films

1999 *Lille Mænsk* (*Little Man*, graduation film)
1997 *Vildfarelser* (*Aberrations*)
1995 *Blodbrødre* (*Blood Brothers*)
1994 *The Last Ditch*

Jørholt: Did you always want to become a film director?

Fog: I grew up in Sønderho on Fanø. Outside the tourist season it was a rather boring place where you could let your thoughts wander under the immense skies. As a child I always had many images in my head, and I loved to stage things. I was the kind of boy who performed as a puppeteer or a conjuror at the other children's birthday parties. When my two brothers and I got a computer – it was probably the first computer on Fanø – I took a profound interest in programming and making computer games, because they also provided a world I could really explore. In my universe, the very few pixels a screen had to offer back then could be turned into something quite elaborate.

In the ninth grade, we were to do a week-long internship somewhere. More than anything else, I wanted to become a rock star, but strange as it may seem, there were no internships as rock stars available, so instead I spent a week at Video Vest, a small production company that made television programmes for the regional TV station, TV South. It was absolutely wonderful, and one of the photographers there advised me to apply to the National Film School, if I wanted to work with moving images. Some time after that, my father borrowed a VHS camera from work, and I began to make gory and hardboiled urban dramas among the idyllic, thatched houses of Sønderho. The kids loved my films, and maybe it was this taste of success that made me continue to make films when I later went to school in Esbjerg. With a friend I made a 30-minute film that won second prize in a competition, but somehow it was absolutely crazy for a boy from Fanø to think that he'd be able to make films for real.

Jørholt: What kind of films did you watch while growing up? Is there a cinema in Sønderho?

Fog: No, not in Sønderho. There's one in Nordby, but the bus schedules for Sønderho usually made it impossible to return home in the evening. So, I really hadn't seen that many films by the time I began fiddling around with filmmaking myself. It was more of a fantasy game that then developed into something more. But when I started secondary school, I saw as many films as possible. At the same time, I took a vivid interest in philosophy, so I preferred films that dealt with interesting subjects. The library in Esbjerg once showed Carl Th. Dreyer's *La passion de Jeanne d'Arc* (*The Passion of Joan of Arc*, 1928) and Trier's *The Element of Crime* (1984) in one double billing – that was a truly great day in Esbjerg! But actually, I was crazy about anything related to film, anything that reached beyond the classic Esbjerg set-up; that is, a good education and material success. We were a bunch of guys who played music instead of football or handball and who, on the whole, didn't do what was expected of us. Film became a sort of refuge that convinced me that life could be different.

After secondary school I gave myself a year to try to make a film. Initially, the main problem was getting anywhere near some kind of equipment, so when they established a new media centre in Esbjerg – a place where the unemployed could work with radio and TV – I immediately registered myself as unemployed. For the first three or four months, however, the only equipment available was a coffee machine, but when they finally got a tape recorder, I sneaked into a convention for cinema owners in Odense, where I interviewed Jens Jørgen Thorsen about his Jesus film.[1]

I soon left the media centre for a folk high school in Kolding with more equipment, and there I made a very personal film, *Unavngiven* [*Unnamed*]. It was a melting pot of philosophy and other stuff that occupied my mind at the time, but I guess it was basically about finding the courage to define oneself as an artist. It was all very pretentious for someone from Jutland. I don't think anybody has ever understood that film, but having made it gave me the courage to move to Copenhagen. I was accepted by a media school in Lyngby, and I also worked behind the camera on Gabriel Axel's *Prince of Jutland* (1994). And I did a few music videos and a lot of local television.

But I needed something that would keep me mentally engaged. I wanted to study at the university, and since my grades weren't high enough to get into Film and Media Studies at the University of Copenhagen, I ended up in Theatre Studies. Especially the history of the theatre was exciting, but after a year it was clear to me that I had to work with film again. I wanted to go to film school and ended up at FAMU for Foreigners in Prague. As the school thought I might be too experienced for the international programme, they suggested that I do a longer film under supervision. As far as I was concerned, that was perfect, because it gave me the opportunity to realize – on celluloid! – a film script entitled *Livstid* [*Lifetime*] that I'd written for a dramaturgy class at the university. It was a very fairytale-like, art nouveau-ish story, with characters based on Kierkegaard's 'life types', oddly enough also with a 'pity tyrant' like the one in *The Art of Crying*. I never made the film, though, because my brothers and I didn't succeed in raising the necessary money. So, I attended the international programme where I made a five-minute film, *The Last Ditch*, about two soldiers who struggle to survive in the trenches.

Jørholt: What were your four years at the National Film School of Denmark like?

Fog: For a Fanø kid like myself, working with actors whom I'd seen on TV was very anxiety provoking, but Lone Scherfig, who was in charge of aspects of the programme, made sure we worked a lot with actors during the first two years. That was really wonderful; working with actors is perhaps the part of filmmaking that I love the most. Finding one's way with the actors is immensely interesting. But of course Mogens Rukov was also very important to me, especially when I was writing the script for my graduation film.

Other than that, I find it very important that the school, unlike many other film schools, offers different streams. This makes it possible to develop a cinematic language in close collaboration with people who are specializing in some of the other key filmmaking roles.

But I also had a hard time at film school. I've been raised to be polite, and I'm used to listening to other people's points of view, so it was very difficult for me to stay on my own course. Even then, content mattered more to me than form, and it took me a long time to transform an idea into a narrative with images and people. My approach did not really harmonize that well with the School's emphasis on tight deadlines and very short formats, the latter being best suited to little jokes or visual exercises, neither of which interests me as such. That was one of the reasons why I made the twenty-minute long *Aberrations* outside the context of the School. *Aberrations*, which was heavily influenced by Antonioni, was shot during the autumn holidays, in my parents' summer cottage on Fanø.

To sum up, I think the most important thing I learnt in film school is perhaps to say no and to stick to the content I've decided to explore. When I undertake a project, I very quickly determine the bull's eye of the story, and, having found it, I'm quite stubborn about resisting anybody who tries to move the bull's eye. But I do of course recognize that a number of different roads can lead to the same goal.

Jørholt: Where did the story of your graduation film, *Little Man*, come from?

Fog: Just before we were to start on our graduation projects, Arne Bro, the Head of the Documentary and TV Department, organized a few days' of teaching that were devoted to personal subject matter. That was the first time we talked about personal material, so it was quite intense. All of a sudden, it was no longer about making films that looked like films but about making films that looked like us, like ourselves. When Arne Bro heard me talk, he said it sounded like I might have grown up in Frederiksberg [an independent and rich municipality within the larger area of Copenhagen], and that made me rewind a bit. When I'd moved to Copenhagen, I'd decided quite consciously to learn to howl like the wolves I was with, for if I wanted to become a film director, I couldn't have people repeating everything I said because it sounded funny. So, I'd divested myself of my West Jutland dialect. Through an almost hysterical form of self-control I'd erased my own background. But I realized that that background should perhaps be my starting point as a filmmaker.

Actually, I didn't move to Fanø until I was seven years old. My family and I were newcomers from Esbjerg, and since you're not accepted as a true 'Sønderhoning' until your family has lived there for three generations, I always felt a little outside the community in Sønderho. Throughout my childhood on Fanø I had a feeling there was a door I couldn't enter. I don't feel I ever got to be one of them, but this idea of pondering how to become part of a small community that you'd like to belong to was the starting point for my graduation film.

My first idea was based on a short story by Andreas Sørensen, about the first black man to arrive in Sønderho some time in the nineteenth century. It was a

Under the immense skies of Fanø in *Lille Mænsk* (*Little Man*). Frame grab.

story about a Brazilian of African descent who'd been best friends with a young man from Sønderho. They'd been sailing on the same boat, and when the young Sønderhoning fell ill and died, the Brazilian set out to fulfil his promise to him: to deliver a letter to his mother. The idea was to make a film about his attempts to get close to the mother and to be accepted in the small community. But that story was too expensive to make. However, even though the original story is quite far removed from the final film, it's a good example of the bull's eye thing that I mentioned earlier, for both the short story and the film are about a person who tries to enter a small community that doesn't know how to relate to someone from beyond its own clearly defined boundaries.

Because the film only lasts 40 minutes, I had to move the protagonist closer to the community, so I made him someone who'd previously been a member of it, before being expelled for having killed a child in a car accident while under the influence of alcohol. I systematically went through and analysed all the stories I could remember about people who'd fallen out with the community, and I based the film on those analyses. But I'm relieved to say that this story has never actually happened on Fanø. That was quite important to me.

In some weird way, returning to Fanø to make that film felt oddly liberating. I realized that I had spent much of the time in film school driving around Amager [island that is part of the larger Copenhagen area and where both the Film School and Copenhagen Airport are located] looking for locations that had some of that particular Fanø atmosphere, although that's not what I was calling it. I felt some kind of need to use those landscapes. But at the same time I guess it was also a bit like in Gabriel Axel's *Babettes gæstebud* (*Babette's Feast*, 1987), where Babette tries to earn the acceptance of the closed community by inviting everyone to a feast so magnificent that no one dares to refuse her. When the finished film was shown in the cinema in Nordby, it was also a kind of feast that no one dared to reject. But even though *Little Man* was probably the greatest film success on Fanø since the populist comedy *Styrmand Karlsen* (*Helmsman Karlsen*; dir. Annelise Reenberg, 1958), it didn't really help me get any closer to anyone. Now I was just that filmmaker guy.

Jørholt: *The Art of Crying* is an adaptation of Erling Jepsen's novel and is set in the southern part of Jutland. You wrote the Fanø story for *Little Man* yourself, yet the two films seem closely related. In both cases, the story unfolds in a closed community where huge human problems lie smouldering beneath the surface of what can be explicitly said, the result being violent physical outbursts from time to time. And although the downplayed, black humour that is so characteristic of *The Art of Crying* is less pronounced in *Little Man*, it is nonetheless there.

Fog: One of the things I appreciated most about Erling's novel was precisely its particular tone, the somewhat grotesque and cynical way of taking up a very serious subject. What you get is this very special, almost oblique humour. Actually, it was my

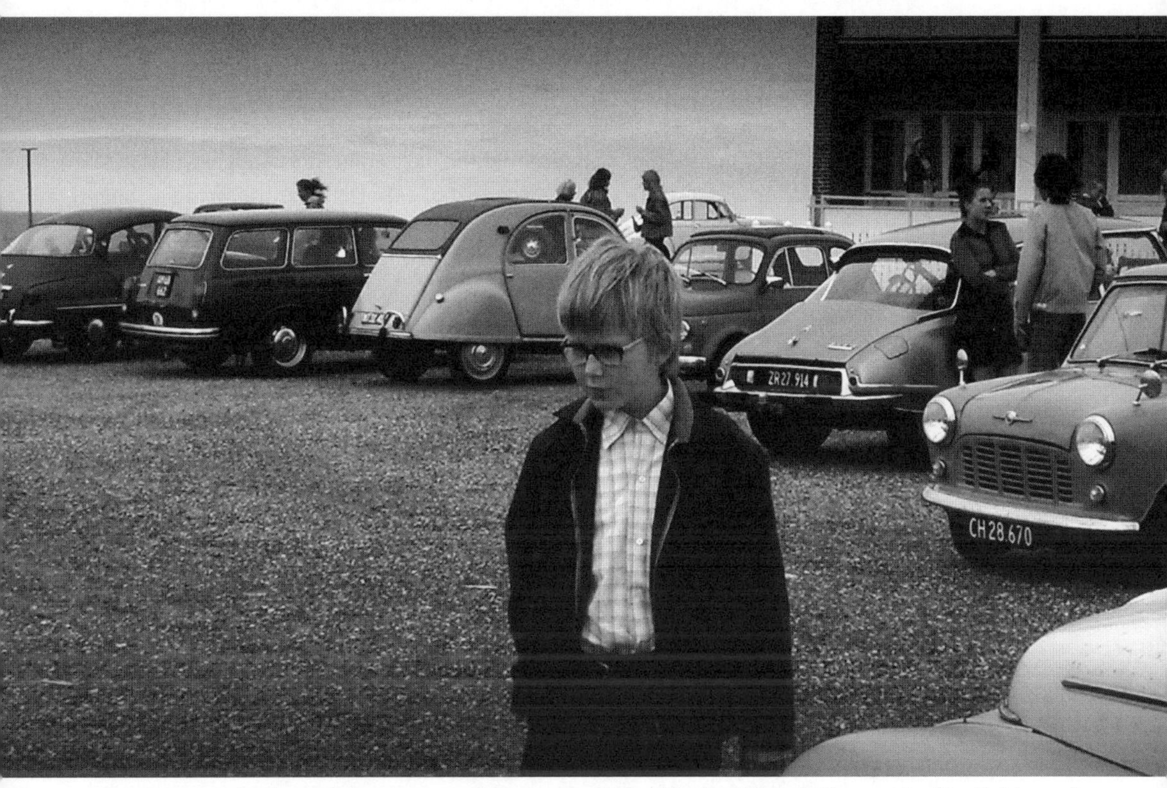

Jannik Lorenzen as the young protagonist in *Kunsten at græde i kor* (*The Art of Crying*). Photography: Henrik Schønau Fog.

intention that *Little Man* should have exactly that tone, because I wanted to use my experience of Fanø – the particular way in which the inhabitants of Fanø use humour when life is at its very toughest – as the instrument on which the melody is played. But that was one of the fights I lost at the Film School, where they found this kind of humour to be in bad taste.

Another thing I admired about the novel was the fact that it addressed the abuse of children in a way that wasn't unbearable, because the story is told through the boy. It is through his eyes that we look out on an oblique world that he himself does not see as oblique. I felt that if we could make that work in a film, if we could get at the subject in a way that underlined the fact that these things take place among people – that it's not the work of the devil – it would be absolutely fantastic. It was, therefore, very important to me to ensure that the particular, obliquely humoristic tone that I was after was a result of the boy's way of experiencing the world – that it was linked to his perspective rather than simply being the tone of the film more generally.

Jørholt: In both films you use both professional and non-professional actors. Why?

Fog: I want the films I make to have a certain realism, and that's a bit more difficult to achieve if the actors are known from some commercial and if the audience is already somehow satiated with regard to a certain face. I suppose I might have found an eleven-year old boy with more film experience for the main part in *The Art of Crying* if I hadn't insisted that he should be able to speak the local dialect from Southern Jutland. Actually, very few children today speak that dialect, which is kind of sad. Anyway, the film is set in Southern Jutland, and therefore the characters need to speak South Jutlandic. I don't think we would have been able to make the story and the humour work if the film hadn't played in a realistic and therefore credible world. When Jannik (Lorenzen) auditioned for the part of Allan, I felt for the first time that we'd found what we'd been looking for: a very particular mix of being eleven years old, from Southern Jutland, precocious and a bit cynical. Somehow these things all came together.

Having very young and inexperienced people like Jannik and Julie (Kolbech) play parts that are as serious as they are is of course quite a delicate matter. But we went to great lengths to give them the tools that would permit them to maintain a third person relationship with their characters. When we shot the scenes, we discussed what 'he' or 'she', i.e. the characters, should do, and once the film was finished, they were totally aware of the fact that it wasn't them up there on the screen but their characters.

Jørholt: It is sometimes said that it's the truly local films that have the greatest chance of attracting a global audience.

Fog: Yes, but I don't necessarily agree. If a film attracts a global audience, it's probably because it's about something important and tells a human story. If spectators from Japan or elsewhere can relate to the film, it's because we worked unbelievably hard to reach the pure human story and to mix humour and seriousness in such a way as to respect the seriousness of the subject while presenting it in a way that wouldn't make the film unbearable to watch. We use the local as an instrument of everyday realism that is meant to enhance the credibility of the film. If there was nothing more to the film than images from Southern Jutland and the local dialect, it would probably not interest anyone other than people from Southern Jutland.

Jørholt: *The Art of Crying* was five years in the making. Why did it take so long?

Fog: We started out with a Danish Film Institute consultant who wanted to change the script and make the father violent but that would have been totally at odds with the film's tightly knit psychological web. The next consultant did not want Jesper Asholt in the role of the father. He had another suggestion that would have resulted in a completely incoherent film. He did give us money to make a pilot with Jesper Asholt, though, but because he didn't believe in Jesper in that role, he didn't like the pilot, so that was that. By then, we'd already been in touch with 300 boys from Southern Jutland, and in the meantime they'd grown too old for the role of Allan. Then Nikolaj Scherfig was appointed as consultant, and he liked the novel, the pilot and me, but not the script, so he asked us to start from scratch and divide the story into chapters. The scriptwriter Bo hr. Hansen then worked on the script for about a year, and after that, we both worked on it for eight months.

Jørholt: Based on your own experience, would you say that these are difficult times for auteur filmmaking in Denmark?

Fog: Consultants are not all the same, of course, and Bo hr. Hansen and I are not experiencing the same kind of difficulties in relation to the project that we're working on now. But the consultant system creates a needle's eye that you have to get through, and you can be forced to change your project to accommodate the consultant's personal taste. It is, of course, quite OK for a consultant really to engage with a project, but there's a limit to how many times you can change a story. In the end, we did follow the third consultant's instructions, but it's extremely tough simply to have to dump a script that has been eighteen months in the making. I don't mean to criticize the consultant system which is fine in many ways but it does create that needle's eye where it really comes down to the consultant's personal preferences.

Jørholt: You also experienced certain problems with the film's producer, Thomas Stenderup.

Fog: Just before we started shooting, he decided that the film should be a shallow, absurd comedy. Otherwise nobody would watch it, or that at least was his argument. But it's of course absolutely impossible to make that kind of U-turn so late in the process, and there are definitely limits to how much comedy you can put into a story about incest. When you work on a subject like that, you have to have a lot of respect for the people who've actually experienced this kind of abuse.

But the problems continued into the shooting phase itself, the editing phase, sound phase, music phase, launch phase, etc. At several points I was threatened with having to give up my right to final cut, and only thanks to legal aid from the Association of Danish Film Directors was I finally able to finish the film as its director and to prevent it from being transformed into an absurd comedy in bad taste. I had to put a lot of energy into that conflict, energy I'd have preferred to put into the film. The process was so tough that I still find it hard to talk about that film. I'm extremely proud of the success it's enjoyed, but I cannot say that sentence without adding the phrase 'in spite of'... That kind of conflict is just not in any way constructive.

Jørholt: How do you manage to survive when a project drags on like that?

Fog: That's a very good question. I haven't done any TV, nor have I made any commercials. Presumably because *Little Man* is so Jutlandic, I haven't been able to fit into any of those boxes. I received a two-year so-called 'activating scholarship' from the Danish Arts Foundation, and during the early phases of the project I lived on those 2 x 70,000 DKK. Later on I also received a bit of some slate funding that the production company had obtained for three projects, including *The Art of Crying*. Being a filmmaker is most frustrating when there's no money to fund a new project. Then you can either try to limit your expenses or do something else. I chose the former in order to be able to concentrate on making the best possible film.

Jørholt: Have you received any offers after *The Art of Crying*?

Fog: No, not after *The Art of Crying*. But I'm working on a project I started immediately after film school. It's a period film, a genre that was somewhat out of fashion by the time the Dogma wave peaked. The film addresses what Søren Kierkegaard calls 'the 70,000 fathom leap', that is, the choice of faith. Bo hr. Hansen and I have now received funding to write a script, so hopefully it will end up as a film.

Jørholt: It's a common assumption that a filmmaker's second film is more difficult than the first one. What's your experience in this regard?

Fog: The overwhelmingly positive response to *Little Man* was totally unexpected and kind of knocked me off my feet for a long time. After that film, I received a number of offers, some more serious than others, and I found it quite difficult to navigate between them. Among other things, I was invited to develop an American feature film remake of *Little Man*, and a French producer wanted me to make a western about Calamity Jane. So I guess you could say that I've already had my 'second film crisis', and it was *The Art of Crying*. I have a lot of difficulty with the more public aspects of being a film director. I don't like playing the part of the cryptic artist, and I sometimes find it hard to know how to situate myself in relation to all the gods and bigwigs of the film world. There's a lot of showing off and bravura in this business, but perhaps that's a necessary condition for getting one's projects off the ground.

Jørholt: Are you in contact with other directors?

Fog: I still keep in touch with some of the people I went to film school with, but I guess I have the same relation to the film milieu that I once had to Fanø; a sense of standing outside a community that I'd actually like to belong to. Perhaps I'm a bit of a loner, but in many ways I don't feel that I'm a part of the Danish film environment. I'd never call another director to ask him or her for advice.

Jørholt: Has Danish film become too mainstream? How do you see the future for Danish film?

Fog: I must say I was quite astonished to find that *The Art of Crying* produced so much fear and trembling. If a film like that produces such a high level of resistance, then there can't be much room to manoeuvre in, in the Danish context. But perhaps it was just an isolated case. Actually, I think the biggest problem faced by Danish cinema today is that success made people think they'd figured everything out. And this made them repeat things, the same thing over and over again. What was once new and refreshing has simply been worn out. The audience is fed up with everyday realism as a form of expression.

I guess we'll need to use more keys on the cinematic keyboard if we're to regain the confidence of viewers who are interested in drama films. Of course shooting on locations outside of Copenhagen is something that costs money, and the same goes for dressing actors in costumes other than their own clothes. But if Danish cinema is not given the economic possibility of using a larger cinematic spectrum, we risk losing the audience that we currently have.

Maybe we also need to work at branding Danish cinema better, internationally. Dogma 95 was a brand, but I'm not sure that Danish film as such is. What is it that Danish film is good at? I don't know. I don't represent Danish cinema as such. I'm just a guy from Fanø.

Note

1. In 1973, the situationist artist and filmmaker Jens Jørgen Thorsen (1932–2000) received support from the Danish Film Institute to make a film about the sex life of Jesus Christ. The project stirred up some controversy on account of its allegedly blasphemous content, and was abandoned after Thorsen had been declared guilty of offending the droit moral of the Evangelists. The verdict was later revoked, and in 1992 Thorsen's Jesus film, *The Return of Jesus*, finally opened in Danish cinemas.

Chapter 6

Henrik Ruben Genz

Henrik Ruben Genz. Photography: Thomas Marott.

Born 1959. Henrik Ruben Genz trained as an illustrator and graphic artist at the Kolding Design School, before, at the age of thirty-one, being accepted into the director's stream at the National Film School of Denmark. His black and white graduation film *Omveje* (*Cross Roads*, 1995) has been singled out as one of the best in the School's history. The film paints a subtle portrait of the encounter between the Jutlander Bjarne (Henrik Lykkegaard), who is having trouble adjusting to the capital, Copenhagen, and his old friend Troels (Jesper Asholt), who has no problem being from the provinces. Genz received an Oscar nomination for the short film *Bror, min bror* (*Theis and Nico*, 1998), which is about a nine-year-old boy who is in love with Gjinja, the local beauty on his block, and who becomes jealous when his brother is invited to her birthday celebration. Genz's feature film debut was a screen version of the popular author Bjarne Reuter's novel *En som Hodder* (*Someone like Hodder*, 2003). Focusing on Hodder's world, the film explores the ten year old's real problems, but also his daydreams. In *Kinamand* (*Chinaman*, 2005) the central character is the plumber Keld (Bjarne Henriksen), who gets involved in life at his local Chinese takeaway. He enters into a pro forma marriage with the beautiful Ling (Vivian Wu) in order to get her a residence permit, but gradually falls in love with her. Genz's latest film, *Frygtelig lykkelig* (*Terribly Happy*, 2008) won the main prize at the international film festival in Karlovy Vary and has had great success with Danish critics and at the box office. In 2009 the film won the larger part of the year's Bodil and Robert awards for its visually intense depiction of the dramatic conditions encountered by Robert (Jakob Cedergren), a policeman from the capital, when he becomes a village policeman in a small town in Southern Jutland. The film is based on a novel by Erling Jepsen, with whom Genz grew up in the southern Jutlandic village of Gram.

Feature films

2008	*Frygtelig lykkelig* (*Terribly Happy*)
2005	*Kinamand* (*Chinaman*)
2003	*En som Hodder* (*Someone like Hodder*)

Short films

1998	*Bror, min bror* (*Theis and Nico*, Oscar-nominated)
1995	*Omveje* (*Cross Roads*, graduation film)

Television

2009	*Lulu & Leon* (Two episodes)
2007	*Forbrydelsen* (*The Killing*, four episodes)
2004–2006	*Krøniken* (*Better Times*, five episodes)
2003	*Forsvar* (*Defense*, three episodes)
2003	*Nikolaj og Julie* (*Nikolaj and Julie*, two episodes)
2001	*De udvalgte* (*The Chosen 7*, four episodes)

Redvall: You started at the Film School's directing programme after having finished your training as an illustrator and graphic artist at the Kolding Design School. Where did the desire to make films come from?

Genz: Originally, I wanted to be a painter, and I went to the Design School in order to become a painter. But I quickly realized that the education on offer there was very industrial. We were taught how to do pictograms and logos, which I basically thought was boring. I then thought I'd attend the school and paint on the side, but painting requires tremendous self-discipline. It's hard to motivate yourself to do it. It's hard to get up in the morning and to make sure you go over to the canvas and start pressing the tubes. It's a lonely activity, and it didn't work for me.

While I was at the Design School TV 2 was established. As a result there was suddenly TV programming that was being financed by commercials, and so the school decided that we should do commercials. That's why the video installation artist Niels Lomholt was hired and in my case that encounter was important. Instead of making a commercial I made a seven-minute, depressing 80s-style portrait of a human being with no sense of direction in life, and filming with a camera turned out to be an epiphany. Suddenly the images just produced themselves. All I had to do was push the button, and spend time with other people while I was doing it. It was like that camera just stuck to my eye, and all I did the following year was film everything that could possibly be filmed.

Among other places, I ended up at the Video Workshop in Haderslev, but I wasn't thinking about becoming a film director. That idea only occurred to me when I met the director Arne Bro in what was a second crucial encounter. He'd trained at the National Film School of Denmark, in Copenhagen, and had ended up at TV South in Haderslev, but he was actually more interested in what was going on at the Video Workshop. He saw some of my weird productions and encouraged me to apply to the Film School. To me the idea of going to the Film School was the same as dreaming about being the first man on Mars. It was just as unrealistic. But I applied and got in, even though I'd never set myself the goal of going there, and even though I'd never been especially interested in film. I still don't watch very many films, and I don't know the names of the directors or actors.

Redvall: What was it like going to the Film School?

Genz: It was a complete upheaval and a very shocking experience to me. Both starting at a new school and living in Copenhagen. I also had to overcome my shyness. Luckily I soon found some likeminded people, because there were actually quite a number of students who were from Jutland, as I was, and from other places, and who weren't already part of the film industry. To me the Film School was like being born into a milieu that I'd otherwise never have made my way into. I wouldn't have known which doors to knock on, and I'd never have dared knock on them if I had. The Film School led me into that milieu quite naturally. I made some important friends and contacts, and then Nimbus Film was established in the same period, and I ended up being affiliated with them.

Redvall: Nimbus Film went on to become an important production company in the Danish context. What did it mean to you to be affiliated with this company from the moment you left the Film School?

Genz: I made the short film *Theis and Nico* while I was at Nimbus Film, but I never managed to make the transition to feature filmmaking while I was there. I actually think that the fact that the company was based on friendships was a bit of an obstacle. We had a difficult time sorting out the job descriptions, and the atmosphere was generally very friendly. I needed a boss who'd put his foot down and say 'We've got a deadline so you'd better get going.' That milieu didn't do anything for my creativity. I suppose I need an employer. At least, that's one of the things that works for me now. I have these tumultuous debates with my producer, and in the process of all that I get what it is I do and don't want to do articulated. You can easily get smothered by a kind of friendliness that's about avoiding conflicts and thus ultimately not very constructive. Some people thrive in that kind of environment, and are so self-motivating that if they're left in peace they produce a script. I need to be challenged, and to have to defend myself. It's the same as with painting; I can't just go into a room alone and make things up. Somebody has to make demands on you, or to have certain expectations of you, or to be a witness to your existence.

Redvall: *Theis and Nico* is a story about the rivalry between two brothers and the first encounter with a girl. The script was written by Michael Horsten, who also wrote the script for your graduation film. How did *Theis and Nico* come about?

Genz: Michael came to me with this little idea for a short film, and the tone and the theme of the story touched me. It was about loneliness, about longing to feel connected to other people, about the desire for community. I didn't know then that I'd later make a number of films with that theme, but I could just feel that it was right. The story made sense to me in a way that the spectacular feature film drafts that I was 'designing' with other writers at the time simply didn't.

When two people are in a room together and have to come up with a film together, it's easy to gravitate towards high tension bank robberies and murder stories. The small, much quieter drama disappears because it can't be sensed in the conversation. It quickly becomes boring when the climax is a look, or a turned back, or a kiss. It's easy to end up emphasizing high drama when you're working collaboratively, because there are all these shared references to very dramatic material. Michael brought me this script that he'd written alone, in his own space and based on his own quiet sense of the first encounter with a girl. I was then able to absorb this in my own space. The story came from a single place, and had a soul from the beginning.

Redvall: *Theis and Nico* won the Crystal Bear at the Berlin Festival and was also nominated for an Oscar. What did these honours mean for your work as a director?

Genz: They meant a lot at the time. My self-confidence had been undermined by a series of failed projects. Getting an Oscar nomination boosted my faith in my abilities. But things were, paradoxically enough, completely quiet after the Oscar nomination. It's never been as quiet as in the six months following the nomination. Perhaps I suddenly became the Oscar nominee you don't call because everybody else is probably calling him.

I was at Nimbus Film, writing while receiving unemployment benefits, because they couldn't afford to pay me, and suddenly these two letters were delivered the same day. That was quite a day. One of the letters indicated that I had to do a job placement, because I was no longer eligible for benefits. The other letter had a gold leafed logo, was from 'The Academy' and conveyed the news about my Oscar nomination. One letter had me becoming something like a dishwasher in a cafeteria, whereas the other letter suggested I might become someone important *over there*. In a way it's a very precise image of what being a director is like. You're out of the game for a long time, you sit on the bench watching the others, and then suddenly you're back in the game, scoring goals, but only for a moment, and then you're out again.

Redvall: What was difficult about making the transition to feature film projects after the Film School?

Genz: It was difficult to find the right material. Getting a good working relationship established between a director and a scriptwriter is hard. It's a sensitive area, where it's all about taste and sensibility. It's hard to find someone who's really compatible with you. What you're looking for in that partnership is a kind of shared basic tonality. You have to have the same sensibility. After Film School I was very, very critical and very deconstructive. Nothing was ever good enough. I was quick to reject things, and that's not a good starting point for collaborative work.

You can explain that critical attitude in different ways. Maybe I was afraid of failing, after having made a promising graduation film. This idea that people would think 'OK, so here's this new talent, let's see what he can actually do.' Perhaps I was afraid that I'd disappoint. There are no doubt lots of reasons, but one big difference between the periods before and after the Film School is that the films I'd made earlier had really come from me. They were driven by my strong desire to make them, and by curiosity. And then suddenly you're a 'real' film director, and you're equipped with an office and a desk, and a phone and a fax, and you're teamed up with some very talented person or other. You end up with this very artificial situation, sitting around a table where the idea is that you're supposed to design a new feature film together. Suddenly it's not coming from the inside. It's about what we can agree on, or what we think is cool. I couldn't feel that material at all and I wasn't clever enough to find a way to make it mine. That's why I'd be so quick to react critically. It actually took me five years to figure out how to tackle all this. Having to do TV series helped.

TV series can be of very mixed quality, but by saying yes to doing these series you sort of get beyond your aversions and anxieties, and you escape the pressures of your own ambition. Instead of dealing with all that you just take on a very concrete job. TV helped me get over this idea that I had to be able to feel something before I could start working on it. The good thing about a TV series is that there's no sense of personal responsibility. You step into a concept. Other people have taken responsibility for whether it's good or bad. Your job is to deliver the best possible craftsmanship, and that task helped me to rediscover the joy of making images and working with drama. I realized that it wasn't necessary to work in as fine, clever or sensitive a way as I'd initially thought. TV helped me to get over that anxiety about the production process.

Redvall: In the 90s a number of Danish directors alternated between directing long TV series for the Danish Broadcasting Corporation and their own films. What do you think the Danish Broadcasting Corporation's invitation to younger directors has meant, in terms of the development of Danish film?

Genz: Those TV series were, and still are, a gift to the entire film industry. Even the less good ones. You get to try out some things that you'd never be allowed to get anywhere near if you were doing that one feature film every three years, after having finally been granted permission to make another film. The TV series have made it possible for filmmakers to risk doing something stupid, to experiment, and there's of course a sense of calm that comes from knowing that you're guaranteed work for a certain period of time. The series have been a gift, and not only from the perspective of the directors. The same is true for everyone involved, for the cinematographers, the editors, the actors and so on. The TV series helped me to open up, and to accept the idea that other practitioners could contribute to one's project. As a director at the Film School you're very focused on doing the writing yourself, or on expressing yourself. Simply taking on somebody else's script feels impoverished, because you have that auteur concept inside you. I think it would be good if the Film School could focus more on having directors learn to work with and direct scripts by others. Because what you graduate into is an industry. It's no longer art. The art lies in keeping your integrity, although you're shaped first by the Film School and then later by the industry.

Redvall: You were at Nimbus during the years when Thomas Vinterberg made *Festen* (*The Celebration*, 1998) for the company, and when Dogma 95 was the latest new thing. Were you in any way involved with Dogma?

Genz: Yes, Dogma came along while I was at Nimbus, and I was at one point asked whether I wanted to do a Dogma film. In the midst of all the euphoria I said yes, but deep inside I could feel something saying no. I only found out later that what was unappealing to me about Dogma was that there was no visual language. The rules were virtually about ruining the image. The actors had to find their own clothes. There was no set design. You weren't allowed to stylize anything. To me the rules seemed completely ridiculous. You weren't allowed to compose an image. The camera had to follow the players. The rules couldn't have been further from my own starting point, in terms of the composition of images.

I can almost only see the world in images. I can never remember what films are about, because I'm always looking at the images. I look at how they cut the faces. And although those faces are talking, I can barely hear what they're saying because I'm preoccupied with other things. Why did they choose that patterned wallpaper? Dogma didn't work for me because it involved mostly technical rules that were about limiting the possibilities of the image and the sound. I just didn't find it inspiring, so the Dogma film project didn't go anywhere; and the same was true for many of my other projects in that period.

Redvall: Your three feature films *Someone like Hodder*, *Chinaman* and *Terribly Happy* are all far removed from the realism that Dogma invites. With its carefully composed images and sensual universes, your visual style has been described as a sort of timeless and classic, magical formalism. How do you feel about the everyday realism that became almost a Danish brand in the wake of Dogma?

Genz: I get tired of realism when it becomes one to one. Films are best when they get close to something that is reminiscent of dreams. When they break with reality or the real world, while still making it possible to understand what's going on. Films have to be sensed and interpreted by the viewer and not explained by the director. Relationship problems shouldn't, for example, be represented in a direct way. That's just not interesting. I prefer it when I have to understand things on a different level.

In *Terribly Happy* we could have shown, in a very realistic and dramatically effective way, how Jørgen beats up Ingelise. Instead we hear the sound of a pram driving by. When we hear the sound of the pram, we know that Jørgen is hitting Ingelise. And we have our own ideas about what that looks like. That way of narrating the story is pure film, real film narration. It's about veiling things to some extent, so that the audience becomes part of the storytelling process. There's a veil between the spectator and the actual events, and the spectator has to find a way through it.

There's no problem looking for an element of truth, even if it's in a context where the cat can say 'morning'. No, a cat can't really say 'morning', but inside the central character's head it can, and perhaps that's exactly where we need to be. We also called the village in the film Skarrild, like *skærsild* [purgatory], because it's a sort of purgatory where certain people have stranded. It's about a parallel reality or a dream reality, maybe even a nightmare reality. It's not about authenticity, but about a mental or existential truth.

I oppose the tendency to drain film of magic. Films are images, and I think it's important to put effort into the composition of the images. There are some classic shapes and proportions that have traditionally been thought of as appealing to the eyes. You can always break with them, but you have to be aware of when and where you do it. I always try to remove everything that's irrelevant from the image, so I can control what people will experience and sense. I don't allow anything to disturb the composition. The expression has to be clean in relation to my intention with the image. In that sense I work with a kind of classic, timeless style.

Redvall: Many Danish directors make a children's film as their feature debut, but then abandon the genre. How did *Someone like Hodder* end up being your first feature film?

Genz: After I'd made *Theis and Nico*, I thought I'd made enough children's films, but Bo hr. Hansen's script for *Someone like Hodder* moved me as I read it. It was once again this business of there suddenly being music that somehow awakened me. It didn't matter that it was a children's film because, as a character, Hodder struck me, and I could envisage the images and the moods. Of course, it's also the case that there wasn't any other good material around at the time, and making a children's film does remove some of the anxiety one has about needing to achieve. You sort of sneak around the fear-provoking red carpet, and in through the backdoor. To me it was a great relief to get that script, because it was really the eleventh hour. I'd reached a point where it was becoming really hard to tell myself I was going to be a director, because there were simply so many shipwrecked ideas in my wake, and they were starting to pull me down. With *Someone like Hodder* I left all the shipwrecked ideas behind me, in order to tell the story of this little creature who runs around trying to belong, while nobody really thinks he's good enough. He doesn't fit in. His whole struggle to win some sort of approval and to find a place in the world spoke to me.

Redvall: Your next film, *Chinaman*, creates an alluring universe centred on a Chinese takeaway restaurant, exotic ideas about China and love that transcends language. Wong Kar-Wai's *In the Mood for Love* (2000) seems to have been a source of inspiration in this case. Where do you find the visual inspiration for your films?

Genz: Before I made *Chinaman* I saw *In the Mood for Love*, and I was quite bored. I didn't understand what it was about at all, but the images were absolutely wonderful. I can be inspired by looking at the shape of other films. *Terribly Happy* has been compared to the films by the Coen brothers. I just saw *Fargo* (1996) and again I was very bored. I can see that there's a funny scene or character here or there, but I probably feel a general sense of restlessness with respect to the duration that a film has. Often I nearly can't get through them, especially if I don't get the story, and I'm just sitting there, staring. But visually I'm naturally inspired by other films. By moods and sensuality. I'm always looking for the right key in which to play. *Chinaman* is clearly inspired by Wong Kar-Wai's film. I think that *Chinaman* is a fine film, but the drama is probably so inward that you have to be very intimately present to get caught up in it, and the larger audience didn't have the patience or sensibility for that. If the conflicts are to catch the attention of a large audience, they apparently have to be clearer, more explicit, almost noisy, or just plain funny. A softspoken and poetic film about an emotionally reticent man who opens up as a result of love wasn't seen as particularly dramatic. Viewed purely in terms of ticket sales, that film is a real failure, which is a pity, I think.

Redvall: *Terribly Happy*, by contrast, was a big success in those same terms. The film is based on a novel by Erling Jepsen, whom you grew up with, in the village of Gram, in Southern Jutland. How did you two end up working together?

Genz: Erling and I actually lived on the same street when we were children. Our worlds started in the same mudhole, so in some way we have the same tonality and humour. We've been shaped by the same cultural and spiritual poverty. We've ended up with a certain view of the world, and so clearly I'm able to recognize what he's on about when he writes. But Erling moved to Copenhagen when he

Opposite: Bjarne Henriksen and Vivian Wu in *Kinamand* (*Chinaman*). Photography: Robin Skjoldborg.

was about eighteen, and he had success with his plays, whereas I stayed behind and messed around and only got to Copenhagen much later. I had no contact with him when I first got to Copenhagen, probably because we'd both become so snooty we didn't want to contact each other. But then he wrote *Kunsten at græde i kor* [*The Art of Crying*], which takes place among all the people on the road in our village. At that point it seemed like I'd best step forward, so I could ask him whether I could adapt his book to film. But by the time I did the book had already been given to Peter Schønau Fog, who, incidentally, turned it into a really good film.

However, Erling told me he had another idea, about a policeman from Copenhagen who moves to Southern Jutland. It sounded interesting and we ended up agreeing to meet twice a week at Café Bizarro on Amager [an island that is part of Copenhagen] in order to talk about the story. Later he sent me chapters for the book, and I then commented on them. When the book was finished it turned out that there were simply too many things in it for the purposes of a film, and that's when I realized I was well served by all that experience I'd had working with scriptwriters on my other films. It was clear to me that I needed a good writer who'd be able to lift the best material from the novel into a script. Saying yes to that book and then allowing myself to hire a writer was an amazing experience.

Dunja Gry Jensen was brought in, and her approach to the book was tough as nails. I know she spared me three years of despair. She cut right to the bone, and her sole aim was to get to where I wanted to go. She did what a good scriptwriter does, which is to dig out what you're looking for, or help you find what you can't see yourself. It's easy to get caught up in absolutely everything. Everything seems equally important, and the result is that you go nowhere with the material. You need a somewhat cynical and precise perspective if you're going to have the courage really to cut, and it was simply a gift having Dunja help with this. Also, by then I'd come to trust my ability to make the material mine again. I knew I'd be able to conquer it again, and that it was just a matter of separating things.

Redvall: *Terribly Happy* was filmed in Southern Jutland where the book takes place. It's my impression that you had to fight hard to be allowed to take a film team that far away from Copenhagen. Is it difficult to make films outside the capital?

Genz: There's a tendency to want all films to have more or less the same budget. This is worrying, because the result is a certain standardization of the films. The effect of the limited budgets is that directors are often forced to tell a present-day story that unfolds in two or three locations, has four actors (usually cast as two young couples) and all of that within a very small radius of the relevant Copenhagen-based production company. It kills variety. Of course it's expensive to put up a team somewhere for three weeks. It costs money and it's difficult for the team. People have trouble getting their private lives to work, what with children who

Kim Bodnia with angry support in the marsh land of Southern Jutland. From *Frygtelig lykkelig* (*Terribly Happy*). Photography: Karin Alsbirk.

need to be picked up from daycare, and who need looking after. There are also a lot of logistical production problems, having to do, for example, with getting the actors back to Copenhagen in time for their evening theatre performances. What do you do if the camera breaks? You lose somewhere between half a day and a whole day, because it has to be sent to Copenhagen and then back again.

You should only set a film in the provinces if the story actually takes place there. In *Terribly Happy* the location itself is as significant as any of the actors. My producer wanted to film on the island of Funen because there was money to be had from the regional film fund FilmFyn, and we'd be closer to Copenhagen. But everything is so well tempered in Funen, with hollyhocks and old wood-beamed houses, and people selling cauliflower by the road. That wasn't what we needed. We didn't need an idyllic postcard-style Denmark. We needed the marsh land of Southern Jutland, and when I took my producer down there, and we stood together in that treeless landscape, under the open skies, he saw my point. So he gave me three weeks down there.

Redvall: Like a number of other Danish films, *Terribly Happy* draws a sombre image of the Danish provinces. Why do you think there's a darker tone in the films set in the provinces?

Genz: Well, the provinces are defined by being remote from the capital, and thus civilization. We're out there where the rules have dissolved, or where there are rules that fit the place better than those originating in the big city. Otherwise there'd be no reason to be there. The provinces are by definition backward, as compared with the capital, which is where the spiritual life unfolds; the provinces represent what's primitive in human beings, the place where desires and decay are just under the surface. I've thought about quite a number of those 'far out in the sticks stories', and whenever the provinces are in the picture, the decay surfaces automatically. It's not something you can control. There's all the sexuality, and then there are the fights and the violence. It's difficult to come up with a tempered and well-mannered story that takes place in the provinces. When you opt for the provinces you also opt for the dark side of society. Morally and spiritually speaking you enter a completely different field.

Redvall: You've worked with many different scriptwriters, just as you've hired different cinematographers and editors for your films. Why do you almost always work with new people?

Genz: There are recurring figures, such as the composer Kåre Bjerkø and the set designer Niels Sejer, but it's true that there's been a high turnover. That actually surprises me too, because I'm someone who looks for a comfort zone. In the case of *Terribly Happy* it would have made sense to work with people I know well. But familiarity can also be a pillow to rest your laurels on. The photographer Bo Tengberg is very good and he's my friend, but we'd done so much TV together that I was afraid we'd incorporated an automatic drive into our way of working, and that we'd have approached the film as though it were a TV series. I had to tear away the carpet from underneath my feet, and break with that sense of security. It's easy to end up with habits and routines in the context of a well-established partnership, and I think it was good to shake things up a bit.

Redvall: What do you see as Danish film's greatest challenge at the moment?

Genz: We've become so good at story structures and turning points that we've sort of mashed everything into that structure and forgotten about the more 'weird' stories that involve an element of fabulation. Fortunately, in the last two or three years filmmakers have started once again to allow themselves to thwart the conventions. Some directors are looking for new paths, and that's why I'm still optimistic about the diversity of Danish film.

On the other hand, I do worry about certain political developments regarding film. We're seeing the power of the Danish Film Institute being diminished, and power being transferred increasingly to the TV stations. And the TV stations are mostly concerned with viewer ratings, and mistakenly think that spectators want film art based on the lowest common denominator. We have to protect the Film Institute's film commissioning system. We've never ever had as many competent film consultants as we do right now. It's not a coincidence that most of them are film editors. They've spent years, as editors, cursing all the missing elements and all the moments that don't work in a story. They're incredibly good readers, and really good at seeing the potential of a script. In earlier times the film consultants were typically cultural critics and pipe-smoking socialists. Now they're persons with a wealth of experience and huge insight into what they're doing, so it's only right that they should have some real influence. You can certainly leave the Film Institute feeling frustrated and angry. *Terribly Happy* was also given some heavy kicks along the way, but they helped to lift the film by about 25 per cent.

Another problem is that there's probably a tendency to go into production too early. Several contemporary Danish films would have benefited from some additional re-writing. There's a lack of precision and refinement, and there's been an eagerness to start filming as soon as possible, and the illusion that problems would be solved during the shooting of the film, or in the cutting room. But all you're doing in thinking that way is deferring the problems until later, and in the end they sit there as glaring weaknesses in the finished film. Even though it's tough, you have to turn every stone ten times before you start making your film, not least of all for your own sake.

Chapter 7

Anders Thomas Jensen

Anders Thomas Jensen.
Photography: Rolf Konow.

Born 1972. In 1996, the self-taught Anders Thomas Jensen directed the first of his three Oscar-nominated short films. *Valgaften* (*Election Night*, 1996) earnt him the statue for a story about an idealist (played by Ulrich Thomsen) who has to relate to racist statements in various cabs on the way to the polling station shortly before closing time. As the scriptwriter for popular 'lad comedies', such as *I Kina spiser de hunde* (*In China They Eat Dogs*; dir. Lasse Spang Olsen, 1999), Anders Thomas Jensen established a new genre in Danish film, focusing on humour and action. His scripts for the Dogma films *Mifunes sidste sang* (*Mifune*; dir. Søren Kragh-Jacobsen, 1999) and *The King is Alive* (dir. Kristian Levring, 2000) brought him international recognition. His first feature film as a director, *Blinkende lygter* (*Flickering Lights*, 2000) tells the story of four petty criminals who are on the run. They hide in a dilapidated inn in a forest where they gradually discover some of life's previously unknown dimensions, the value of earth-cooled beers, for example, as an instance of national heritage. With witty dialogue and a cast of prominent young actors delivering top performances, *Flickering Lights* became a national hit. Anders Thomas Jensen has since directed his own scripts for *De grønne slagtere* (*The Green Butchers*, 2003) and *Adams æbler* (*Adam's Apples*, 2005), both of which are characterized by a raw sense of humour, played out in highly stylized cinematic worlds. In *The Green Butchers* the two orphaned butcher's assistants (played by Mads Mikkelsen and Nikolaj Lie Kaas) open a shop in a small provincial town, where human meat in a special marinade quickly becomes popular. In *Adam's Apples* the unorthodox country vicar Ivan (Mads Mikkelsen) gives the neo-Nazi Adam (Ulrich Thomsen) the task of baking an apple pie, and the prosaic project develops, with coarse humour as a recurring element, into a drama about both self-deception and Christian charity. With the script for *Elsker dig for evigt* (*Open Hearts*, 2002) Anders Thomas Jensen began what would become a long-term collaborative partnership with filmmaker Susanne Bier. Both *Brødre* (*Brothers*, 2003; remade by Jim Sheridan in 2009), and the Oscar-nominated *Efter brylluppet* (*After the Wedding*, 2006) received international attention. At the same time, Anders Thomas Jensen has worked in a consultative capacity for both Danish and international directors, most recently in connection with the scripts for Lars von Trier's *Antichrist* (2009). In 2003, Anders Thomas Jensen received an honorary Bodil from Denmark's National Association of Film Critics along with scriptwriter Kim Fupz Aakeson and the Head of the Scriptwriting Department at the National Film School of Denmark, Mogens Rukov.

Feature films

2005 *Adams æbler* (*Adam's Apples*)
2003 *De grønne slagtere* (*The Green Butchers*)
2000 *Blinkende lygter* (*Flickering Lights*)

Short films

1998 *Valgaften* (*Election Night*, won an Oscar in 1999 for best live-action short film)
1997 *Wolfgang* (Oscar-nominated)
1996 *Ernst & lyset* (*Ernst and the Light*, Oscar-nominated)

Scripts for feature films

2009 *Ved verdens ende* (*At World's End*; dir. Tomas Villum Jensen)
2009 *Antichrist* (credited as story supervisor; dir. Lars von Trier)
2009 *Brothers* (dir. Jim Sheridan, remake of Susanne Bier's *Brothers*, original screenplay)
2008, *Den du frygter* (*Fear Me Not*; dir. Kristian Levring)
2008 *The Duchess* (dir. Saul Dibb, co-written with Jeffrey Hatcher and Saul Dibb)
2007 *Hvid nat* (*White Night*; dir. Jannik Johansen)
2007 *Til døden os skiller* (*With Your Permission*; dir. Paprika Steen)
2006 *Sprængfarlig bombe* (*Clash of Egos*; dir. Tomas Villum Jensen)
2006 *Efter brylluppet* (*After the Wedding*; dir. Susanne Bier)
2005 *Mørke* (*Murk*; dir. Jannik Johansen)
2005 *Adams æbler* (*Adam's Apples*; dir. Anders Thomas Jensen)
2005 *Solkongen* (*The Sun King*; dir. Tomas Villum Jensen)
2005 *Vet hard* (*Too Fat, Too Furious*; dir. Tim Oliehoek)
2004 *Brødre* (*Brothers*; dir. Susanne Bier)
2003 *Rembrandt* (dir. Jannik Johansen)
2003 *Skagerrak* (dir. Søren Kragh-Jacobsen)
2003 *De grønne slagtere* (*The Green Butchers*; dir. Anders Thomas Jensen)
2002 *Wilbur Wants to Kill Himself* (dir. Lone Scherfig)
2002 *Elsker dig for evigt* (*Open Hearts*; dir. Susanne Bier)
2002 *Gamle mænd i nye biler* (*Old Men in New Cars*; dir. Lasse Spang Olsen)
2001 *Grev Axel* (*Count Axel*; dir. Søren Fauli)
2000 *Blinkende lygter* (*Flickering Lights*; dir. Anders Thomas Jensen)
2000 *The King is Alive* (dir. Kristian Levring)
2000 *Dykkerne* (*Beyond*; dir. Åke Sandgren)
1999 *I Kina spiser de hunde* (*In China They Eat Dogs*; dir. Lasse Spang Olsen)
1999 *Mifunes sidste sang* (*Mifune*; dir. Søren Kragh-Jacobsen)
1998 *Albert* (dir. Jørn Faurschou)
1998 *Baby Doom* (dir. Peter Gren Larsen)

Redvall: Danish film is very much dominated by directors from the National Film School of Denmark. You're a self-taught director and scriptwriter. Where did your interest in film come from?

Jensen: I've just always watched films, and always wanted to make films. We got a video player very early on, and I saw all kinds of things. I met Tomas Villum Jensen at my secondary school in Frederiksværk, and we started doing a lot of things together. We had an incredibly good headmaster, who gave us an enormous amount of support. We were a bit wild, and he recognized that we had the potential to make films. Back then, secondary schools could start up new classes, and our school put on a film and media class and purchased lots of equipment. So during my last two years in secondary school, I almost only made films. I think it means a lot that certain people recognize your abilities and really support you.

After secondary school a door opened into the film business when Tomas got a role in *Drengene fra Sankt Petri* (*The Boys from St Petri*; dir. Søren Kragh-Jacobsen, 1991). I finished secondary school a year after Tomas, and then actually became a postman, working in the countryside, for a year. I tried to get into both the Film School and the Department of Film and Media Studies at the University of Copenhagen, but with no luck. Instead I started studying Rhetoric at the university. I moved to Copenhagen and, alongside my studies, I took on some small jobs through Tomas. I read scripts and finally I got up the courage to present three of my own scripts to different producers. I sent scripts to Per Holst, Tivi Magnusson and Peter Aalbæk Jensen. The only one who responded was Tivi. He just said: 'Here's an office.' And that's how it all started. We started making short films together.

Redvall: It sounds like a relatively painless entry into the industry. Did you have a plan for how you wanted your career to evolve, or have things happened in a more haphazard way?

Jensen: You might say that I was aware that I wanted to start by doing something on a modest scale. It's hard to get into the industry and you have to start small. The first short film we made cost nothing at all, and that's where you have to start. We borrowed everything. Of course this was possible because Tomas had a lot of connections.

Redvall: You started your career by making three short films, all of which were nominated for an Oscar; and *Election Night* won an Oscar. The films show a very certain feel for telling short stories. Where did that come from?

Jensen: You can say that the structure of a short film is pretty much the same as that of a feature film, but you have to work in a very concentrated way. Short films are sort of miniature films, or at least you have to try to think of them in this way. The ones I've made are almost like sketches because they're only ten minutes long. Seven minutes is the ideal length, as far as I'm concerned. You can do three acts in that time, if you're working with simplified characters. A good example is *Ernst and the Light*, where it's a gift to work with Jesus as a character, because you don't need to spend time on characterization; we know who he is. The hard thing about short films is when you get to 50 minutes. That's too long for a sketch and too short to explore things in any real depth. But to me a good short film is sort of a sketch for a feature film.

Redvall: You've never trained as a scriptwriter, yet at this point you're considered one of Denmark's best scriptwriters. The film historian David Bordwell has even called you 'one of the finest script craftsmen in world filmmaking today'. How did you learn to write scripts? Have you read some of the classic 'how to' books, or has it been pure learning by doing?

Jensen: I've read some things by people like Syd Field. But in reality the art of telling a story is something that everyone has intuitions about. It's not something you have to learn as an adult. By then it's an in-built capacity, unless you're a bit slow. Everyone has an inherent feel for those acts. Now that I have children, I can see how my daughter is learning to tell stories. Of course we're talking here about well-stimulated children whose parents can be counted on to laugh at all their jokes, no matter how bad they are. But my daughter is clearly learning to structure her stories. She knows that if she starts with the point of the story, she won't get any attention at the table. Even though she's only four years old, she already knows that she needs to conclude with the point of the story. And that's already the beginning of dramaturgy. Some of the things I wrote when I just wrote without knowing anything about dramaturgy were really good. I think that you just have a gut feeling for when it gets boring. Most people do, if they think about it.

I don't think in terms of structure while I'm writing, but I always check it afterwards; now there needs to be a turning point, and now this needs to happen. But there's something dangerous about structure, because it can easily become too mechanical and tight. Almost all the films I like play around a bit with form, and also with genre. They're more a mix of something familiar and something new. For example, I'm extremely entertained and impressed by the Coen brothers' films. They're real filmmakers. I certainly find inspiration there, but in general I'd say that I work very intuitively. Of course there's a little lie in that, because the more you've done, the more aware you are of the effects you have to work with, and of the tools you use. You can't write a lot of scripts and remain unaware of these things. It's actually a bit of a struggle for me to background it all and retain that natural, joyful approach to the process. Naturally it's easier to be unreflective or unaware when you don't know anything!

Redvall: Many of your short films are characterized by tight set-ups. In *Ernst and the Light* the entire film plays out between two characters in a car. *Election Night* has a taxi with various customers as the principal framework for the story. Did you consciously think about limiting yourself in certain ways when you created these stories, in order to make them more manageable to produce? Do you sometimes think in similar ways when you write scripts for feature films?

Nikolaj Lie Kaas, Mads Mikkelsen, Ulrich Thomsen, and Søren Pilmark as four small-time gangsters from Copenhagen in *Blinkende lygter* (*Flickering Lights*). Photography: Rolf Konow.

Jensen: When I wrote short films, I most certainly thought about making them manageable, and I still tend to create very solid frameworks for my stories, especially when I have to direct them myself. I try to stick to a very self-contained universe. Sometimes I try a different approach, but I always end up with that closed universe. Maybe everything has to happen in this one town. It's safer that way, and that sense of security has to do with feeling that you know exactly where the story takes place. You can trick yourself into believing that everything is under control, because it's now all taking place in this one town, or in this room. Of course you never have the full overview, but you have to believe that you do, and for as long as you possibly can.

Redvall: You won an Oscar for *Election Night* and then went on to write a series of feature film scripts for others, among them *In China They Eat Dogs* for Lasse Spang Olsen. This film launched what would be called 'lad comedies' in Denmark. Much like your first film, *Flickering Lights*, the story plays out among small-time criminals and is characterized by irony and witty lines, all in connection with the immaturity and odd personalities of the characters. What attracted you to those stories?

Jensen: In the case of *In China They Eat Dogs* there was a clear intention to be provocative. At the time, a feature film consultant at the Danish Film Institute had pronounced that nobody would get money for a film with a gun in it. His was a position characterized by a lot of contrariness. I remember a meeting I had at the Film Institute on the very same day that three people had been shot in Aarhus, and the feedback was; 'But that kind of thing doesn't happen in Denmark.' It was all about making solid films that would somehow educate viewers, and there was this idea that there were things that couldn't be made fun of and that certain imagined situations were simply remote from Danish realities. Jang [Nicolas Winding Refn] helped change all of this. He provided a serious portrait of criminals with *Pusher* (1996), and then we started to get into those action comedies that were clearly inspired by Tarantino. They were so much fun to make, and they do what they're supposed to do, but you don't want to watch them over and over again.

Redvall: You've continued to write absurd comedies, but your scriptwriting took on another dimension when you wrote the more serious scripts for two of the early Dogma films, *Mifune* and *The King is Alive*. How did you get involved with Dogma 95?

Jensen: With *Mifune*, Søren Kragh-Jacobsen simply asked me whether I'd write the script, based on an idea that he'd come up with. In the case of *The King is Alive*, I'd written some commercials for Kristian Levring, so I knew him from the advertising business. It's true that the Dogma films took me in a more serious direction, but that was no surprise to me. During that period I wrote six films in sixteen months. Some are serious, some are mainly pure entertainment, but I've always been involved with both kinds of projects. The short films I made in high school were very different from each other; everything from a film based on a French poem or a serious short story by Peter Seeberg to a film based on the worst slapstick.

I think I have the same approach to the film medium as many other young directors, where it's all really about the medium. It's about film and feeling a great love for film. You've seen nearly everything and want to do it all. When you get a bit further down the road, then you start choosing what you really want to do. But when you're around twenty-four, you just want to try it all. You want to make a good comedy and a good drama and a good thriller. So I'm just happy I've had a chance to explore so many different genres and to work with so many different directors.

Redvall: How did you feel about the Dogma rules? On the surface your own films are very far from the technically ascetic universe of the Dogma film.

Jensen: To be honest, I didn't even think about the rules while I was writing the scripts. It was the coolest process. What was really cool was that the money was there. The shooting was soon to begin, and there was a director with a vision, and a producer, and then there was me. That's just how it should be, and I think it's why those films are so good. We didn't have to get comments from all sorts of consultants. We wrote the film that the director and I wanted to make, and then we shot it. That energy was amazing. It was simply without parallel. I really didn't think much about the rules. The great strength of those films comes from the people who made them, from their vision and from the deliberate removal of certain institutional constraints. That's what was amazing. There's something to be learnt from that.

Redvall: Are there too many script readers and consultants in Danish film?

Jensen: Yes, there are probably too many people involved in reading, assessing and commenting on projects, but it's different for me now that I've made so many films. Scriptwriters or directors who are new or have less experience probably have to go through a more cumbersome process. My own experience is that if a project is good, then it will always get produced. There isn't another *Apocalypse Now* (dir. Francis Ford Coppola, 1979) lying around on someone's desk. The good films get made, and that's promising. The fact that some people do a lot of damage with their comments, or delay someone with talent, is sad, but we do tend to whine a bit because we've been spoiled in Denmark for a long time. When it comes to scripts, there aren't many people who know how to read them. People tend to read them as prose and they're not. They're a tool, and there are some pitfalls. I've read many Danish scripts that are really amusing to read, but won't make for funny films, because the fun is tied up with the reading experience.

Generally there's a lot of sugar on the spoon, so to speak, when it comes to Danish scripts. I do this too. I write very descriptively, and I paint a pretty elaborate picture of each and every scene. I put a lot of effort into making it all readable; you have to, if you want people to understand what you're doing. On the other hand, if you read the scripts for the big American films, you'll see that everything is very cynically described. The reading experience is ice cold. If you're a good reader you can see that the script works really well, but if you're not a good reader, you'll have a hard time seeing this.

Redvall: You directed your first feature film, *Flickering Lights*, in the afterglow of the success of the Dogma films, and at a time when you were writing scripts for quite a number of other directors. How do you choose which films you want to direct yourself and which you will give to others?

Jensen: When I'm in the process of writing I always want to direct the film myself. It really has to be commissioned work for that desire not to be there. As you become really familiar with the material you necessarily end up wanting to direct it yourself. But then when you put the script aside, and take a step back, you can feel whether the material has stayed with you. With *Adam's Apples* I knew quite early on that I wanted to make it myself. I'd been brewing the story for a long time, but the script did go out to a few others, because I wrote it so early on. After I won the Oscar for *Election Night* I suddenly found myself able to make *Adam's Apples* on a decent budget. But I did rewrite it quite significantly because I needed to make the script mine again. I've ended up giving a story to other people on several occasions, even though I initially thought I wanted to make the films myself.

I'm basically realizing that I'm probably more of a scriptwriter than a director. I like writing more than directing. It satisfies me more. But it's a huge privilege to be able to go out and make films sometimes. It's been three years now, and it might be another three years before I direct another film, because I don't need to work right now. When I go out and make films, it's because I really want to direct precisely this story, with these characters. If there's just a little bit of something missing, I'll try to give the project to someone else.

Redvall: As early as your short films, you've been working with a distinctive visual style, one characterized by an insistence on good lighting, among other things. This is quite unusual given the emphasis in Danish film on a kind of everyday aesthetic. Did you have a clear vision early on of how to make the words on paper come alive on the screen?

Jensen: I've probably had quite a clear idea about this from the start. Again, this is probably because, unlike many of the slightly older filmmakers, I come from a pure film background. To me it was just always about film, and I've always wanted my films really to be films. I remember *Lawrence of Arabia* (dir. David Lean, 1962) playing on 70 mm when I was sixteen or so. I saw it three times. Now that's a real film! I've been offered the opportunity to direct Dogma films, but in some ways the idea of doing a Dogma film seemed stupid to me, especially at a time when all cinemas have good screens and great sound.

I've always had a great fondness for films that really make use of the cinematic medium, and I think a lot of people fail to pay sufficient attention to that part of the filmmaking process. It's easy to make something that's ugly and handheld, but you have to take telling stories with images seriously. You have to take the language of film seriously. Many Danish directors have started doing this in recent years and it's wonderful, because there was a time when everything looked Dogma-like and I found myself thinking 'It's got to stop now.'

Redvall: Your three feature films have distinguished themselves from many other films made during the same period by not being realistic everyday dramas in an urban context. Instead these films take place in surreal small town environments (*The Green Butchers* and *Adam's Apples*) or in a forest (*Flickering Lights*). Why do you seek to get out of the city in your films?

Jensen: I'm from the provinces myself, and ended up moving to Copenhagen. To me setting a film in a city is very confusing. Of course you can also think of that kind of setting as a sort of self-imposed restriction, but for me it's very much about trying to create a universe that really is completely right for the film. If you want to stick 100 per cent to a given style, then it's hard to set a story in a city. There are always annoying little characters in films set in cities, waiters or a friend of a friend. My idea was to keep it clean, and that's so much easier to do when you're in the middle of a forest!

Redvall: Another common feature of your films is the rather rough tone established by the main characters, who are all diligent users of irony, pointedly directed at what is politically correct. Why do your films break with the otherwise dominant niceties of Danish film?

Jensen: I don't see myself as a provocateur. When I talk to academics or journalists that issue comes up, but my audience doesn't think about the issue of political correctness or how my films may or may not challenge it. I've no deliberate intention of challenging niceties. It's not about challenging what's politically correct, but about working with what's really funny. There are some elements in my films that might be provocative – the child with Down's syndrome who's mentioned in *Adam's Apples*, for example – but generally I'd say that I shoot down many ideas along the way because they'd simply be too much. So viewers actually end up seeing a mild version of what I've been working with! If viewers think that what I show them is provocative, then they should try turning the TV on. Ordinary prime time has changed a lot. The humour is quite rough. There's nearly nothing, with the exception of religion, that escapes challenge.

Redvall: We've got Jesus in *Ernst and the Light*, and a rather unorthodox parson and the Book of Job in *Adam's Apples*.

Jensen: Yes, but this is actually all done in quite a sober way. I think that virtually all taboos have been broken at this point. There certainly aren't a lot left.

Redvall: As a scriptwriter you collaborate with many different directors and film people. Do you also work collaboratively as a director, in the sense of drawing on other directors?

Jensen: Very much so. Talking to other directors along the way helps me a lot, and that's an area where it's clear to me that the older generation held their cards more tightly to their chests. Things were more competitive for them. I don't know whether it's a self-reinforcing process, but when you're doing well yourself, it's a lot easier to let other people in on what you're doing. What motivates this kind of sharing is the feeling that if things go well for fellow practitioners, then Danish film will also thrive. I don't think that way of thinking was as widespread before; that if you have a good idea, then you're quite happy to share it with someone else because that ultimately benefits everyone. My sense is that the old dogs thought in a rather different way.

Redvall: Why has that changed?

Jensen: As I see it, the increased collaboration is pretty much down to Trier. He established Zentropa, and Zentropa has quite simply worshipped the concept of collectivism. It's amazing to think about how Trier took his world famous name and got it circulating through Dogma, in order then to let a lot of other people enjoy some of the fruits of what he's achieved. It all started with Zentropa and Nimbus, and it's clear that the other producers have had to learn to do this kind of thing too. Earlier it was all about contracts, and not being allowed to mention anything to anyone, and no one was allowed to see your stuff. But the films become better when you let other people in on the process. Naturally there's an element of competition, but it's important to look other directors in the eye and to remember that they wish you no harm. Or, not only harm!

Redvall: You've collaborated very successfully with Susanne Bier for quite a number of years, starting with the Dogma film *Open Hearts*, and moving on to *Brothers* and the Oscar-nominated *After the Wedding*. What is it about your collaboration with Bier that works so well?

Jensen: Our collaboration actually grew out of a film that Susanne Bier made in Sweden, *Livet är en schlager* (*Once in a Lifetime*, 2000). One day we were talking about this film, and we both started laughing when I cited my list of critical comments on it. And then we decided to do a proper comedy together. That's been our credo ever since, but we always end up doing something else. The first project we worked on together was actually an adaptation of Henrik Ibsen's *A Doll's House*, but what we came up with was really bad. The problem is that when you're working with an original text that's that good, then you can't change anything without making things worse. Ibsen is just better than we are. That film project eventually turned into *Open Hearts*.

In the case of *After the Wedding*, I'd written a proposal for a romantic comedy. I frankly don't know what happens. As we sit there laughing a lot together, we nonetheless become serious, and so we end up with these great human emotions and tragedies. We're actually both comedy people, so there must be something about minus and minus becoming plus, because we never end up with comedies. But we collaborate in a very fruitful and efficient way that allows us to come up with things that neither of us would have thought of on our own.

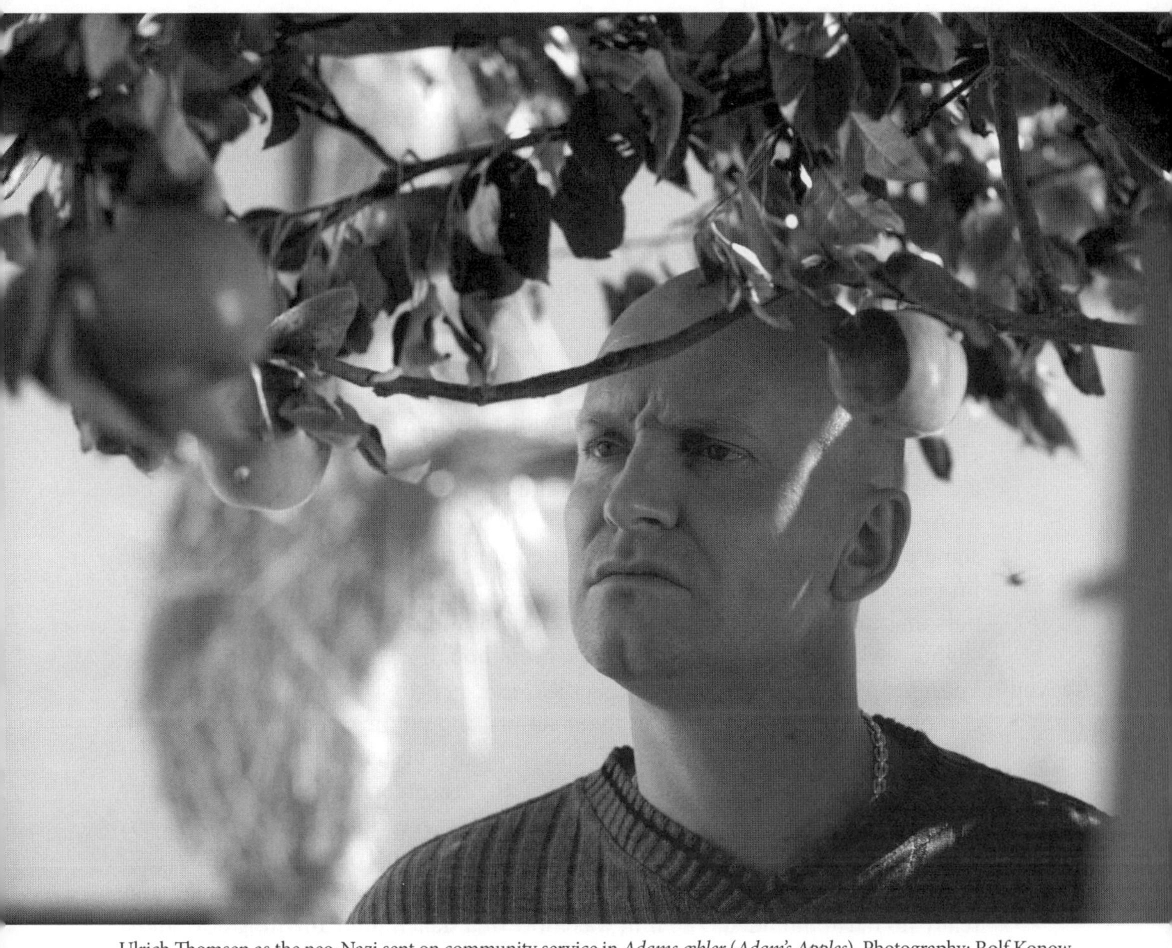

Ulrich Thomsen as the neo-Nazi sent on community service in *Adams æbler* (*Adam's Apples*). Photography: Rolf Konow.

Redvall: You've also worked with Lars von Trier. You wrote the character profiles (with Lone Scherfig) for the Scottish–Danish 'Advance Party' project, and you also helped write the script for von Trier's new feature film, *Antichrist*. But the two of you have also been embroiled in some public controversy, after he criticized scriptwriters like yourself for being effective to the point of actually ruining the films. How does your collaboration with von Trier work?

Jensen: 'Advance Party' was his idea, and then Lone and I wrote some character profiles. But I wrote the first draft for *Antichrist*. He had ten pages or so, and a draft had to be prepared for the purposes of applying for funding. I then wrote a draft, which he re-wrote. I get along very well with von Trier, and I actually always have. He's fun and nice and clever. That's why his criticisms were so absurd. He was a consultant on *Brothers*. He's even on the credit list. Yes, he criticized me, but many of the ideas were actually his own! But his criticisms were also justified to some extent. Basically he just wants better films to be made. He's not just being provocative. There's something to it. He tried to tell me that I need to get more personal in what I do, and he's probably right about that. He just always has a slightly awkward way of putting things, even though he means no harm.

Redvall: Your script for Tomas Villum Jensen's *Clash of Egos* was seen by many as a commentary on this controversy about scripts, and on the state of play in Danish film. In this film you have an angry man seek out a pretentious director in order to demand his money back for a film ticket, the reason being the dreadful quality of the film. With knowledge of Danish film you can see hints at not so few players on the Danish film scene. Did that film spring from von Trier's criticism?

Jensen: Both yes and no. It was fun making a film about those issues, but there was really no harm intended. The film was more of a sketch than anything else, and a somewhat hasty one at that, I'd say. It should have been revised a few more times. But it's much as with a satirical song or a letter that you might write. Often you'd be better off just crumpling it up or sticking it in a drawer.

Redvall: *Brothers* has been remade by Jim Sheridan and you've also co-written *The Duchess*. How do your experiences with the European or American film worlds compare with your work in the Danish context?

Jensen: The big difference is that you don't get a second chance abroad. You get cut down. In Denmark it's okay to present something along the way, as work in progress. You involve other people in the project, get comments and feedback and talk about it all. You can't do that with foreign producers, all of whom read stacks of scripts. I don't really think that the level is higher in American film. We're not behind or anything. But their volume is simply greater. There's more crap and that's why there are also more good films. That's why they have fifteen good films per year and we have one. It's that simple. But I have to say that I haven't had to try to hammer my own scripts through at meetings with studios. I've worked with a particular director, or with a small independent company with a studio above it, and that's a very European thing to do. The other sort of thing is exhausting. I've been at meetings where I've felt that I'd waste eight months of my life, without getting the film made, and I can't be bothered with that sort of thing.

Generally I think that things are changing in both Danish and foreign film. Production is getting cheaper. I think that the crucial connections to be made in the future will have to do with distribution. My hope, really, is that we'll be able to make all kinds of films, because getting something produced is an amazingly good learning experience. You learn the most through that leap from text to film.

Redvall: Do you think there's anything unique about being a Danish director?

Jensen: If I think about Danish film in general, then it's actually shocking how uneducated most directors are. Very few directors have an academic background. I've been with first-time directors in Germany, all of them ten to twelve years older than me, and they almost all had a PhD in something or other, and were talking Schopenhauer and Heidegger. It's a much more elitist system there. If you can sneak someone with a Bachelor's degree into a Danish Top 50 list, then you're lucky.

There's strength in what we have, because there's a devil-may-care attitude and a will to just shoot it off, and to get better and better by doing it. But it would be interesting to see what would happen if you got ten academics into the Top 50 list. We have a very simple approach to filmmaking. What would happen if we got some deeper thinking involved? There's not a whole lot of that in Danish film. You have to go to the theatre for that. But on the other hand, it was clear to me that in Germany the aspiring filmmakers were killing each others' ideas. And they all wanted to keep on polishing their work, with the result that many of them had been writing for seven years or so, trying to get all the symbols into their scripts.

The advantage of Danish film is probably the learning by doing thing, but it would be fun to have a hardcore Danish intellectual making heavy, heavy films after having spent eighteen years chewing through books; or to have an artist come up with something along the lines of what Peter Greenaway does. Because if films like that were thrown into the pot of Danish film, then maybe the rest of us would pull in new directions. In that sense you could say that the Danish film world is nepotistic; it's very much a club, with people who start out lugging cables or at the Film School, and then they work their way up to feature films. They don't have a theoretical perspective. I certainly think that the practitioner's background is best for Danish film, but a bit of the other kind of thing would be good. A mixture of backgrounds and approaches is very healthy.

Chapter 8

Hella Joof

Hella Joof. Photography: Helene Hansen.

Born 1962. Hella Joof graduated from the Odense Theatre Drama School in 1990. By the time she directed her first feature film, *En kort en lang* (*Shake It All About*, 2001) she had a well-established profile as one of Denmark's most talented actresses, especially in the area of satire and comedy. Hella Joof has performed at the Royal Danish Theatre, the Betty Nansen Theatre, the Grønnegaard Theatre and Dr Dante's Aveny Theatre. As a performer, she enjoyed considerable success with her contributions to TV 2's satirical programme, *Lex & Klatten* (1997), which she created together with fellow performers Martin Brygmann, Peter Frödin and Paprika Steen. Joof subsequently established the satirical group *Det Brune Punktum* (The Brown Point), together with Brygmann and Frödin. The group performed regularly at the Bellevue Theatre, on the coast just north of Copenhagen, but also on radio. As a screen actress, Joof played the memorable role of police officer in the satirical children's musical, *Hannibal og Jerry* (*Hannibal and Jerry*, 1997; dirs Steen Rasmussen and Michael Wikke). Here too she performed alongside Brygmann, Frödin and Steen.

Hella Joof made the transition to the director's role with *Shake It All About*, a box-office hit. Featuring Mads Mikkelsen and Troels Lyby as the gay couple Jacob and Jørgen, this comedy explores the consequences of Jacob's unexpected heterosexual desire for Jørgen's sister-in-law, Caroline (Charlotte Munck). In *Oh Happy Day* (2004), Hannah (Lotte Andersen) is given an opportunity to reflect on her life when the leader of an American gospel choir, Moses Jackson (Malik Yoba), ends up prolonging his stay in Denmark, due to an accident that she caused. The comedy *Fidibus* (*Easy Skanking*, 2006) focuses on the middle-class university student Kalle's (Rudi Köhnke) entanglement with criminal elements in Copenhagen, and especially his romantic involvement with jailed drug dealer Paten's (Jesper Dahl) girlfriend, Sabrina (Lene Maria Christensen). In 2007 Joof moved across the Sound, directing *Linas kvällsbok* (*Bitter Sweetheart*) for Svensk Filmindustri. The film looks at the trials of puberty and is an adaptation of Emma Hamberg's novel in diary form. Joof's most recent film, *Se min kjole* (*Hush Little Baby*, 2009) is a road movie and her most serious film yet. Based on considerable research, *Hush Little Baby* asks probing questions about what might allow adolescent victims of abuse to take steps towards recovery and a new life. Joof has also been involved in directing series for television. Produced by the TV station TV 2 *Hvor svært kan det være?* (*How Hard Can It Be?*, 2002) is a sitcom about the lives of three couples in a three-storey house. *Album* (*Album*), produced by the Danish Broadcasting Corporation, features a script by the poet and author Bo hr. Hansen, one of Denmark's most accomplished contemporary scriptwriters. With the exception of *Bitter Sweetheart*, all of Joof's feature films have been produced by the Danish production company Fine & Mellow.

Feature films

2009 *Se min kjole* (*Hush Little Baby*)
2007 *Linas kvällsbok* (*Bitter Sweetheart*)
2006 *Fidibus* (*Easy Skanking*)
2004 *Oh Happy Day*
2001 *En kort en lang* (*Shake It All About*)

Television

2008 *Album* (*Album*, mini series, 5 episodes)
2002 *Hvor svært kan det være* (*How Hard Can It Be?*, episodes 1–4, 6, 8, 10–13)

Hjort: You're one of a small number of bi-racial Danish filmmakers. How would you describe the role that race has played in your development as an actress and filmmaker?

Joof: My father was from Gambia, but I didn't grow up with him. I grew up in Denmark, with my mother, who married a Danish man when I was two years old. She had a daughter with him and we lived in Birkerød [an affluent suburb north of Copenhagen]. They then divorced, and I grew up with my mother and sister, in a small apartment. Quite a standard Danish arrangement. I graduated from high school in Copenhagen, having focused on classical languages, and decided I wanted to study medicine. I have no idea why. I got into university, and was there, I think, for all of three days. When I was twenty or so I was asked to play Josephine Baker in a play that the actor Buster Larsen was involved in. I happened to be friends with his daughter. And through them I suddenly found myself in the theatre milieu, which turned out to be a world that really interested me. So I applied to the Theatre School in Odense in 1986, and got in. I had my daughter while I was at the Theatre School, between the second and third years, and I graduated after four years.

I'd hoped I might be offered a job at the Odense Theatre, but this didn't happen. I was told I was too exotic. I was the first black person in the theatre milieu, and while I was at the school, I used to think to myself 'Surely they wouldn't have let me in if they thought I wouldn't get any work later.' Things were really difficult back then. It's easier to talk about these things, now that I'm older. When I was a young actress, I could tell that my ethnic identity really meant something. People would say things like, 'It would be really *interesting* to have you be part of this', but then nothing would happen. Someone else was always picked instead. I'd be told that audiences would find it too strange, if I were part of a performance. The only person who ever hired me to play major roles was Peter Langdal at the Betty Nansen Theatre. He had me play Electra, and other classical roles. I think it was that sense of hitting a brick wall that made me realize I probably needed to think quite differently about what I wanted to do. I could play somebody's best friend, but I couldn't play the lead, because if the lead were black, then suddenly that's what the story would be all about. Or at least that's what people thought. I'd say, 'Why would the story suddenly be about race? My life isn't about being black. Right now it is, because we're talking about race, but otherwise it's not an issue. The problems I have in my life, with my partner or my child, have nothing to do with the colour of my skin. The problems have to do with my being a thirty-something-year-old woman. The only time I'm confronted with the colour of my skin is in situations like these, where it's about the roles that I can play.'

So I ended up teaming up with Paprika Steen, Martin Brygmann and Peter Frödin. And we produced an enormous number of comic sketches, in which we'd parody some of the great roles from Shakespeare and Ibsen. Since we weren't getting those roles out there in the 'real' world of theatre, we simply gave ourselves the roles we wanted, but with adjustments. We had a lot of success with our first comedy group, *Lex & Klatten*, and even more success with our satirical group, *Det Brune Punktum*. We also produced a lot of music and songs, and had a lot of fun. And then I started working on *Shake It All About*. When I look back I feel like I've had a really interesting career. It's not the career I'd expected, or had hoped for, but it's actually more interesting than the one I first imagined for myself. When I was young I wanted to play Célimène at the Royal Theatre. And I think I would have made a wonderful Célimène. But I was simply never given that role. And I'm sure I could have played some wonderful leading roles in various films, but I wasn't given those roles. So in that sense the colour of my skin has had a huge impact on my career. But when I look at it all now, I can see that the impact was a positive one. But I do think things are easier now, for people like myself. Danish society has changed a lot in recent years. When I was a child there were two black children in Birkerød, where we lived. People would stop and stare at us in the streets, and would want to touch us. It's just not like that anymore.

Hjort: Much like Paprika Steen, you've gone from being on stage and in front of the camera, to being behind it, as a director. Was that transition a difficult one to make in your case?

Joof: I'd been an actress for many years by the time I directed my first film, and I think that made it easier. And things moved really, really quickly. Thomas Gammeltoft, my producer, called me up to propose the idea for *Shake It All About* in September 1999, and we shot the film in November 2000. That was my first experience as a director, and it's a bit like women who have an easy time delivering their first child. They just assume the next delivery will be easy too, although they could end up with a C-section, or who knows what. My first film was really a huge box-office success. And when you've made one successful film, you're always given an opportunity to direct a second film. *Oh Happy Day* was harder, though. The idea for the film came from Lotte Andersen, and there were three of us, Lotte, Jannik Johansen and myself, involved in writing the script. And three's a crowd. I won't ever do that again. But in all other respects making *Oh Happy Day* was a wonderful experience. We were in the US, where we did some research on gospel music and gospel choirs, and where we visited any number of churches. If you've made a film that was a box-office success, then there's this expectation that you'll pull the same feat off again. But *Oh Happy Day* only sold 250,000 tickets; it just wasn't as well received. And the media coverage was really very different. Suddenly what was newsworthy was this idea that I seemed to think I was going to be a director now, instead of an actress.

I should add that I've never really felt particularly welcome in the filmmaking milieu. It's a tiny, tiny milieu, and it's quite incestuous, and if you didn't go to the National Film School of Denmark, you're necessarily an outsider. But I've always felt that being a bit of an outsider wasn't necessarily a bad thing. But in another sense I am of course very much part of it all, because I went to the Odense Theatre School. I have incredible access to the actors. I really feel that I could get any actor in Denmark to accept a role in one of my films. And that's because I'm an actress myself, and I know them all, and have actually studied together with a lot of them. Of course I was able to get Mads Mikkelsen to play Jacob in *Shake It All About*.

Hjort: How does your background as an actress contribute to your understanding of the director's role?

Joof: As an actress you have a huge advantage when you direct. I know the language. I know what I need to say to the actors in order to get them to do a specific thing. I've often had the experience of wondering what on earth a director was trying to get me to do. I've had to say things like, 'Should I be more angry here? Do you want it to take longer before I discover that he's been unfaithful?' And the director would say something vague like 'Uh, nooo. It's more like…' And I'd say 'I really want to help you, and you can ask me to do anything, but I just don't understand what you want. What if I just try out some different interpretations? Then you can tell me which one you prefer. Because if I know which interpretation you prefer, then I'll be able to infer what it is you're looking for.' My experience is that a lot of directors know all kinds of things about the technical side of filmmaking, about narrative structure and images, but they have absolutely no clue when it comes to how they should communicate with actors. In that sense Paprika (Steen) and I have a huge advantage. Also, we're not afraid of actors. Many directors are. I have no qualms about telling my actors that they were absolutely dreadful. They crack up when I do it, because that kind of comment isn't unsettling when it comes from another actor. If a director from the National Film School says something like that, then the actors become unnerved. I can say all kinds of things to the actors. I can say things like, 'Ok, we'll do another take. Could you try not to be so pleased with yourselves this time around? I could tell that you were already thinking about the great reviews you were going to get. Try to eliminate that dimension. Just try to remember that you're playing these characters, and they're not the least bit cool, and you're not going to win some Bodil award, OK?' And they laugh their heads off. And I'm allowed to say something like that because I'm an actress and I know what it's like to stand there and think you're putting on a brilliant performance. Directors often forget that actors feel vulnerable, not when they're told they didn't perform well, but when they're told this in a really vague and imprecise way.

Something else I think is really wonderful about directing when you have a lot of acting experience is the ability you have to tell whether dialogue works. When the dialogue is what I call 'literature', something that should be read, not said aloud, I can tell immediately. I can simply tell when an actor won't be able to deliver a line, because the line is wrong. I also draw on my acting experience in my work with different members of the crew. The cinematographer may have ideas about where he wants the characters to stand, because a certain background is desirable, from the point of view of the aesthetics of the image. And then I'll be able to explain that the character simply cannot stand in a certain spot, because psychologically that spot would produce a completely different response to the conflict in which she finds herself. So it becomes a matter of figuring out how we can get the image we want, without introducing elements that are psychologically implausible.

Hjort: You've been associated with the production company Fine & Mellow for many years. What is the nature of that association?

Joof: Thomas Gammeltoft produced *Shake It All About*, and we ended up creating a production company together, with Jannik Johansen. Nordisk was also involved, and owned a fair share of the company. We eventually sold the original Fine & Mellow to Nordisk, for various reasons. What I'd discovered was that it's really no good trying to have three chief executives. I don't want to be *a* boss, I want to be *the* boss, because I have all kinds of opinions about all kinds of things. So we created a new company, which is also called Fine & Mellow, and the agreement was that Thomas would be the boss, and Jannik and I would be employed as directors. So I still work for Fine & Mellow, and if I come up with an idea for a film, I have to propose it to them in the first instance. If they don't want to produce the film, then I can take the idea to another company.

Hjort: Your most recent film, *Hush Little Baby*, has been very well received indeed. It's at once a very beautiful and probing film about some very serious issues, addiction and abuse. What moved you to tell this story?

Joof: I have a friend who is a social worker, and who was working in Tingbjerg at one point, which is an area with a lot of social problems. She told me how she'd once visited a young mother with addiction problems, and had found one of the two children in the process of trying to fry a head of iceberg lettuce. The child was five and the mother was in every way oblivious to what was going on. That story made an enormous impression on me. It's dreadful when grown-ups treat themselves abusively, with drugs or alcohol. But it's simply intolerable when children become the victims of this kind of self-inflicted abuse.

Hjort: The question as to whether research should play a role in the scriptwriting and filmmaking process more generally has emerged as a central one in the Danish film milieu in recent years. I gather that *Hush Little Baby* involved a fair bit of research. Could you talk about that process?

Joof: I emphasize research much less than, say Annette K. Olesen or Pernille Fischer Christensen. But in the case of *Hush Little Baby* we did do a lot of research. I did, and so did my cast. What we learnt from our discussions with young girls with addiction problems was that their reality is so extreme that you actually can't depict it in a fiction film. The younger actresses spent time at the Hanne Marie Home, talking to the young addicts. And they were really shaken by what they saw and heard. When they first read the script, they all felt that it was full of terrible things. After talking to the real addicts, the actresses all said that each and every girl they talked to had survived at least as many horrendous experiences as all of the characters in the film, collectively. They'd survived things that you can't even begin to imagine. It was crucial for the actresses to meet real addicts, because they came back with enormous respect for these people, and thus also for their characters. Also, the actresses realized they had to play their characters in a non-naturalistic way. Nobody, but nobody, is interested in seeing a fiction film with a naturalistic depiction of addiction.

Hjort: Although it is a grim film in many ways, *Hush Little Baby* is also hopeful.

Joof: Hope is the starting point for *Hush Little Baby*. The characters in the film are between eighteen and twenty-two. And the questions I ask are: is it too late? Or is there still something left, something that they can build on, if they decide to live? When is it too late? Some researchers say that an infant who lives with drug addicts, and experiences no real human contact during the earliest months of its life, can't possibly recover from the psychological scars that neglect inflicts. Where you stand on this issue probably depends on whether you take a more scientific view or a more spiritual approach. I chose the latter approach. I did my research. I read a lot of autobiographies written by girls who had been sexually abused. And I talked at some length with Henrik Ringdom, who's a psychiatrist and specializes in addiction. But, having done my research, I felt it was necessary to set some of what I'd learnt aside. And this is evident in the film. Because if you compare the progress made by some of the characters with that of addicts in the real world, it quickly becomes clear that our film is far more hopeful than is really warranted by the facts. And when we were writing the script Ida Maria Rydén and I wanted *all* the girls to make it. But that's just not workable, because this isn't

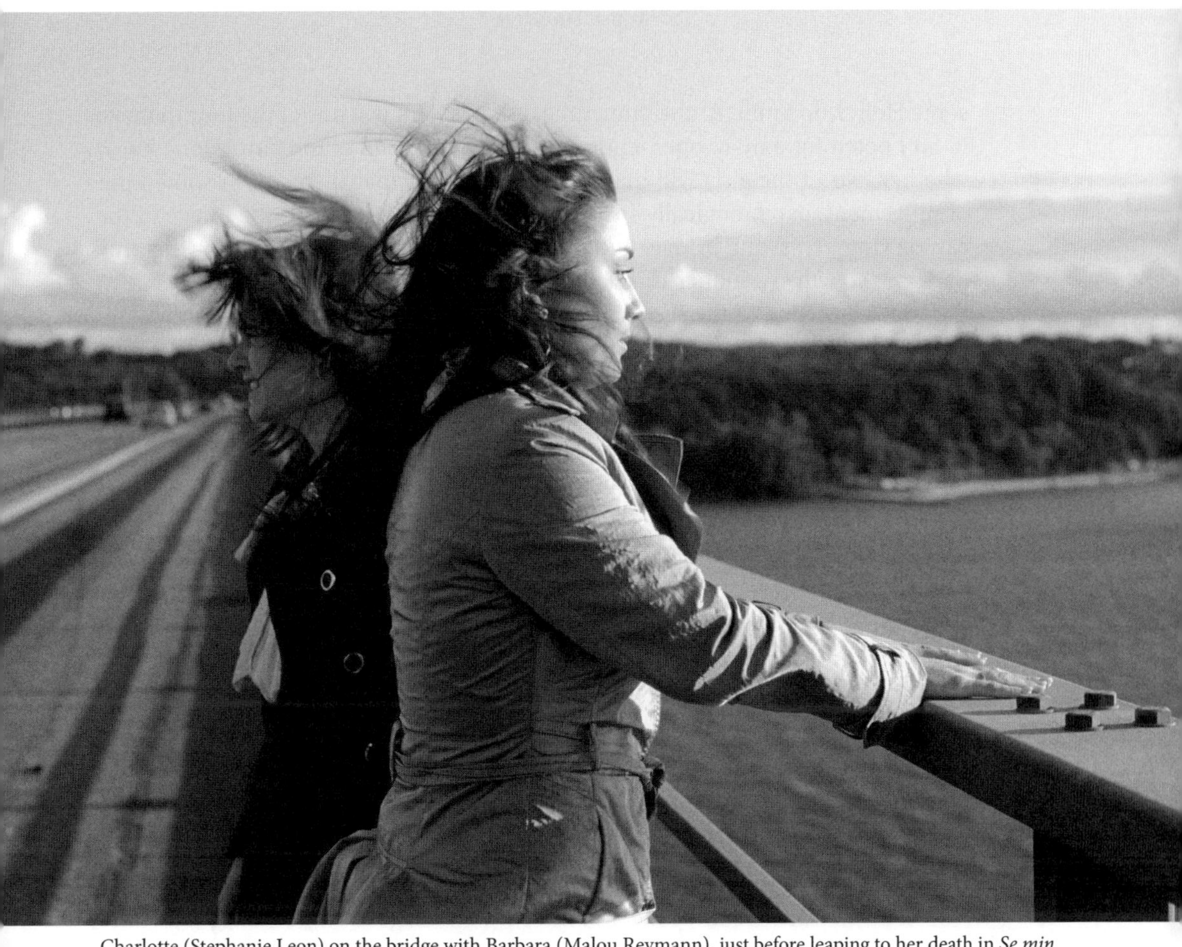

Charlotte (Stephanie Leon) on the bridge with Barbara (Malou Reymann), just before leaping to her death in *Se min kjole* (*Hush Little Baby*). Photography: Kim Høgh.

some Hollywood film. At the same time, I didn't want just one of the four to make it. So I opted for a more open-ended ending. By the end of the film I don't know whether two of the girls will make it. All I know is that there's been some kind of movement, psychologically speaking. And this is reflected in the image of the car, driving across the bridge, and in the emergency lane. I'm sure I'm the only person who will ever notice this detail, but there's a symbolic connection between the two last scenes. In the scene where Charlotte (Stephanie Leon) is standing on the bridge with Barbara (Malou Reymann), and is preparing to jump because she prefers death to a life without dignity due to illness, she lights a cigarette with a little green lighter. And in the final scene, Barbara and the two other girls drive away in that wreck of a Citroën, and in the emergency lane. And in the bottom of the image there's a little green lighter. Nobody will ever notice it, I'm sure, but *I* know it's there. It's a very symbolic ending, and I thought very carefully about that final image. I wanted it to be very subtle, but to have something big about it. And I think it does. They're on that bridge, and they're crossing that enormous expanse of water.

Hjort: *Hush Little Baby* is in many ways a beautiful film, image-wise. What were you and your cinematographer, Kim Høgh, trying to achieve stylistically?

Joof: I've worked with Kim on most of my films, so we've developed a shared understanding and an ability to grasp where the other person is going, without having to engage in a lot of talk. But you're right, we wanted the film to be beautiful. And I wanted it to be grandiloquent at times. The last thing I was after was a kind of 70s style realism. The place where the girls have been housed is actually very lovely, as are the surroundings. And the girls are beautiful, in that fierce and wild way that you often see in younger addicts who manage to stay off drugs for more than three months. But there are two scenes in particular that illustrate what we were after, stylistically, as an attempt to bring beauty into this hard-hitting story. For example, the scene with the closet, when Charlotte opens the door and sees all the shoes and all the dresses, and realizes the extent of the sexual abuse that Barbara has suffered. The image is full of symbolic meaning, it's very carefully framed, the colours are very carefully balanced and the sound/image relations are carefully thought through. There's circus-like music in the background. That scene gives me a knot in my stomach each time I see it. It's really a scene where I've tried to stretch the elastic, so to speak, as far as it can possibly be stretched. I didn't want melodrama, but I did want great drama, and the film's style at that moment reflects this.

Another scene that is really important in terms of the aesthetics of the film, is the one where the girls drive away, after having confronted Barbara's mother (Bodil Jørgensen) with her knowledge of the abuse. There's this incredible long shot, with the car in the distance, and behind it these fields that are on fire. My production designer Mette Rio, who is absolutely wonderful, had been up all night, spreading hay across that field. And then she poured petrol on the hay, and lit it. It was a completely over the top set-up, and all because we wanted exactly those images that are in the film. The film is about people who have been virtually dead, and who are struggling to find the desire to live. So you need to work with some really dramatic stylistic devices. I actually quite like to work that way, more generally. In *Oh Happy Day* there are some scenes that are pretty symbol-laden too, the one with the rose buds, for example (Mette Rio again), or the one where Kirsten (Ditte Hansen), who is very much the lost sheep, shows up in a sheepskin coat.

Hjort: There are interesting parallels between *Hush Little Baby* and *Oh Happy Day*, although the tone of the two films couldn't be more different. Would you agree that there's a message in *Hush Little Baby*, about how social problems are best dealt with?

Joof: There are problems in life that people have to *want* to overcome. People who are obese eat themselves to death. Anorexics starve themselves to death. Alcoholics drink themselves to death. Drug addicts fix themselves to death. And nobody can help them unless they want to be helped. So what can we do to help people reach the point where they make a decision to live? That's the question. And the welfare state provides the wrong answer. It creates an astonishing level of passivity and dependency. And you see signs of this everywhere in our society. Nobody can figure out how to do anything because there's this expectation that somebody will fix things for you, or that society as a whole will, or should. That attitude is extraordinarily common here. We live in a society where people expect to be happy, and they think it's the responsibility of the state to make sure they are. The idea of taking responsibility for your own happiness, and unhappiness, is not exactly encouraged by welfare-state mentalities. And this business of responsibility really interests me. I'm not saying that a child who has been abused, or has spent years in a home, is responsible for what's happened to it. But at a certain point it does become relevant to talk of responsibility. Those eighteen-year-old guys, with their tattoos and pit bulls, who beat people up because they once were beaten themselves, they *are* responsible for their actions. Had you shown me one of those men as a five year old, I would have said, 'It's not your fault.' But to the eighteen year old I want to say: 'You just pulverized that human being. And you haven't taken a long hard look at your own childhood. I know it's hard, but at a certain point *you* have to decide that you really want help. If you don't make that decision, at a really deep level, there's nothing anybody can do.' And that's why Charlotte asks the girls what they want. It's an attempt to get into that core, where there might be something that can motivate a fundamental decision to live.

In some instances, welfare-state mentalities really aren't that helpful. You can't, for example, just pump a whole lot of money into Africa and expect the problems to go away. What you *can* do is support a lot of enterprising people by lending them money. But in Denmark people just don't get it when I say 'Don't give, lend.' They start talking about how I don't think it's important to have schools in Africa, or about how I clearly don't care about the plight of African children. And then I'll say, 'But the point is to help get the market forces going, so that enterprising people will build schools.' People then look at me with considerable horror, and say that I'm reasoning like a supporter of the Liberal Party, and not like a Social Democrat. Well, yes. But all I can say is that it's a pity the Social Democrats aren't saying these things. In Denmark people on the left have simply been too busy labelling people as weak, and as requiring assistance. But that approach produces a crippling passivity and dependency.

There are too many safety nets in Denmark, and they're part of that Social Democratic legacy. I was on Zanzibar at one point and spoke to a young man who wanted to go to university. And I told him that schools and universities in Denmark are free. And he said, 'So everybody goes to university?' And I said 'No, they don't.' And he said, 'Why not?' To which my response was, 'That's a long story.' But the answer is, because everything is free, because you know that you can get by without going to university, because you know you'll never starve. Nothing has consequences. And as a result there's very little joy or happiness in Danish society. There's a huge underclass in Denmark, and it consists of people who were given a lot of opportunities and did absolutely nothing with them.

By the way, I spend every evening on a micro-loan site, investing money in different projects in Africa. Mads Kjær started this site and it's called myc4.com. And I mention the site every time I give a radio interview. We keep collecting and donating money. What we need to do is invest money in Africa, and invest in the projects the women put together. My point, in terms of what *Hush Little Baby* is all about, is that you have to find ways to help that don't create passivity and dependency.

Hjort: That's fascinating! What kinds of projects are you supporting, and where, more specifically, are these projects in Africa?

Joof: They're in Senegal, in Tanzania and in Kenya. It's always the women I support. Well, there's one man. He wanted to use solar cells to generate electricity in Uganda. He wrote that there was so much sun there during the day, and so much darkness at night, and he wanted to generate some light at night, so the children could do their homework.

Hjort: *Oh Happy Day* is also rather critical of Danish society. When Moses Jackson (Malik Yoba) asks Hannah (Lotte Andersen) what she and her friends do in the evenings, she says 'Nothing.'

Joof: I think I'm opposed to the whole concept of welfare, at some very deep level. I remember being on a radio programme at one point and asking why politicians didn't pursue a platform involving less welfare, rather than more, which is what politicians in Denmark normally do. And everybody burst out laughing, and I had to say, 'But

Moses Jackson (Malik Yoba) and Hannah (Lotte Andersen) in *Oh Happy Day*. Photography: Lars Høgsted.

I mean what I'm saying. It's not a joke.' But in Denmark you can't be opposed to the concept of welfare. If you are, you can forget the idea of being a politician.

Hjort: While *Oh Happy Day* and *Hush Little Baby* share a critical perspective on aspects of Danish culture and society, some critics were somewhat harsh in their assessment of the former, whereas the latter has generated a very positive response. How do you explain the difference?

Joof: You have to keep in mind that I started out as an actress. And much of what I've done as an actress has been satirical and comic. The shift from acting to directing is a significant one, and people could sort of accept the idea of my directing one film. But *Oh Happy Day* was my second film, and it signalled a serious intention to keep on directing films. And I think its reception was shaped by that, and by questions as to whether this was really what I should be doing. Also, because I was already a pretty established public figure by the time I made *Oh Happy Day* people had all kinds of ideas about me and what I stand for. I've been very outspoken over the years, in interviews, in radio programmes and so on. That said, the lukewarm critical reception is actually rather telling, because it is definitely linked to the film's religious themes. There's an extreme and quite dogmatic secularism in Denmark, and the idea of exploring religion cinematically is actually almost offensive to a lot of Danes. And I can't help but think, 'OK, so it's alright to show someone's brain splattering all over a car, as in *Pulp Fiction* (dir. Quentin Tarantino, 1994). That's somehow hilarious. But I'm not allowed to show how someone changes, in all kinds of positive ways, as a result of faith?' It makes no sense to me, frankly. I think a lot of those fifty-something male critics just couldn't reconcile their hardcore leftist, secular commitments with the openness to spirituality and to faith that is clearly present in the film. The strange thing is that you can ask Danes about all kinds of things: how much they earn, what the size of their mortgage is, what their sexual orientation is, just to name a few examples. But you can't ask them whether they believe in God. I happen to be a relatively religious being. I've been that way since I was a child. It's not that I was raised as a believer. That religiosity is present in my films, necessarily so, because I cannot live without a sense of hope. I may make films about all kinds of dreadful things, but I'll always make sure there's a little green lighter in them somewhere.

Hjort: In 2007 you directed *Bitter Sweetheart* in Sweden. How did that film come about, and how do you see the possibilities for collaboration across the Sound?

Joof: I was contacted by the production company SF. They'd seen *Oh Happy Day* and really liked it. They wanted to work with a female director, and they're in short supply in Sweden. Bergman no doubt casts long shadows! It was in every way a delightful project, and I'd very much like to work in Sweden again.

Hjort: You've directed films for TV, both for the National Broadcasting Corporation and for the commercial TV 2. Has this TV work had any impact on your work as a film director?

Joof: I don't really see the two activities as being that different.

Hjort: What are you working on these days?

Joof: I'm writing a script together with my friend Anna Neye Poulsen. It's political, and we're thinking of it as a spoof on Nikolaj Arcel's *King's Game* (*Kongekabale*, 2004). You know that party that was created? Ny Alliance? Well it's sort of a satirical take on that initiative. I want to make a film that is set in a political milieu, and since *King's Game* has already taken a really serious look at that kind of milieu, our film will need to be a lot less serious. I've also got a children's film in the works. I didn't write the script myself, Morten Dragsted did. It's a story about children who have no choice but to take the law into their own hands. And I have any number of scripts on my computer. But I've told people that I'm quite happy to show up and play a small part from time to time, because I really do love acting. In fact, I like it a lot more now than I did before, and I think I'm a lot easier to work with. I just say, 'What would you like me to do? Where do you want me to stand? Where is the camera?' Before I was much more opinionated, and would make all kinds of remarks about my character and what I thought she would and would not do or say.

Hjort: Have you ever thought about making a film in Africa, in South Africa, for example, where there's a vital film industry, or in East Africa, where the Danish Film Institute has been involved in capacity building through the Zanzibar International Film Festival?

Joof: I would really love to do that. When I read Alexander McCall Smith's *The No. 1 Ladies' Detective Agency* I immediately called Thomas [Gammeltoft] and said, we have to take out an option on McCall's books. Those books should be adapted, and I *really* want to direct the films. So he made a few inquiries and it turned out that Anthony Minghella already had optioned the books. And I said 'No, no, the director really should be black. I know I don't live in Africa, but I really feel I know something about the world of those books.' And then Minghella ends up dying, just when his TV series is ready to be shown. Terrible. So somebody has to take over the project of adapting those books, and *maybe* that somebody is me?

I'd much rather shoot films in Africa than in Hollywood. I don't know of any Danish director who has gone to Hollywood and come back happy. The good films Danish directors have made have all been made here, not there. What's good about the Danish context is the way in which we work. Nobody from the Danish Film Institute is ever going to require me to re-cut a scene, or to change it. Someone like Ingolf Gabold, the Head of DR TV Drama, might say something like, 'By emphasizing this scene this much you make it really difficult for us to leave the cinema happy. So if your idea is that we should be unhappy, then you've achieved what you're after. But if you'd like us to be happy at the end of the film, I think you might want to take another look at that scene, because it's quite long and it's quite massive.' What you get is a lot of really good constructive criticism. But nobody would ever dream of insisting on changes. You can't work that way in Hollywood.

Chapter 9

Ole Christian Madsen

Ole Christian Madsen.
Photography: Jan Buus.

Born 1966. Ole Christian Madsen graduated as a director from the National Film School of Denmark in 1993. With its story about a young second generation immigrant in the Vesterbro neighborhood of Copenhagen, his first film, the medium length *Sinans brullup* (*Sinan's Wedding*, 1997), was also one of the first Danish films to address the issue of immigrants in Denmark. Madsen's first feature film, the award-winning low budget film *Pizza King* (1999), was also set among immigrants and featured a group of young second generation immigrants who get embroiled with Copenhagen's underground crime scene, with a tragic outcome. The six-hour-long, film-noir-inspired historical TV series *Edderkoppen* (*The Spider*, 2000), about organized crime in a moral no man's land in the years immediately after World War Two, secured the director a popular national breakthrough.

Madsen's Dogma film, *En kærlighedshistorie* (*Kira's Reason: A Love Story*, 2001), is a drama about a couple who go through an excruciating crisis in their marriage. The stylistically eclectic *Nordkraft* (*Angels in Fast Motion*, 2004), an adaptation of Jakob Ejersbo's eponymous novel about lowlives in the provincial town of Aalborg, was a rather expensive production, whereas *Prag* (*Prague*, 2006) was another portrait of a marital crisis made on a very modest budget, this time set in the Czech capital. Madsen's latest film, the World War Two drama *Flammen & Citronen* (*Flame & Citron*, 2008), about two young Danish resistance fighters, is the most expensive Danish-language film ever (it cost 47 million DKK). With 670,000 tickets sold in Denmark alone, *Flame & Citron* topped the Danish 2008 list of films, Danish as well as international, and it is the last ten years' best-selling Danish film. Since *Pizza King*, all Ole Christian Madsen's films have won national and/or international awards.

In addition to his feature films, Madsen has worked for television. Besides the mini-series *The Spider*, which is almost like a feature film, he has directed a number of episodes of the TV series *Taxa* (*Taxi*, 1997) and *Rejseholdet* (*Unit One*, 2002–2004).

In 1993, Ole Christian Madsen was among the founders of the production company Nimbus Film which has produced all of his films.

Feature films

2008	*Flammen & Citronen* (*Flame & Citron*)
2006	*Prag* (*Prague*)
2004	*Nordkraft* (*Angels in Fast Motion*)
2001	*En kærlighedshistorie* (*Kira's Reason: A Love Story*)
1999	*Pizza King*

Short films

1997	*Sinans bryllup* (*Sinan's Wedding*)
1993	*Lykkelige Jim* (*Happy Jim*, graduation film)

Television

2002–2004	*Rejseholdet* (*Unit One*, four episodes)
2000	*Edderkoppen* (*The Spider*, mini-series, six episodes)
1997	*Taxa* (*Taxi*, two episodes)

Jørholt: With Thomas Vinterberg and Per Fly you were part of the so-called 'golden cohort' at the National Film School of Denmark. How would you describe the significance of the school, personally, but also in relation to the Danish film boom of the last ten years or so?

Madsen: The Film School has been decisive for the way I think about films, and for the way in which Danish cinema has developed. It's my impression that our class was a kind of experiment where we were taught more about narration than about any other aspects of filmmaking, including more aesthetic matters, and that was crucial for us. I'd made films before I entered film school – experimental films and documentaries – but I would never have been able to approach filmmaking in the mature way that is necessary in order to operate in the film industry, if I hadn't been to film school.

Actually, when we graduated from the Film School, there really wasn't much of a film industry in Denmark. There was the brand new Zentropa, and of course there was Nordisk Film. Nordisk Film was very much the enemy, the company that made all the films we didn't like. They provided a kind of negative example and thus forced us to invent something else. We created Nimbus Film and focused on more anarchistic productions, the Dogma films being a case in point. We took the established film industry by surprise, and all of a sudden we found that the power had been transferred to directors, scriptwriters and actors. That was a real shift.

The Danish film boom, if you can call it that, is based on two things: a generation from the Film School that graduated at the right moment and wanted to tell new stories in a different and more dynamic way; and Lars von Trier, who had singlehandedly managed to win prestige and recognition for Danish cinema. The Dogma rules were instrumental in our being able to communicate with the film world internationally. But a precondition for the success of Danish cinema was, of course, the political goodwill that we enjoyed. There'd been nothing really going on in Danish cinema for decades, and people had been waiting for something finally to happen.

Jørholt: *Sinan's Wedding* and *Pizza King* were among the first Danish films to deal with the issue of immigrants. How did you get the idea of making those films at a time when the Danish film milieu seemed almost phobic about taking up immigration issues?

Madsen: That sense of phobia is still there. But the reason I turned to these issues was that I'd been trying to come up with a story that I was personally invested in, a story about things I'd experienced myself. After a couple of years of searching in vain, I decided that instead of transposing an inner story to the outside world, I would take a story from the outside and move it in. I had Turkish friends and I also knew other people from the immigrant milieu, and I was struck by the fact that their problems weren't different in type, but in degree. They were dealing with the kinds of problems we all have to deal with, but these problems were more extreme because of the immigrant dimension. Also, I was very excited about what was happening in England at the time, and about Hanif Kureishi and his novel *The Black Album* – the whole movement that came out of the wave of immigration to Europe. To me, that was basically the only story worth telling. Besides, it was good dramatic material. Since the problems were so pronounced, the dramatic conflicts would also be quite clear. I then embarked on a fairly long research process, spent time with the immigrant communities and tried to make friends with as many people as possible. *Pizza King* is based on about 20 to 25 interviews that were then absorbed into one story.

Initially, however, none of the Danish cinemas would show the film, because there was this fear that it would attract violent young immigrants who would create a row. So the film sat on the shelf for a year and a half before it opened in the cinemas. It was simply too controversial, which is totally bizarre. We finally brokered a compromise, which was that *Pizza King* would be screened at separate times. This meant that the viewers for *Pizza King* wouldn't be in the cinemas at the same time as the viewers for other films. *Pizza King* was shown, for example, at 8.30pm, whereas the other films started at 9.30pm. The idea was to prevent the two groups of spectators from bumping into each other.

Jørholt: *Pizza King* is indeed quite a radical film for its time. For instance, there are practically no actors from non-immigrant backgrounds in the film.

Madsen: We deliberately decided that all the actors would be from an immigrant background. The whole idea was to paint a portrait of this community, of what was almost a kind of parallel subculture, and to do this from the inside. We had a distributor who would only handle the film if two of the protagonists were 'white', so Danes would be able to identify with them. I couldn't accept that, of course, so we ended up making the film on a much smaller budget. And yes, the environment depicted in the film is tough, but not nearly as tough as it is in real life today. Actually, even then the immigrant community found that our depiction of the milieu didn't show enough conflict and violence.

Jørholt: In many ways, *Pizza King* bears a strong resemblance to Martin Scorsese's *Mean Streets* (1973), but whereas Scorsese was talking about his own environment from the inside, you were an outsider to the Danish immigrant milieu. What were your thoughts about your own outsider position?

Madsen: As a matter of fact, I was very inspired by Scorsese at the time, but my own position as an outsider was of course something that I thought about a lot. However, the problem was that nobody else was making films about immigrants, and in spite of everything, I did know something about this environment, having already explored it in *Sinan's Wedding*. So my attitude was, let's give it a try and see what happens. The difficulties we encountered came, not from the immigrant community itself – they accepted me with open arms and showed me a lot of trust – but from the politically correct left. Those people were really negative about the project, and criticized me for being a fucking Dane who made films about immigrants. But they were the only ones to do so.

Jørholt: Originally, you planned to make an entire immigrant trilogy. Have you abandoned that idea?

Madsen: I also wanted to make a comedy about immigrant women. This whole immigrant debate is so fraught with problems that I decided to try to lighten things up a bit through some humour. But by the time I started writing the story things were moving so fast that each time I thought I'd written something that would work, people immediately told me stories that suggested otherwise. So, in the end, I shelved the project because I just couldn't find my way to the heart of the story. Besides, I found it tiresome that it was so hard to get people to take an interest in these films, and I was tired of constantly being criticized for making them. Those difficulties kind of put me off. Nobody in the established Danish milieu ever told me that it was great that I'd made these films. That just didn't happen. It is really regrettable that people in Denmark aren't more open to films about immigrants. The fate of Omar Shargawi's *Ma Salama Jamil* (*Go With Peace Jamil*, 2008) tells you something about just how hard it is to get people to take an interest in these stories. But I haven't abandoned my idea of an immigrant comedy. We'll just have to see what happens.

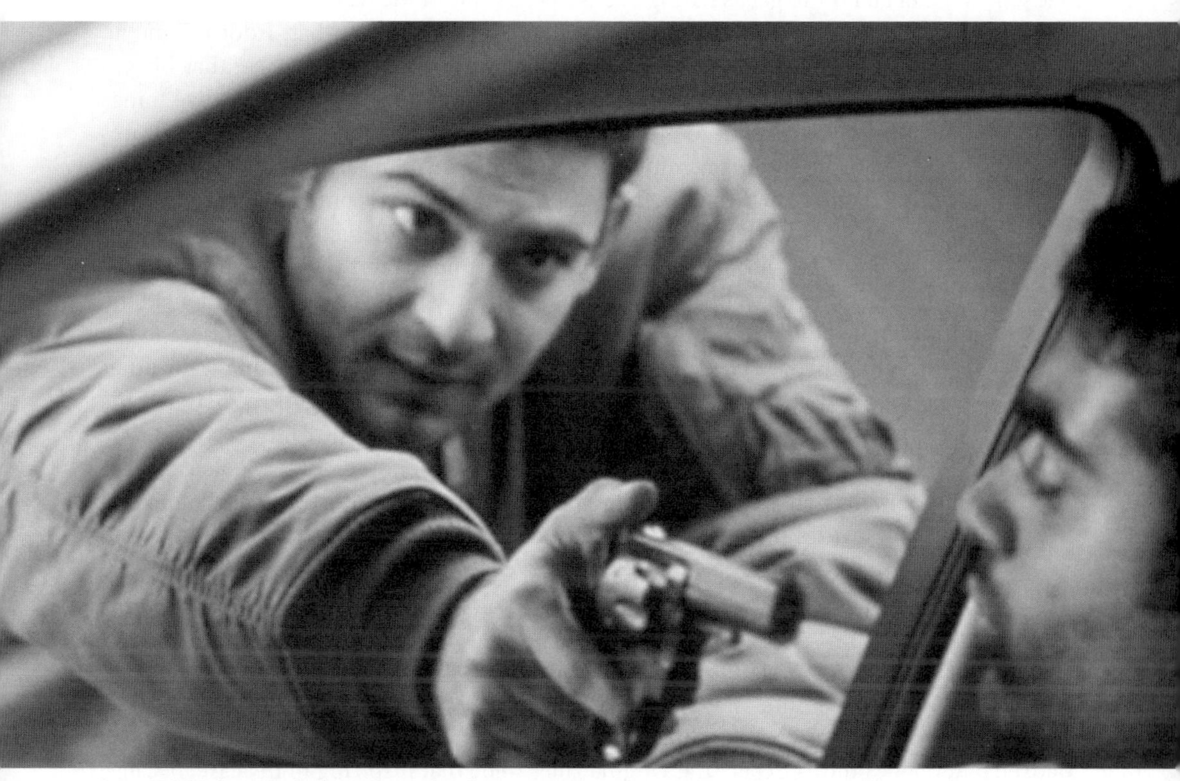

Janus Nabil Bakrawi and Ali Kazim as second generation immigrants in *Pizza King*. Frame grab.

Jørholt: Even though *Angels in Fast Motion* isn't about immigrants, it has certain similarities to *Pizza King*. Both films side with outsiders; both are multiprotagonist films, and in both cases, the characters are moving towards an unavoidable tragedy. But whereas *Pizza King* has an element of improvisation, *Angels in Fast Motion* is a tightly controlled and highly stylized film. What kind of stylistic questions do you consider before making a film?

Madsen: First of all I try to get as strong a sense as possible of the reality I intend to portray, and then I settle on a particular cinematic style based on that. I don't come up with specific shots in advance. It's not until we're actually on the set that I begin to think about what would look interesting on the screen. I tend to stylize things quite a lot as I work, but to me style is only an instrument for making the features of a given reality more prominent. In that sense my films are not in fact like those of Guy Ritchie, to which *Angels in Fast Motion* has been compared.

I'm not intimately familiar with the environment depicted in *Angels in Fast Motion* but I do know something about it. I understand the anatomy of abuse, the feeling of being trapped inside a bubble from which you cannot escape. In the film we tried to express that particular feeling by strapping a small camera to the actors, and since we already had the camera, we ended up also using it for other purposes. So, in that sense, I suppose you could say that style gets the better of me every now and then. But the starting point is always a given reality.

Also, I almost always draw inspiration from still photography. I look at a lot of photographs that are related to the milieu we're about to portray, and I often add a certain texture that I'll have found in the work of a very specific photographer. The texture of *Angels in Fast Motion*, for example, was strongly inspired by the American photographer Nan Goldin.

Jørholt: Compared to *Angels in Fast Motion*, your two films about marital crises, *Kira's Reason: A Love Story* and *Prague*, are much smaller productions. *Kira's Reason* is even a Dogma film. Why did you decide to make a Dogma film? Did you see the Dogma rules as creative challenges?

Madsen: Actually, I didn't expect the Dogma rules to be that inspiring in my case, because I felt that *Pizza King* was a Dogma film 'avant la lettre'. So to me, the idea of reducing filmmaking to locations, actors and story – and of excluding style because there was no money – was not new. Eventually, of course, Dogma itself turned into a style, albeit a different kind of style. Just before *Kira's Reason*, I'd made a mini-series for TV, *The Spider*, which was a very large and stylistically refined production. The style was very film noir, and we worked with this closed claustrophobic universe. But as far as the work of getting to the heart of the story is concerned, it turned out that *The Spider* and *Kira's Reason* weren't actually that different. I didn't experience Dogma as some huge liberation.

As far as the Dogma concept of letting creativity grow from constraints is concerned, I'd say that that way of thinking informs everything I do. We always try to articulate the most compelling vision possible, within the limits of the available resources, but there's never enough money – not even when you make a film as expensive as *Flame & Citron*. I actually see limited resources as a necessary condition for creativity. It's very important to aim a little higher than your resources allow, and then to push things as far as you possibly can. If you adjust your ambitions to your financial means and come up with a nice, bureaucratic production process that has everybody going home at four o'clock every day, you simply will not convince the audience. There's got to be that element of working against constraints. Constraints produce a certain dynamic. So to me, economic resources, or constraints, and creativity are very closely related.

Jørholt: In your two historical dramas, *The Spider* and *Flame & Citron*, you take on official Danish history about the creation of the Danish welfare society in the years after World War Two and the resistance movement during the German occupation of Denmark, respectively. Was it important for you to correct the official version of these moments in the national history of Denmark, or did you see the historical events primarily as dramatic material?

Madsen: As far as *Flame & Citron* is concerned, I'd say that, yes, it was quite important to me personally to confront the wretched history classes I'd been exposed to in school: the story about the small country that's occupied by the evil Germans, and where the entire population, cool and undaunted, joins the resistance movement, eventually forcing the evil Germans to give up. Even as a child I was aware that this wasn't what actually happened. My father was an officer and he was very interested in the resistance movement. Ever since I was very young, I've always read a lot about the German occupation, so I was well aware of the fact that only very few Danes fought against the Germans. And as an adult I've never understood how we Danes could live with this false understanding of ourselves, how our national identity could become so untrue to reality. So, in *Flame & Citron*, it was immensely important for us to present a more truthful image of the resistance movement.

The scriptwriter Lars K. Andersen and I started research for the film back in 1999, and during our work we ran into more and more people who knew something about the period. It was as though we kept opening up more and more boxes, until we ended up with an entirely open Pandora's box. From this material we tried to create a story that made sense. What did this special resistance unit look like? How did it operate? Here was this group of resistance fighters who saw themselves as a kind of secret service; it was very important to me also to show this aspect of the resistance movement. There's something scary about Flame and Citron as actual persons. There's a kind of idealism there that eventually gets caught up in the machinery of power. Two people who end up losing their way.

Jørholt: In the film the German intelligence officer calls Flame and Citron 'soldiers without an army'. This description would probably also fit many of those who are referred to as terrorists today. Were you thinking about contemporary terrorism when you made the film?

Madsen: Not necessarily in the sense suggested by your question. I would definitely not want to compare the Danish resistance movement during World War Two to the terrorism we see in the world today. On the other hand, every underground or guerrilla army works in the same way, and in a guerrilla war the weaker element usually has to resort to more and more brutal means, because it just doesn't have the same resources as the stronger element it's up against. In principle, that's what happened in Copenhagen between 1943 and 1945. In this sense, you might say that the German occupation of Denmark is a grand narrative because it reflects all the conflicts of the world today. So, the issue of terrorism was clearly in my mind when I made the film, but I wouldn't want to draw any direct parallels between then and now.

Jørholt: *Flame & Citron* was shot primarily in Berlin and Prague, which makes the film's Copenhagen look a little strange to a Copenhagen audience. Did you deliberately try to represent Copenhagen in a less obvious way, or was shooting in Prague and Berlin dictated by budgetary considerations?

Madsen: Most of the films' large exterior scenes are actually shot in Copenhagen. But it's very difficult to shoot a historical film in Copenhagen, because everything is so modern. As a matter of fact, I wish we'd shot it all in Prague or Berlin. I realize one could get the impression that the urban environment is more like 'some place in the world' than the actual city of Copenhagen, but we were trying to balance two aims. We wanted to revise the official version of a particular period in the history of Denmark while also making a film with a universal human dimension.

Jørholt: You also made *Prague* in the Czech Republic. What is your experience of working in German and Czech production environments compared to making films in Denmark?

Madsen: I love making films abroad. There may, of course, be certain cultural barriers that need to be surmounted, but other than that, the work discipline and seriousness you find in the German and Czech production milieus are very different from what I experience in Denmark today. In Danish film production, the work days are far too short. Nowadays a full work day in the Danish production milieu is only seven hours and 45 minutes. One reason is probably that salaries have gone up to such an extent that the production companies simply cannot afford to pay people to work ten hours a day. I don't mean to say that the film workers are making too much money – compared to the overall salary scale and prices in Denmark, there's nothing unusual about the film industry – but Danish cinema has woven itself into a bureaucratic web of regulations dictated by the trade unions, all of which makes filming extremely difficult. My view is that if we choose to make films for a living, then we have to be willing to accept working hours that don't fit the standard nine to five model.

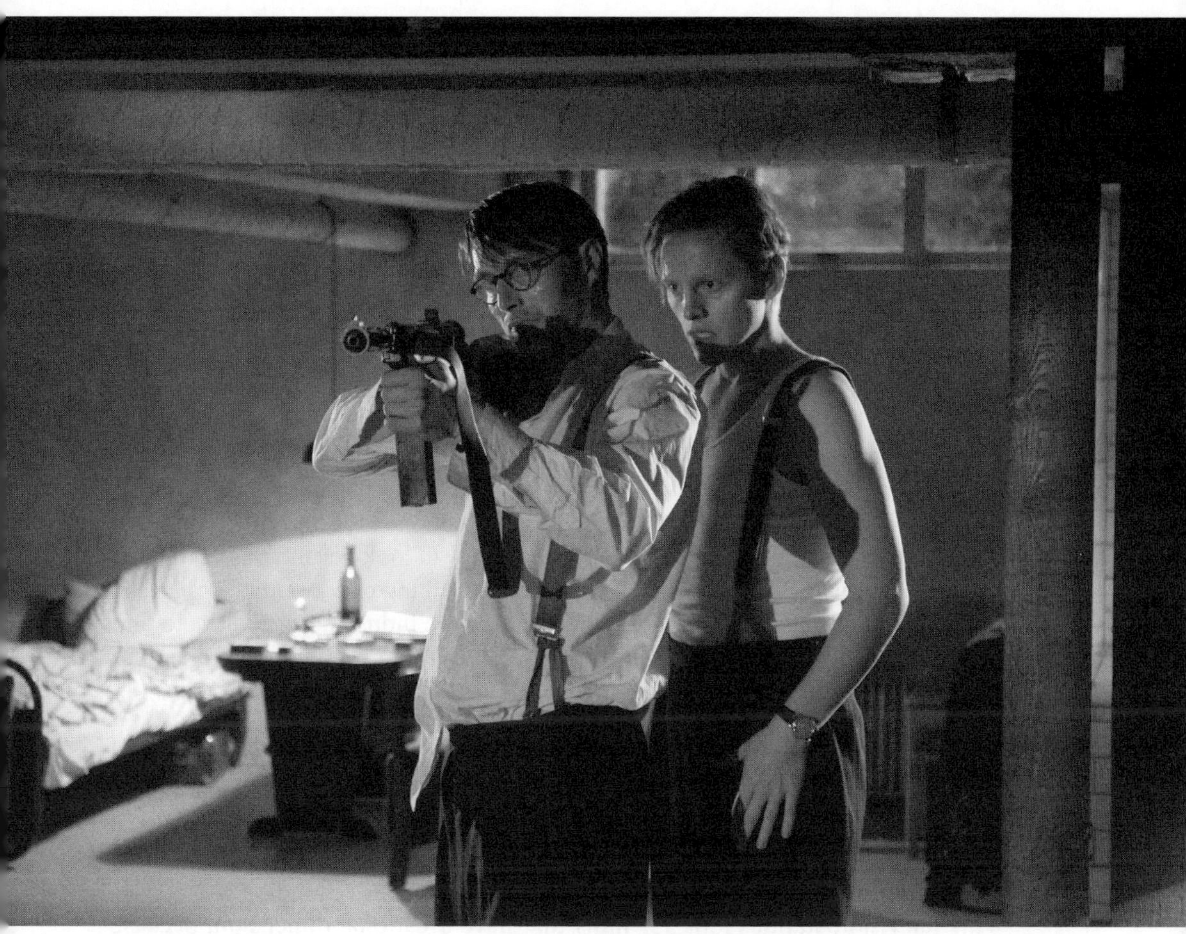

Mads Mikkelsen and Thure Lindhardt as WWII resistance fighters in *Flammen & Citronen* (*Flame & Citron*). Photography: Britta Krehl.

Jørholt: Have you ever received any offers from abroad?

Madsen: I've had several offers from both Germany and the US. Actually, it's my agent who has turned down the offers I've received from Hollywood, because he thought they would flop. I have to be confident that he understands that game better than I do. I understand the Danish system; over there, I don't understand anything.

Jørholt: You've sometimes suggested that Danish cinema ought to be more international. Your point has been that Danish companies with an established presence abroad would be able to tap into foreign support. In Germany, you've pointed out, there are five large film funds, three of them the size of our Danish Film Institute. In your view, has Danish cinema become too provincial, or perhaps too nationally oriented, given the globalized nature of the world in which we live?

Madsen: The main problem is that there's not enough money for making films. And it's absolutely certain that we won't be getting more money for film in Denmark in the foreseeable future. Danish cinema simply has to look beyond our borders in order to survive. After all, you can't go back to making only twenty films a year. That's just not possible. It would sabotage the entire industry. So, we have to find more money, and it can only be found abroad. Germany is right next to us, and the Germans have a lot of money. Why shouldn't Danish production companies shoot a German film in the German language? There are lots of possibilities.

As I see it, the Danish Film Institute continues to promote a very sensible path for Danish cinema. The problem is that the last four-year Media Policy Accord with the film sector conferred more power on the television stations, and this has had the effect of making Danish cinema much more provincial and more nationally oriented in terms of the milieu's self-understanding. Obviously, the television stations look for films that have a national dimension, because their aim is to show these films to a national audience. It seems to me that there's really been a process of turning in on ourselves here. The most recent contract with the film sector gave the television stations the power to decide which feature films will and will not be produced in Denmark. If the television stations turn down a project, the film simply won't be produced. Within the last five years, it's also become very hard to find cinematographers and scriptwriters who are willing to take the risk of collaborating on a project that may not get produced. Whether or not a project will actually get produced is decided by the television stations, and they don't come into the process until quite late in the game. If Danish cinema is to have a future, it's absolutely crucial to disclose the huge problems that have been created by the last two Media Accords. The influence of the television stations must be downgraded to a more reasonable level. Even the television stations are unhappy about the degree of responsibility they've been given. But of course, the fear is that if the financial contribution of the television stations is reduced, there will simply not be enough money.

Jørholt: You've made quite a lot of television yourself. Wouldn't you say that television also has contributed in a positive way to Danish cinema? I'm thinking of some of the new and award-winning TV series like *Taxi* and *Unit One* which were to a large extent created by directors, scriptwriters and actors from the film scene, including yourself.

Madsen: It all started with *Taxi*, and basically I'd like to say that Rumle Hammerich and Sven Clausen at the Danish Broadcasting Corporation were absolutely right to put directors and scriptwriters in charge of these new series, because they brought renewal and innovation to both the visual look and the narrative content of Danish TV fiction. At the same time, the directors and actors profited from the opportunity to gain new experience. When you have to shoot several scenes a day, you have to make decisions very quickly, without thinking too much. Perhaps it wasn't that stimulating from a creative point of view, but those working conditions really toughen you up, and teach you a certain professionalism that is extremely important. Besides, the fact that people actually wanted to see the things we produced was a fantastic experience. Many of us have advanced much faster in the film industry because of our work for television, not least Niels Arden Oplev and myself. We owe Danish TV a lot, but the converse is also true, because we helped to make Danish TV dramas much more professional.

The flip side of all this is that some of us may have become a bit too good at working this way, which means that our own feature film production methods get undermined. We learnt to work extremely fast, and all of a sudden we could shoot a film in half the time we were used to. Ever since the television stations started using filmmakers in a serious and sustained way, the typical shooting period for a feature film has been reduced from nine to ten weeks to only six weeks. Moreover, our feature films have come to resemble TV series more and more. Shot within the framework of a production form that is meant to be fast, they've simply been shaped by the aesthetics of the TV series. At the outset, the television stations adopted what they found useful from the language of film, and now cinema owners and distributors tend to think that our feature films should look like the TV series, so that there'll be an audience for them. Actually, these people are right up to a point, because the TV series do address the audience in a very accessible visual language. Thinking along box-office lines is quite new to me, though. I've never thought about my films in terms of how many tickets they'd sell, but I now have to do this.

When we made *Taxi*, it was the only Danish TV series of this new and more professional kind, but now the Danish Broadcasting Corporation, TV 2 and TV 3 are constantly producing several series concurrently. That means that many creative people leave the film industry for television. If you need to get in touch with a scriptwriter, it's almost certain that you'll find him or her working for the Danish Broadcasting Corporation, and at a good salary. The Danish Broadcasting Corporation and

TV 2 can offer a guaranteed salary for maybe two years, something the film industry simply cannot compete with. So, television is essentially shaping an entire generation of actors, cinematographers and scriptwriters, the result being that TV further influences the language our feature films are told in.

In fact, Danish films are no longer selling as many tickets as they did just a few years ago. The opening of a new film is just not accompanied by the same kind of jubilatory optimism that we experienced even a year ago. I'm not sure, but it looks like we may be heading into a period that is more like the 80s, when Danish viewers didn't care to watch our films, and the critics quite simply hated them.

Jørholt: However, *Flame & Citron* did sell more than 670,000 tickets on the Danish market alone.

Madsen: Of course, I can't complain, but I am also concerned about my next film, and the conditions under which I'll be making it. *Flame & Citron* was made in the slipstream of the good times. It was shot in 2007, after we'd spent nine to ten years financing and pre-producing it. Of course, nothing is easy when you're in the midst of it all, but looking back now I can see that we're incredibly fortunate to have been part of the milieu at a time when there was more money, because we've been able to make a more diverse range of films as a result. And that's what has become much harder. And given the success of *Flame & Citron*, I can't help but wonder how the others are doing if I'm finding the going tough these days. It's a really bad sign if the director of the bestselling film is having trouble financing his next film.

Jørholt: As far as I understand, you're working on no fewer than three new projects right now. Is this just a coincidence, or is it some kind of deliberate strategy to work on different projects simultaneously?

Madsen: The three films have very different budgets, and the strategy is to start by making an inexpensive film that hopefully can be made quite quickly, and to try to find the means to make the other two films at the same time. If everything works according to plan, I'll have succeded in financing the medium-cost film by the time I finish the cheapest film, and while I'm making the medium-cost film, I'll be looking abroad for money for the most expensive of the three films. The trick is always to be thinking strategically.

Right now I'm working on my third relationship film, a comedy which we will shoot in Buenos Aires in October. At the same time, I'm engaged in a historical project about Eik Skaløe and the Danish rock group Steppeulvene which I made a documentary about before entering film school. Since then, I've dreamt about going back to that material and making a feature film about it, if the necessary financial backing could be found and if sufficient interest could be generated in the project. It looks like that's all finally happening. I'm also working with Per Fly on a project about Denmark's military engagement in the war in Afghanistan.

Jørholt: Such close collaboration between two directors is quite rare, I suppose. Or would you say that Danish directors tend to network a fair bit, and to draw on each other for creative inspiration?

Madsen: The collaboration between Per and myself on this Afghanistan project is indeed absolutely unique, but there *is* a creative network in Danish cinema, only it's neither as large nor as closely knit as people sometimes claim. There are lots of directors with whom I have nothing to do, and with whom I feel I have nothing in common. But here and there, there are a few alliances – like the one between Per Fly and myself. At the same time, Per and I are best friends, which is probably what makes our creative collaboration so strong. We know that we won't end up fighting, and that we'll be able to solve any problems that might arise rationally. Thomas Vinterberg is not part of that particular project, but since film school, he too has been one of my close partners.

So I would say that there is indeed a network, or perhaps, more accurately, there are shifting creative alliances. But there's also an element of competition, because we're all trying to get a share of the same money. That doesn't really have much of an impact on our way of being together, though.

Jørholt: Lately, Danish film has been criticized for being too mainstream, for not experimenting enough. What do you think of that kind of criticism?

Madsen: I totally agree. We must definitely become better at making smaller and more experimental films. But to me, it's perhaps primarily a question of not being good enough at identifying the kinds of films we're making. The result is what you might call 'muddied' films that don't belong properly in one of three categories: genuine artistic experiments; art films with some mainstream characteristics and appeal; popular family films. Those are essentially the three types of films we're working with in Denmark, and they more or less thrive synergistically on each other. The artistic experiments are doing best at festivals and abroad. The art films targeting a mainstream audience help to give Danish cinema a distinctive identity. And the family films for the general public like *Far til fire* [*Father of Four*; a series of popular films by various directors] help to ensure that we have a domestic cinema market that functions, and earns a lot of money. To me, it's unthinkable that those three types of cinema should not work alongside each other.

Our main problem is that we don't produce enough. And if we don't produce enough we don't get better at our craft and we don't refine our skills. There was a period when many of us were able to produce a lot, and that's really crucial, because we need to become really outstanding, in terms of how we express ourselves and how we tell our stories. I'd like to make a film a year and to work with different genres and different aspects of human existence. If that's possible in Denmark, I'd love to make films here until I'm eighty. But if it's not possible in Denmark, I'll probably go somewhere else.

Chapter 10

Anders Morgenthaler

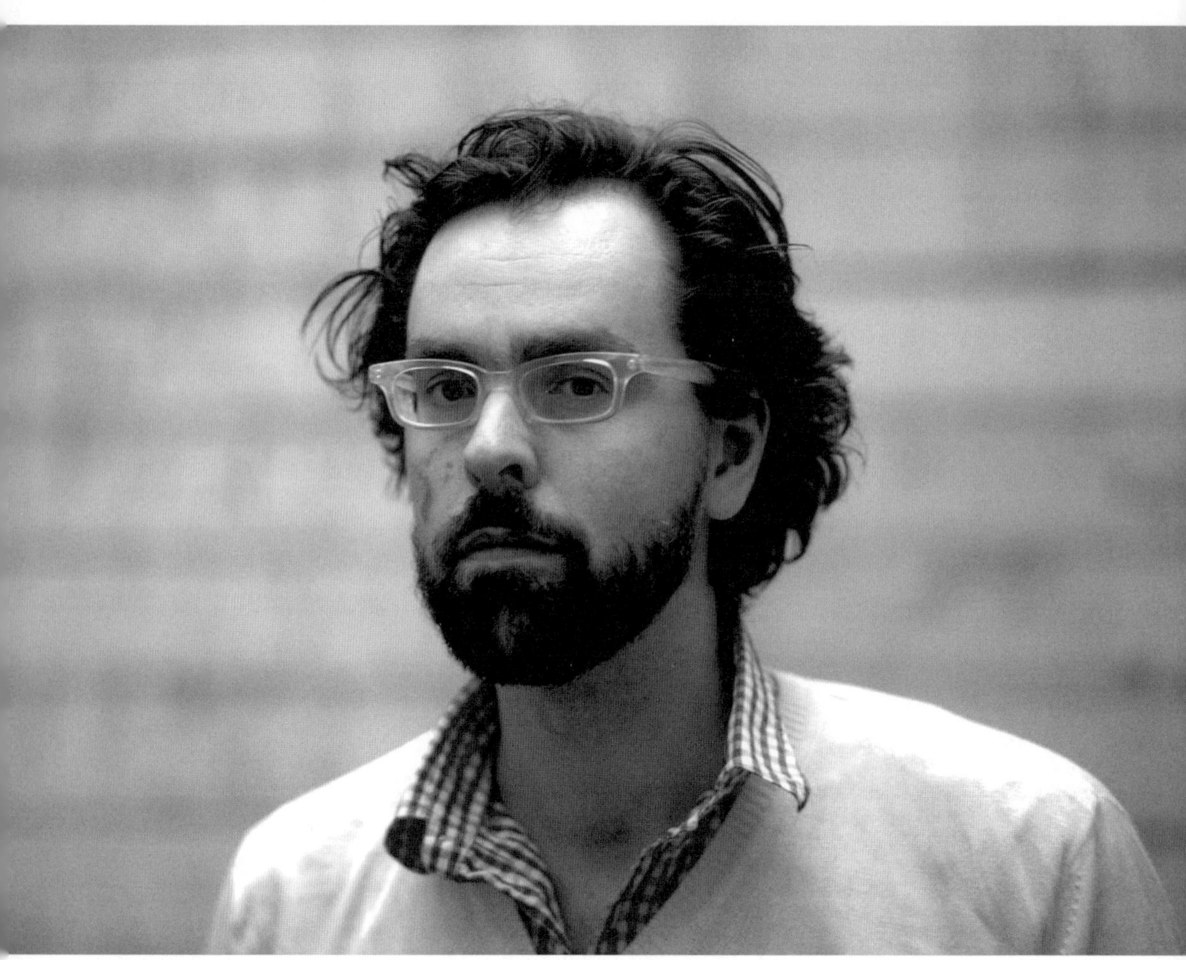

Anders Morgenthaler. Photography: EGO.

Born 1972. Morgenthaler graduated from the Design School in Kolding in 1998 and from the animation stream at the National Film School of Denmark in 2002. His award-winning graduation film, *Araki: The Killing of a Japanese Photographer*, is an eight-minute animated film about a man's bloody revenge against the sex industry, personified in the Japanese photographer Araki Nobuyoshi. Morgenthaler achieved an international breakthrough with his first feature film, the animated and equally award-winning *Princess* (2006), which takes the revenge theme from *Araki* to a poetic level. His first live-action film, *Ekko* (*Echo*, 2007), is a stylistically eclectic story about a desperate father who kidnaps his own son and takes him to an abandoned summer cottage in a summerly Danish province. With *Carsten & Gittes filmballade* (*Carsten & Gitte's Movie Madness*, 2008) and *Æblet og ormen* (*The Apple and the Worm*, 2009) Morgenthaler returned to animation, this time for very young children. In 2006, he created the production company Copenhagen Bombay with former Zentropa producer Sarita Christensen. The company's profile is based on films and multimedia products for children and young people.

Anders Morgenthaler is also known as a cartoonist, as one half of the Wulffmorgenthaler duo (with the standup comedian Mikael Wulff) that provides the Danish newspaper *Politiken* with a both crazy and controversial cartoon on a daily basis. Morgenthaler has also made politically incorrect children's television for grown-ups with Wulff: *Wulffmorgenthaler* (2005). Among other things *Wulffmorgenthaler* introduced the quasi-fascistic rhinoceros Dolph to the Danish mediascape. At this point Dolph enjoys cult status in Denmark.

Feature films

2009 *Æblet og ormen* (*The Apple and the Worm*)
2008 *Carsten & Gittes filmballade* (*Carsten & Gitte's Movie Madness*)
2007 *Ekko* (*Echo*)
2006 *Princess*

Short films

2008 *Eat Shit and Die*
2002 *Araki: The Killing of a Japanese Photographer* (graduation film)

Television

2005 *Wulffmorgenthaler* (eight episodes)

Jørholt: Who is Anders Morgenthaler? You are involved in so many different things that it may be difficult to put a label on you.

Morgenthaler: I don't even know myself. That's my problem, and it's a source of confusion in my work as an artist. Who the f… makes both *Princess* and 26 episodes of *Børnetimen* (*The Children's Hour*), which I'm doing for television right now? To me, it is all equally interesting, equally rewarding. I've invented a kind of children's television which is aimed at stimulating children's thought processes, and encompasses everything modern children lack in their daily lives. I'm the father of small children myself, so this kind of stuff interests me, and that's why I involve myself in projects like these. But I sense that some people see these projects as an admission of failure. Apparently, it's not artistic to take an interest in your own life situation. Trier, for example, has never made television programmes for children.

There are so many things that I want to do, and I sense that at the moment I'm moving away from film as a purely narrative medium. Stories told on a variety of different platforms have always interested me, but I kind of abandoned this line of work in the 1990s because the whole CD-ROM market made it all so banal. In the last three years, however, I've come up with one concept after the other. Something called *Energy Hunters*, for instance. It's a toy concept for children and it requires them to run around and shoot each other. What it's really about, however, is energy. What is energy? And how much energy do you consume in different situations? The idea is to give children an understanding of the concept of energy.

They run around and tap each other for energy, and the whole thing is embedded in a story about an ancient monastic order, which I wrote with Kenneth Bøgh Andersen, who writes stories for children and young people. The basic idea is that the earth already existed 250 million years ago in the form and with the cultures we know now, and we're back there again. At the time, the energy hunters didn't succeed in eliminating all the fossil fuel monsters and spirits that have been set free by our energy consumption. So it's a kind of Jedi order. I simply love that kind of stuff. And it will all be told on a lot of different platforms. There'll be a real-life game, toys that can be plugged into the computer (which will make it a computer game) and the possibility of playing the game on a cell phone. The toys that will be produced for *Energy Hunters* include a bag with solar cells and a gadget for your bicycle that will permit you to charge things and make your own energy. So the children will get an understanding of energy. And all of this is to be embedded in this overriding story about ancient monks.

Many of my own points of reference come from *Star Wars*, and if you ask an engineer why he became an engineer, he just might say that it's because he watched *Star Trek* as a child. You must respect children and their universe, for you can really influence them and thereby possibly contribute to making the world a better place in ten years. I'm also developing a food concept for children where they have to mix their own food from a variety of different kinds of dried food. I simply took muesli, dismantled it and turned it into a fantasy universe, a role-play environment where the children come to see these different instances of dried food as magic.

Other than that, we're now going to do pandas. We just closed a deal with the Danish Broadcasting Corporation about sixteen Simpson-like episodes about a fucked up suburban panda family. It's going to be great fun.

But to some people I'm still primarily a director of art films that are only seen by very few people. By and by, I guess most people know my name, only they find it hard to label me. How can he make a film that goes to Cannes and then a 45-minute film for children between two and a half and six years old? In the case of Trier or Christoffer Boe you always know more or less what to expect.

Jørholt: You speak of your diverse interests as a problem. Why?

Morgenthaler: When you try to finance a film, you have to adopt some kind of attitude, and in the film business, you basically have two options. Either the Trier attitude, which is introverted and unapproachable (the couple of times I've met Trier, he's actually been very pleasant and interested in other people) or the Per Fly/Thomas Vinterberg attitude, that's to say the persona of the extroverted, humane and happy filmmaker. I can't see myself in either of these two roles exclusively. I'm both terribly introverted and manic, and at the same time I can be almost insanely happy. My biggest problem, but it may also be a gigantic advantage, is how to tell the story it takes to create the financial network necessary for me to be able to do my work.

Besides, each time a filmmaker makes something a little out of the ordinary, people expect that person to repeat Trier's success story. When I made *Princess*, all the journalists wanted me to be the new Trier. When Christoffer made *Reconstruction* (2003) everybody wanted him to be the new Trier. But when the next films we made weren't selected for the main competition in Cannes, we were all of sudden ruled out of the game.

Jørholt: Has Trier come to rest as a kind of shadow over Danish cinema?

Morgenthaler: I think Trier is fantastic, so he's definitely not the problem. The problem is all the professional opinion makers – reporters and academic researchers – who have turned him into a kind of standard for success. That's so wrong. I am me, and I have no intention whatsoever of trying to repeat the things he's done.

Jørholt: But do you keep in touch with other filmmakers? Is there some kind of network that allows you to draw on each other?

Morgenthaler: If there is a directors' network, I don't use it, but I honestly don't think there is any network. The tendency in Danish cinema is rather to hide things from one another, because we all compete for the same money. But even in that respect, I'm kind of an outsider, because I'm also a producer. I have a few good friends whom I talk to, like Christoffer Boe, but we hardly ever discuss any specific films. What we discuss is more the business side of it all. How the business dimension can supply an interesting framework for our artistic endeavours. I suppose all good artists are also good business people – after all, they must sell an idea, a vision, a product. Only, this is not something people talk about very much.

You cannot be a naïve artist who just makes something. It simply doesn't work that way. My role models are the great American auteurs, Francis Ford Coppola et al., who were always extremely conscious of the entire business dimension of filmmaking. Coppola still insists on his status as an auteur although he knows very well that he had to make *Jack* (1996) in order to make ends meet. Martin Scorsese, too, is terribly shrewd. Take *The Aviator* (2004), for instance, which he made at a time when he really needed cash on the table. These are not bad films, but my point is that art is not something that just happens because you sit in a café smoking cigarettes with a couple of people. Filmmakers are businessmen and women. I would claim that the best artists have a special talent for business. That goes for Trier as well. Trier knows so much about business. After all, Dogma 95 is a business concept. People shouldn't be naïve and believe that it's only an artistic concept. And if he makes *Antichrist* (2009) now, it's because

Zentropa needs a film that will make the international headlines in a big way. I don't think Trier separates art from business. None of us do.

I can give you an example from my own work. Right now I'm writing a children's film about death and loss but presented in a hopefully funny and touching way and inserted into a visually fantastic universe. I'm quite confident that we can raise money for this film, to the requisite budgetary level. But prior to that, I wrote a ruthless film for grown-ups, and I conceived of it from the outset as a much less expensive production and as an attempt to challenge the conventional wisdom about what a film team should be. And I did this because I knew from the beginning that there would only be a small audience for this film. I really admire Steven Soderbergh and Lukas Moodysson for the way they think art and budget together, as a whole. That's what I want to do too.

My point is that budgetary constraints work as an interesting creative motor. The business part is extremely important for the artistic drive. I don't think business is more important than art. They are two dynamic unities feeding each other. And both parts are equally fun.

Jørholt: Why did you and your producer Sarita Christensen create your own production company, Copenhagen Bombay?

Morgenthaler: Basically, there were two reasons. On the one hand, the market was suffering from a fatal lack of stimulating media products for children and young people, and this was something we wanted to do something about. Media products for children have quite a low status. They're the things you produce when you have no other options. In my case it's exactly the other way around. During my film school years, I already had a company with 35 employees, TV-Animation, and we produced entertainment for children and sold it to television stations all over Europe. The company no longer exists, but it was a good learning experience. Making films and television for children is really giving something back to the world.

Besides, it was important for us to insist on the fact that storytelling is at a crossroads. If we look a few years ahead, film will probably no longer be an independent art form but rather part of a storytelling multimedia puzzle. Future generations will have grown up with computer games and may not have watched that many films.

You can choose to take an interest in this multiplatform development because you want to stay in business, and therefore have to go with the times; or you can take a genuine interest in it. Sarita and I have opted for the second approach. We find it interesting that film can just be part of a larger story, a particular shading of it. There aren't just films and television series, but *lots* of platforms. We're not, of course, the first people to have noticed this. Just think of the creator of *Lost*, J.J. Abrams, who is one of the most multiplatform-conscious creators ever. *Lost* is a television series with all kinds of strange storytelling offshoots on the internet. I find that immensely interesting.

Jørholt: What is your own role in Copenhagen Bombay?

Morgenthaler: I'm the company's creative director. I invent these things and find people – writers and directors – who can help realize my various concepts while I myself go back to my own projects. The biggest problem is to find people who are both sufficiently skilled and willing to work under these conditions. In Denmark, there's a tendency to educate people who think that they can start out as artistic directors. I need to recruit people directly from film schools, and what's striking is that at the Film School in Copenhagen it's almost impossible to find anyone who's willing to work the way I've described. The graduates all want to own a given concept themselves. We don't have the same tradition as in the US, where very skilled young people are eager to work under the creative direction of somebody else, because they regard it as a learning process. Up until now, I've only succeeded in finding two people who are willing to work under these conditions. It's clear to me that they really do profit from the set-up, as do I, of course, and perhaps even more than they do. To me, it's very strange that it has to be so difficult to find young talent willing to work in this way. If I were young, I'd be thrilled to be allowed to work under somebody like myself. But perhaps my name simply isn't sufficiently well known. I play at being Spielberg before actually *being* Spielberg, which is a problem, of course.

Jørholt: Let's talk about your own films. Even though they're extremely different – some are for children, some for grown-ups; some are animated, others live-action films – there is a common denominator, which is children, and the world of the child.

Morgenthaler: Yes, I think almost all my stories contain both an unconscious religious dimension and something that has to do with children. I wish I could provide a clear and explicit explanation for this, but I can't. I'm very much guided by my intuitions. I just act without really being able to explain why. I can articulate most other things, but not that. It probably has to do with the fact that in a certain sense, I'm still very childlike myself. A very large part of me is still a child, and I insist on being a child in my way of seeing the world. I have the enthusiasm of a child for certain things, and I am childish, bordering on the naïve, when I come up with new projects.

Jørholt: *Araki* and *Princess* seem to be strongly inspired by Japanese anime.

Morgenthaler: Actually, my Japanese inspiration is very limited. My interest in anime and manga is limited to their technical platform which I found useful. But I do take an interest in Japanese culture in a more general sense and, not least, in the way the Japanese tackle things from a purely business-oriented,

Precision and poetry in *Princess*.

aesthetic and technical point of view. The Japanese and the Koreans, Asia more generally, are now at the forefront of the development of the film medium.

Jørholt: In both *Araki* and *Princess* you mix animation and live-action sequences. The shaky, handheld live-action images in *Princess* almost seem like a commentary on Dogma. Are they?

Morgenthaler: No. A lot of people find this mixture of animation and live-action sequences very unique, but as far as I was concerned it was only a question of animation not being able to obtain the desired emotional effect on the audience. There had to be real faces with eyes capable of telling you a billion different things. What works in *Princess* is the way the live-action sequences give life to the relatively simple drawings. Unconsciously, the audience supplies the animation with more nuances than are actually there.

Jørholt: Could the entire story have been told as a live-action film?

Morgenthaler: Yes, I think so, but in that case it would on the one hand have been almost unbearable, and on the other hand it would have had trouble showing the beauty of life. Take, for instance, the scene on the poster where the two protagonists are sitting on a bench, looking at a lake immediately after killing another human being and fighting between themselves. In a scene like that, animation is a fantastic tool for placing the characters very precisely on a bench while cherry leaves float around in the air. This is the kind of poetic touch that's much harder, and usually much more expensive, to create in a live-action film. In animation, the pauses are extremely important.

An entire animated film can be fantastic but it can also become boring because there's no emotional image to place it next to. The problem with animation is that it creates a certain distance between the spectator and the story. But in *Princess*, we succeed in breaking down this distance, and that's pretty cool. If the entire film had been animated, you would have been able to keep the film at arm's length. And if the entire film had been made as live action, it would have been too naïve. In that case, it would have to have been more complex.

Jørholt: Where exactly is *Princess* set, geographically speaking?

Morgenthaler: Everywhere. Using a cliché, but in the best sense of the word, you might say that it is a global film. The story can take place anywhere. We place the Assistens Cemetery [large cemetery in Copenhagen where both Hans Christian Andersen and Søren Kierkegaard are buried] between the skyscrapers of Manhattan, and we have both Japanese and Danish architecture, and so forth. All backgrounds are constructed from collage-like images from a large number of cities all over the world. There are no African huts, but if you look closely, you'll see Middle Eastern colours around the Assistens Cemetery, inspired by imperialist French renditions of Morocco.

Jørholt: Why this global dimension? Because you're telling a universal story, or because you want to address an international audience?

Morgenthaler: Because it's a universal story. But then I also knew very well that one of the advantages of animation is that it can easily be translated into a lot of different languages. So, if it worked, the film would be easy to sell, which, indeed, it turned out to be. It performed exactly as it was supposed to. It was all entirely by the book. When I have a vision of what I want to do, I always think of the concept in relation to a particular platform, right from the beginning. That's how I enhance my chances of a good outcome.

Jørholt: Despite the live-action sequences in *Araki* and *Princess*, it must have been quite a readjustment when you went from animation to the live-action film *Echo*. How much experience did you have with directing actors?

Morgenthaler: There's not that much difference between directing actors' voices for an animated film and directing actors for a live-action film. It's all about creating a comfortable ambience, so the people who work for you will believe in the vision you have. But looking back, I realize that I didn't

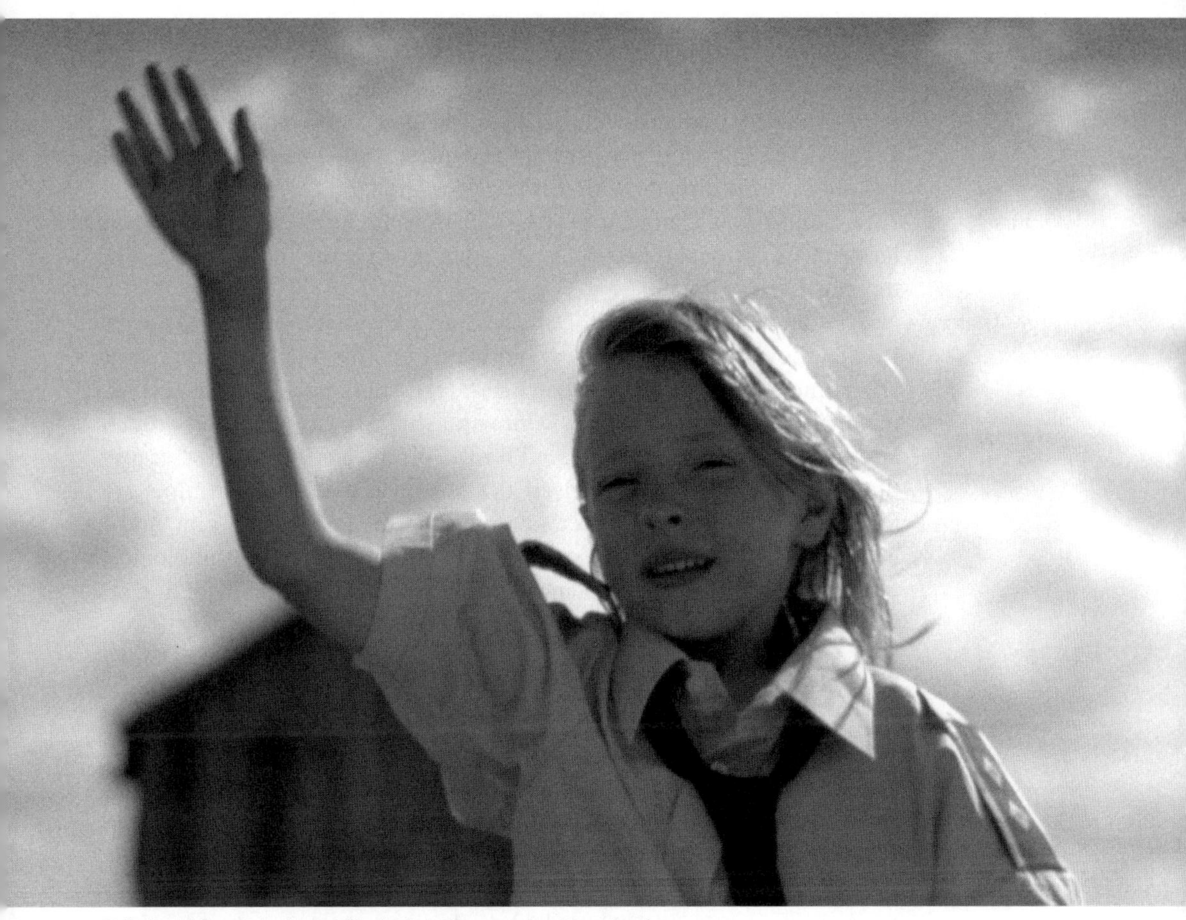

Villads Milthers Fritsche in *Ekko* (*Echo*). Photography: Bjørn Bertheussen.

have enough experience with the practical 'glue' between sequences. For example, walking sequences that get a character from one place to another. I'm not the only director with this problem, though.

Jørholt: How would you characterize your relationship to Danish cinema, in terms of its national aspects? Do you identify with the term 'Danish film director'?

Morgenthaler: No, not any more. Not at all. Danish cinema has sort of missed the boat. I don't know if the politicians are to blame for this, but the most recent government Media Policy Accord certainly didn't create fertile soil for making more artistic films in Denmark. This is partly because a much larger share of the risk was placed on the producers, and partly because the television stations were given the power to decide which films are to be made. The Dogma directors reinvented the language of film, and I believe it's time to do it again, but in a different way. The new technological platforms present both a challenge and an invitation. It's about coming up with something that's hyper-beautiful but doesn't cost any money. If you want to make artistic films, they shouldn't cost more than what the Danish Film Institute is able to pay, without the support of the television stations.

Jørholt: Danish cinema has also been criticized for having become too populistic. What's your view on the matter?

Morgenthaler: I agree. Danish cinema has become far too populistic, far too mainstream, far too proper. Danish cinema has become all that it was not supposed to be and has now left the more interesting scene to the Norwegians and the Swedes. I just saw a new Swedish film, *Ping-pongkingen* (*The King of Ping Pong*; dir. Jens Jonsson, 2008) which is absolutely amazing. And Joachim Trier's Norwegian film *Reprise* (2006) is simply a masterpiece. I bet he's seen Christoffer Boe's films, and what he's added is an emotional connection to the audience. The paradox of it all is that the Norwegian Film Institute and the Swedish film industry are now trying to pick up a few tricks from the Danes, which is why they've created the very same structures that are now being abandoned by the Danes. It's completely absurd.

But I don't want to whine about these things. One of the purposes of Copenhagen Bombay is to get out of the hell of spending your time complaining about there being no money. We just don't want to waste our time on that. What we want to do is make good on our excitement about making media products for children and young people, and thereby generate a pool of rights which may eventually result in a certain degree of financial independence. Our goal is to be able to put our own money on the table, at least to a significant extent, when we wish to engage in artistically innovative projects. We're still very far from reaching that goal, but some day we'll get there. We invest very consciously in certain kinds of projects – *Carsten & Gitte's Movie Madness*, for example – where what's important to us is reaching a certain level of quality with a product that's not as commercial as most entertainment for children is today.

We're loaded with concepts for children, and we can sell anything. Very soon, we'll also be taking these concepts to the international market, and then the rights may turn out to be worth quite a lot of money. That, at least, is what we're hoping. But I'm convinced we'll eventually succeed. Just imagine if the pandas could be the first Danish animated series to hit American television screens. Wouldn't that be fun? Artistically as well as from a business point of view. We may have bitten off more than we could chew when we first created Copenhagen Bombay, but after having trimmed the company to about half of its original size, we're doing quite well.

It's no longer possible to finance films the way they've been financed for the last eighteen years. We who are still young, and especially the newcomers, will never again be able to work on productions that are fully financed from the outset. There will be no additional government subsidies for Danish cinema. It's the end of an era. We had some truly wonderful years, but now we have to find a new way of going about it. That's the challenge, but it's also what makes it exciting. Finding new ways will be our contribution to the resurrection of Danish cinema.

Chapter 11

Annette K. Olesen

Annette K. Olesen. Photography: Morten Holtum.

Born 1965. Annette K. Olesen graduated as a director from the National Film School of Denmark in 1991. Her award-winning graduation film, *10:32 tirsdag – en kærlighedshistorie* (*10:32 Tuesday – A Love Story*, 1991) is an experimental art film that examines a young woman's scepticism about love, even as she moves in with her lover. Olesen subsequently directed the short films *Julies balkon* (*Juliet's Balcony*, 1992) and *Ritualer* (*Rituals*, 1993) as part of a National Film Board of Denmark initiative. Combining fictional and non-fictional elements, these films clearly prefigure Olesen's later feature films. Before making the transition to feature filmmaking Olesen also directed *Tifanfaya* (1997), a children's film based on a short book by Henrik Nordbrandt. Jesper Christensen had a part in this story about the orphan Tifanfaya and her evil relatives, and Olesen's encounter with the actor was to prove decisive. *Små ulykker* (*Minor Mishaps*, 2002) was initiated by Christensen and a number of other actors who had been inspired by a Mike Leigh-style approach to filmmaking. Through this first feature, which won the Blue Angel award at the Berlin International Film Festival in 2002, Olesen developed a strong partnership with the Zentropa producer Ib Tardini and with the prolific scriptwriter Kim Fupz Aakeson. That partnership has put the concept of research, and of learning through filmmaking, on the radar of Danish film. Working with Aakeson as her scriptwriter on all of her four features to date, Olesen has developed her research-based approach further, adjusting it to the dictates of Dogma (*Forbrydelser* [*In Your Hands*, 2004]), to the challenges involved in working with amateurs (*1:1*, 2006) and to the high-risk conditions of the world of human trafficking and sex work (*Lille soldat* [*Little Soldier*, 2008]). Although politics and art are two distinct phenomena as far as Olesen is concerned, she has emerged as a public intellectual in Denmark, particularly in response both to the Danish People's Party's insistence on a certain conception of culture, and to conflicts surrounding ethnicity and the now multicultural nature of Danish society. For example, when the Muhammed cartoon crisis was at its most intense, Annette K. Olesen organized a public demonstration in favour of dialogue and mutual understanding, together with Najat El-Ouargui from the Betty Nansen Theatre. With more than 4,000 people participating, the women's public response to the crisis was covered by the BBC and Al Jazeera, among many other TV stations. In the wake of that demonstration, Olesen was drawn into various working groups and think tanks devised with crisis resolution, both in the short and longer term, in mind. Annette K. Olesen has taught at the National Film School of Denmark, and in Cairo as part of an innovative form of documentary training involving Middle Eastern partners.

Feature films

2008 *Lille soldat* (*Little Soldier*)
2006 *1:1*
2004 *Forbrydelser* (*In Your Hands*)
2002 *Små ulykker* (*Minor Mishaps*)

Short films and documentaries

2007 *45 cm*
2001 *Y*
1997 *Tifanfaya*
1993 *Ritualer* (*Rituals*)
1992 *Julies balkon* (*Juliet's Balcony*)
1991 *10:32 tirsdag – en kærlighedshistorie* (*10:32 Tuesday – A Love Story*, graduation film)

Television

2000 *Selvsving* (TV series, two episodes)

Hjort: You spent a year in Madrid before getting into the National Film School of Denmark, and you also worked in the TV milieu for a bit. How would you describe your path into film?

Olesen: I was a bartender while I was in Madrid, but I hung out with friends who were artists and I suddenly realized that it was possible to make a living that way. That was a real eye opener for me. I'm from a very typical middle-class Danish family, and I grew up in the suburbs. When I came back from Madrid Kanal 2, the first private TV station in Denmark, had just been established. And Kanal 2 had recruited all these pioneering and visionary people. Lotte Larzen and Camilla Miehe-Renard, among others. Young people with incredible energy and drive. It's not like I knew a whole lot about what was going on in that milieu, but I'd just returned from Madrid and I needed a job. I ended up with a substitute job at Kanal 2, through an agency. My job was to sort and file tapes. After I'd been on the job for a few months I started to explore a bit. I was curious about what was going on around me. I was allowed to observe some editing, and I also tried my hand at being an assistant to one of the producers. My first experience of the editing process was really incredible, because I felt I'd discovered something I simply had to explore further.

Hjort: How did you get into the National Film School? What was the strength of your application?

Olesen: We had to submit two samples of our work. But this was before digital video. Technologically speaking, we're really talking about the dinosaur age! So we weren't expected actually to have produced anything. I'd always been very interested in photography. My father is a really passionate amateur photographer, so photography was something I'd learnt about at home. I'd also enjoyed writing from an early age. So I submitted a story and a series of photographs of the person I was living with when I applied to the school.

In terms of the admissions process, there's someone I really ought to mention, and that's Arne Bro. Arne is now Head of Documentary at the Film School. I happened to meet him around about the time when I was thinking of applying to the school. I hadn't a clue who he was and he didn't know anything about me, but we got talking and I told him that my plan was to become a director. I hadn't even entertained the idea that I might get rejected. I had no idea how competitive the admissions process was. Thank goodness. My sense is that Arne sort of decided that I belonged at the school. So every time I was summoned for some test at the school, I'd go by Arne's place first, and he'd kind of coach me. He quite simply took me under his wing, and he's always taken a real interest in my work.

Hjort: Jørgen Leth and Mogens Rukov are listed as consultants in the credits for your graduation film, *10:32 Tuesday*. What did they contribute to this film?

Olesen: Rukov taught dramaturgy at the school, and when I was there he'd just discovered Syd Field. He'd seen the light, and was completely enthralled by linear dramaturgy. So he'd go on and on about these plot points. Looking back now, I have no trouble seeing why he thought we needed to know about these things. But at the time I found that approach quite simply deadly. As far as I was concerned, that approach was really remote from the essence of art, and turned filmmaking into something almost mathematical. I wasn't particularly interested in linear stories back then, and was much more interested in exploring various phenomena in a thematic way. But Rukov and I got on just fine, and were perfectly diplomatic with one another. When I handed in my proposal for my graduation film it quickly became clear that the film I intended to make was structured in an associative way. *10:32 Tuesday* is about a young woman who reflects on her relation to love and men. And she does this while unpacking her boxes in the home of a man she's in the process of moving together with. It's a story that has very little to do with the concept of a 'natural story'. Rukov's response to my initial proposal was: 'I really don't understand this, and I can't help you with this. So we'll have to find someone who can.' And he suggested Jørgen Leth who was perfect, because he's exactly the kind of storyteller that my film proposal called for. I'm really grateful to Rukov and the other teachers at the school, for not simply rejecting my idea, and for actually going to great lengths to facilitate my project and help me make my film.

Jørgen was incredibly generous and kind, and a really good listener. Among other things, he suggested that we should see a whole lot of Godard films together. I'd seen one or two films by Godard, and I'd liked them just fine, but hadn't really thought about them analytically, in terms of visual style or narrative structure. So Jørgen ordered every single film that was available from the Film Museum and the two of us sat there in the Museum's big cinema, which was right next to the Film School back then, and we watched Godard films for two days solid. We saw almost all of his films, and it was an extraordinary experience. I really felt like a child in a candy shop, also because Jørgen really understood my ideas and took them seriously. Jørgen really meant a lot to me. And he gave me some really concrete advice, which I followed.

Hjort: What kind of advice did he give you?

Olesen: Jørgen's advice was that I should write a list of scenes. He said 'Write down as many scenes as you can think of. Don't worry about how you're going to organize them, not at this stage. Just brainstorm.' So I wrote and I wrote and I wrote. Jørgen then read everything, and when we met to discuss the material he said: 'Now you have to choose the most important ones.' His advice was very simple and straightforward, but based on his own characteristic approach to filmmaking. Another thing he said was: 'Trust your own inclinations, your own sense of what is interesting. Look for what interests you, instead of trying to calculate things in a tactical way. Come up with some very basic rules for yourself, rules that will make possible your *own* passionate engagement with the material.' And that is exactly how Jørgen works. I eventually came up with a framework that integrated all these different scenes I'd produced. I wrote a text that was added to the images as a voice over that expressed the woman's thoughts, and I think that was actually Jørgen's idea. The result of all this was a very colourful and kaleidoscopic film, with animation and all sorts of strange things.

Hjort: You've been involved in some of the lifelong learning/continuing education/professional development courses that the National Film School of Denmark organizes. What have you taught and how important are those offerings for the Danish film milieu?

Olesen: I get email alerts about those offerings and I often see courses or workshops that really interest me. It's not often that I have the time actually to attend these things, but I think the school puts on an incredibly interesting programme. My impression is that the organizers try really hard to keep abreast of what people in the industry are interested in and feel they need to know about. For example, I attended a two-day seminar with Ken Loach some time ago, together with Ib Tardini and Per Fly.

I offered a two-day session at one point, with Torben Skjødt Jensen, called 'The Short Story'. I think we ended up with something like 300 participants. Our aim was to try to identify what a short story is, what its structure is. It was a lot of fun because we did this from all kinds of angles. We brought in directors from the advertising business. And we brought in musicians and poets, people who work with short stories as a kind of genre. We wanted to learn about their various practices, and about how they structured their material. We also saw an enormous number of short films.

I've also done some regular teaching for the Film School. My teaching has focused mostly on concept development, on getting the students to the point where they can articulate what it is they want to tell their viewers. I've also taught courses on how to work with actors. I've now started teaching a course like this for the students specializing in documentary filmmaking. And that's very interesting, because they don't really see it as obviously relevant to their area. So I end up talking a lot about what a director is, and trying to get the students to see that although they're not going to be working with actors, they're nonetheless going to be working with people who will be on camera. These aspiring directors have to understand that the minute you walk into a room, as a director, you become the centre of attention, whether or not you're working with actors. So you have to be very aware of the kinds of messages you're sending, and of the extent to which whatever you do or say registers as directing. Arne and I are developing this course further at the moment. It's a really interesting course, precisely because it's got that cross-over element.

Hjort: Ib Tardini at Zentropa has produced all of your feature films, each of them with a script by Kim Fupz Aakeson. How did you meet these two people and what is the basis for your continued collaboration?

Olesen: I haven't actually worked with the same people that much, but it's true that I've had two steady mates, Ib and Fupz. I think that that partnership is based on a shared understanding of what makes for interesting films, and what makes for an interesting way of making films. I feel very lucky, because I didn't actually seek either of them out. In many ways my life as a filmmaker has been shaped by a lot of lucky encounters; there's this sense of lovely oranges just sort of landing in my turban, so to speak. I'd made the short film *Tifanfaya*, and Jesper Christensen had had a part in that. He was the first actor, with the exception of my good friend Charlotte Sieling, who didn't scare me. I really enjoyed working with him, so when he called me a few months after we'd finished *Tifanfaya*, I was interested in what he had to propose. What he proposed was a project that ended up becoming *Minor Mishaps*. Maria Rich, Jannie Faurschou and Jesper had been part of a workshop with Paul Clements [author of *The Improvised Play: The Work of Mike Leigh*], somewhere north of Copenhagen. And Jannie was living in the same house as Fupz at that point in time, so he'd been drawn into their project. Maria, Jannie, Jesper and Fupz had then contacted Ib, about getting some money to develop a story based on some characters the actors had worked on in the context of Clements' workshop. Ib's response was that they first needed to find themselves a director, because he saw the director as providing a kind of anchor for the whole process. Jesper then called me. They no doubt had a long list of names, and I'm sure several people turned their project down before they got to me. When Jesper called me I was actually in the process of applying to the School of Midwifery, and I was quite ready to turn my back on filmmaking. But when he started telling me about the way they were developing the characters, it was crystal clear to me that this was a project I wanted to be part of. They were bringing documentary elements into the fiction filmmaking process, and I really liked that. So I thought, to hell with it, let me have a go at this.

I hadn't met Fupz before all this. I just knew he'd written the script for *The One and Only* (*Den eneste ene*; dir. Susanne Bier, 1999). But we just clicked. I think we're very similar people in many ways. We've both got that mix of existential curmudgeonliness and silliness that makes for a certain sense of humour. And Ib's approach to things is also one that I like. He called me up, told me he'd heard I was to direct the film, and suggested that we meet. So we met up for some coffee, and Ib slammed a whole lot of cigarettes on the table and said, 'I've produced x number of films, commercial films, and I'm sick of producing films like that. I'm too old to keep on doing the same thing. I want to produce a film that has some real substance to it.' He hadn't actually produced as many as he said he'd produced, but his point was clear, and I just thought 'This is my man!' So there was Ib with all of his bluntness, and Fupz with his black humour, and then me. And I wasn't really that worried about anything, because I assumed that I'd probably end up becoming a midwife anyway. Somehow that mix of attitudes just worked really well.

Hjort: You developed your characteristic approach, with its emphasis on research and improvisation, through *Minor Mishaps*.

Olesen: Yes, I learnt so much from making *Minor Mishaps*. I learnt all the things about working with actors that I needed to know but had never learnt during my years at the Film School. By the time I graduated from the Film School I'd spent all of ten days with actors, and that's over a period of four years. Things have really changed, but back then the emphasis was on teaching directors about stories, cameras and lighting arrangements.

Hjort: So after *Minor Mishaps*, you, Ib and Fupz simply decided you'd continue working together?

Olesen: *Minor Mishaps* started out as an interesting hippy-like project and ended up becoming a film that we're all really, really proud of. It went straight to Berlin and won a major prize. That experience was really fantastic. And when you've experienced something like that together and have remained good friends all along, then there's absolutely no reason not to continue working together. After Berlin, Ib, Fupz and I sat down and we put into words what it was we wanted to do together. We came up with a kind of mantra, this idea that we wanted to *learn* something from the very process of making films. We'd learnt so much from making *Minor Mishaps* and simply wanted to continue the learning process. Filmmaking is a lot of fun when you pursue it in a way that allows you to explore and examine reality, as well as the actual practice of filmmaking itself.

Hjort: Are there times when the improvisational and collaborative processes threaten to derail your own plans for your story and film?

Olesen: Yes, definitely. The best example of this is from *Minor Mishaps*. In that film Fupz and I had expected Søren (Jesper Christensen) and Hanne (Karen-Lise Mynster) to split up. Søren was this very sceptical, self-satisfied character, who couldn't work on account of an injury and who had no desire to do or change anything. We felt he was too boring to work with as a dramatic character, so Hanne was supposed to leave Søren. So we talked to Karen-Lise Mynster about her character probably having an affair, and put this into an impro. And Jesper Christensen, as Søren, was furious. And after the impros we'd de-brief them, and they'd say 'I can't leave her' or 'I can't leave him' or 'We love each other.' So we had to make a decision. We'd already lined up an actress to play the role of the real estate agent who was to sell their house once they got divorced. We had done an enormous amount of background work, and had a veritable army ready to move in to produce the scenes following their divorce. But the actors/characters refused to leave each other. We finally decided that the story actually would be more interesting if we avoided a more obvious narrative development, and so we stuck to what Jesper and Karen-Lise were insisting on in the impros, namely the inherent interest of their characters' perpetual marital crisis.

Hjort: *In Your Hands* is one of the official Danish Dogma films. While Dogma produced something resembling a group style at a certain point, the Dogma challenge can in fact be taken up in quite different ways. Why were you interested in making a Dogma film? Did you see a natural fit between your Mike Leigh-inspired approach to filmmaking and Dogma's emphasis on authenticity and truth?

Olesen: Yes, the idea of making a Dogma film made perfect sense to me. Fupz and I had already started working on *In Your Hands* when Ib and Lars [von Trier] talked to us about making a Dogma film, so we weren't initially thinking about the film in those terms. There were several reasons why making a Dogma film seemed like a natural next step for me. Through *Minor Mishaps* I'd developed a way of working with actors that harmonized perfectly with the Dogma approach. *Minor Mishaps* taught me that an actor's deep connection with a character almost always is more interesting than whatever opinions I might have about that character. If the actors have worked very thoroughly with their characters, then their understanding of their characters becomes my way of guaranteeing that the film's performances, and thus the film, have a certain truthfulness and authenticity. *Minor Mishaps* taught me that I don't have to be omniscient as a director. I don't have to know everything about each and every character, or about the story. The Dogma rules support this approach to directing. Take Kate, for example, and the supernatural capacities that she seems to have. Normally we would have been inclined, through music, or through lighting, to settle the question as to whether she did or did not have certain supernatural powers. But the Dogma rules proscribe all such manipulations, and as a result Fupz and I were allowed *not* to settle the question.

Hjort: Could you outline the steps in the process of directing the actors in your Dogma film?

Olesen: Having learnt some crucial lessons from *Minor Mishaps* we decided not to give the actors the script, although we had in fact written it. Fupz and I sat down together and matched five to seven key traits with each character, and we gave each actor one of these trait clusters. We explained that we couldn't give them the full script at this stage, but hoped that they'd nonetheless want to be part of the film. They were then supposed to take this trait cluster and match it with three people whom they'd actually known or still knew. Having done this, they reported back to Fupz and myself, one by one. And then we chose the real person whom we felt was the best match with the character. We didn't always choose the most obvious match. For example, Trine [Dyrholm] actually came back with a junkie, but the match that we chose in her case was with a very proper suburban housewife. The psychological profile of that woman was much closer to the Kate character that Trine plays than the junkie's. We then did a series of impros with these characters, and based on what we learnt through that process we then finalized the script. Once the actors had seen the script they were given the opportunity to comment on it, so that further adjustments could be made. It is my conviction that the performances have the kind of authenticity and truth that Dogma calls for, precisely because they're anchored in the actors' real encounter with actually existing human beings.

Hjort: Trine Dyrholm is considered to be one of Denmark's most accomplished and courageous actresses. Trine had leading roles in *In Your Hands* and *Little Soldier*. What is it about Trine that you admire, as a director?

Olesen: What is special about Trine? I can only get at that with a story. When I was young I was a top-level gymnast. And some of the things I did as a gymnast were simply deadly. I mean, you quite simply risk your life. I acquired a kind of mental discipline that allowed me to sort of lobotomize myself, to block certain thoughts. You simply decide that the idea of death isn't a consideration, to the point where you don't even think about the risks. I used to bungee jump too, and when you're standing at the top of a crane, some 56 metres above the Copenhagen harbour and are getting ready to let yourself fall, you have to block the knowledge you have of possible death. This is what Trine is like, as an actress. Trine is able to tune out all kinds of mental obstacles, so that she has this uncluttered relation to what she is doing, this capacity to be entirely in the moment and utterly present. She's able to block the kinds of thoughts that stem from vanity, or from the fear of professional death, that is, the fear of performing really poorly. She's also able to remove a possible feeling of not quite knowing or not quite understanding what she's doing. She's extraordinary. Most of us simply cannot do this kind of thing. It's very liberating to work with Trine, also because she really thinks of herself as part of a team.

Hjort: Women play central and somewhat unusual roles in your films. I'm thinking, for example, of the prison priest, Anna (Ann Eleonora Jørgensen), and the soldier, Lotte (Trine Dyrholm), in *In Your Hands* and *Little Soldier* respectively. What are your thoughts on the cinematic representation of women?

Olesen: I've often felt that cinematic narratives tend to show us men, not only as gendered beings, but also as non-gendered beings and thus as representative of a kind of universal humanity. Cinematic representations of women have always been strongly gendered. Women's screen presence has been defined by gender, with women for the most part representing femininity, sexuality, motherhood and so on. I'm a filmmaker and a woman, and I like to think seriously about things. So it's hard not to notice the extent to which women have been excluded from the non-gendered modes of representation that are used to evoke aspects of humanity as such. I'm interested in representing women in the more gender-neutral way that is usually reserved for male characters. But there's no systematic reflection on this in my films. In that sense I don't see myself as being political about gender.

Hjort: Your third feature, *1:1*, was released at the height of the Muhammed cartoon crisis. How did that crisis affect its reception?

Olesen: Yes, *1:1*, which is set in an immigrant milieu and focuses on ethnic conflict, came out just as all these things were happening. So the film was easily interpreted as a film about immigration issues. But I tend to want to keep my politics somewhat separate from my filmmaking, in the sense that the emphasis in my filmmaking is on the artistic process, on film as a form of artistic expression. This doesn't mean that my films aren't informed by my political views, but *1:1*, for example, is a film about fear, and not a journalistic commentary on immigration issues and the problems of integration. The timing of the film's release made it quite difficult to make that conception of the film stick. The difference I'm getting at has to do with where the emphasis is placed, whether the emphasis is on emotionality or on politics. In my films I emphasize the emotional tenor of the stories I tell. As a politically engaged citizen, I emphasize other things.

Hjort: With the exception of three of the characters, *1:1* is a film that features performances by amateurs. Was your approach in this film similar to the one you used in *Minor Mishaps* and *In Your Hands*?

Olesen: In terms of this business of always wanting to learn something through the filmmaking process, *1:1* was about seeing whether the approach from *Minor Mishaps* and *In Your Hands* could be made to work if the characters were played by amateurs, not actors. *1:1* was a bit like moving onto slippery ice, and it was about pursuing the approach I'd defined to its logical conclusion. We had a full script, but I didn't allow the cast to see it. I then developed the characters, little by little, with the players. We focused on very banal situations, like having dinner or coming home from school, things that were close to their lives. But we gave the characters a different name right from the start, to establish a boundary between the story world and the performers' actual lives. Once I felt they'd come far enough, we started staging scenes, but still without disclosing the entire script. They would then improvise in response to the situation they'd been given, and Fupz would be sitting there, taking notes and revising the script as we went along. The really extraordinary exchange between Mohammed Al-Bakier [Shadi], Subhi Hassan [Tareq] and the father, that came out of an impro. Once the script was finished, we gave it to the cast and everyone then had to learn their lines. I sometimes think this was a mistake. The amateur actors suddenly became very nervous, very worried about their lines, even though they'd invented a lot of them themselves. It would have been easier, in the final analysis, not to have given them the script, but just a treatment. You can ask a professional actor to improvise on an emotion, but amateurs don't have the tools needed to start improvising again once they've been given a script.

Hjort: *Little Soldier* deals with human trafficking and prostitution. Was the research process you normally engage in with your scriptwriter and actors constrained by the nature of the reality you were exploring?

Olesen: Yes, definitely. Trine Dyrholm, who plays Lotte, didn't, for example, work with prostitutes when she was researching her role, because that was simply impossible. The Nigerian women who work in Denmark as prostitutes don't want to be official in any way, and they protect themselves, to the point where even getting in contact with them is very difficult. I finally managed to meet a couple of them in the houses where they worked, but Fupz was never allowed anywhere near them, because he's a man. We spent months trying to find a way into the milieu. Although Trine never made contact with the milieu, Lorna Brown, who plays Lily, did. We managed to set up a contact for her, so that she could go into the city at night and meet some of the women. My point is that I don't need to be part of the *entire* research process. If I can help facilitate a meeting between Lorna Brown and these women, then I don't need to be there myself. And that's because I simply know that her seeing the real conditions under which these women live will give depth to her performance and thus to her character. That's essentially why I work the way I do. It's about confronting the clichés we all have with reality. I don't have to confront all my own clichés directly, but I do have to facilitate that process in the case of the actors. And when I see what they come back with, I realize, again and again, that they've shown me things I would never have come up with on my own.

Hjort: Do your current projects involve further collaboration with Fupz?

Olesen: Fupz and I are taking a break, professionally that is. We're chatting a lot over coffee, but I know that I need to move on to something new at this point. I need to situate

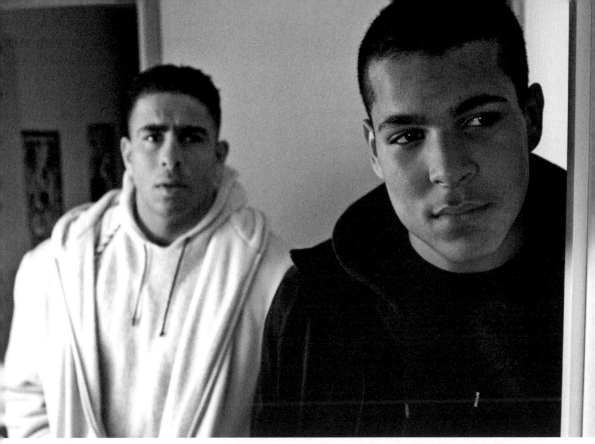

Mohammed Al-Bakier as Shadi and Subhi Hassan as Tareq, the two brothers in *1:1*. Photography: Per Arnesen.

Lotte (Trine Dyrholm) removes the drugged sex worker Lily (Lorna Brown) from the home of a necrophiliac in *Lille soldat* (*Little Soldier*). Photography: Mike Kollöffel.

myself on unfamiliar ground. I'm working on a couple of projects. One of them is an adaptation, which is something completely new for me. And the other is a period film set in 1972, which means I'm moving away from my usual emphasis on the here and now. In the case of the adaptation I'm working with a Norwegian scriptwriter, Erlend Loe, who was educated in Denmark, at the National Film School, but lives in Norway. And in the case of the period film I'm collaborating with both a Danish and an American scriptwriter, Dorte W. Høgh and David Weber, and in ways that are consistent with Syd Field's approach. So I really am moving in new directions. I know Fupz so well at this point that working with him is a bit like working with one's spouse. The minute Fupz walks through the door I can tell whether he's happy or sad!

Chapter 12

Niels Arden Oplev

Niels Arden Oplev.
Photography: Claus Peuckert.

Born 1961. Niels Arden Oplev graduated as a director from the National Film School of Denmark in 1989. While in film school, he made an award-winning documentary portrait of his father, *Hugo fra Himmerland* (*Hugo from Himmerland*, 1987). His equally award-winning graduation film, *Kyndelmisse* (*Winter's End*, 1989), was nominated for an Oscar in 1991. His first feature film, *Portland* (1996), a visually stunning film about lowlife youths in the provincial town of Aalborg, charted a new direction for Danish cinema, aesthetically as well as thematically. It was also one of the first films of the so-called New Danish Cinema. The cult film *Fukssvansen* (*Chop Chop*, 2001) further explored the provincial outsider theme, this time in a crazy comedy format indebted at once to traditional Danish folk comedy, cartoons and the oddball universe of the Coen brothers.

With *Drømmen* (*We Shall Overcome*, 2006), Arden Oplev proved himself to be both a serious and mature director. This partly autobiographical film about a twelve-year-old boy's rebellion against an authoritarian school master in the late 1960s became Arden Oplev's popular breakthrough, and earned him a Crystal Bear at the Berlin Film Festival as well as more than 25 other international awards. Youthful rebellion was also the subject matter of *To verdener* (*Worlds Apart*, 2008), which is about a young girl who breaks with her family and the Jehovah's Witnesses community in which she grew up. Although a smaller production than *We Shall Overcome*, *Worlds Apart* was a major box-office hit. Arden Oplev's most recent film, *Män som hatar kvinnor* (*The Girl with the Dragon Tattoo*, 2009), is a Swedish adaptation of the Swedish writer Stieg Larsson's bestselling eponymous novel. With its carefully produced crime story about some of the less appealing aspects of the Swedish welfare society, this film is likely to beat all Scandinavian box-office records.

In addition to his film work, Arden Oplev has also directed a number of episodes for the Danish television series *Taxa* (*Taxi*), *Forsvar* (*Defense*), *Rejseholdet* (*Unit One*) and *Ørnen* (*The Eagle*). In the case of *Defense*, *Unit One* and *The Eagle*, Arden Oplev also helped to articulate the concept for the series. In 2009, Arden Oplev moved to the United States with his family.

Feature films

2009	*Män som hatar kvinnor* (*The Girl with the Dragon Tattoo*)
2008	*To verdener* (*Worlds Apart*)
2006	*Drømmen* (*We Shall Overcome*)
2001	*Fukssvansen* (*Chop Chop*)
1996	*Portland*

Documentaries

1997	*Headbang i Hovedlandet* (*Headbang on the Mainland*)
1987	*Hugo fra Himmerland* (*Hugo from Himmerland*)

Shorts

1993	*En succes* (*A Success*)
1992	*Nøgen* (*Naked*)
1991	*Tusmørket* (*The Twilight*)
1989	*Kyndelmisse* (*Winter's End*, graduation film)

Television

2004–2006	*Ørnen: En krimi-odyssé* (*The Eagle*, concept and seven episodes)
2003–2004	*Forsvar* (*Defense*, concept and four episodes)
2000–2003	*Rejseholdet* (*Unit One*, concept and three episodes)
1997–1999	*Taxa* (*Taxi*, nine episodes)

Jørholt: Right now you're enjoying more success at the box office than any other Danish director, both domestically and internationally, and you may be standing on the threshold of an international career. Did you dare even hope for this kind of success when you made your first film, *Portland*, in 1996?

Arden Oplev: No, it all feels like a fantastic adventure. Completely unreal. *The Girl with the Dragon Tattoo* has sold about 2.9 million tickets in Scandinavia, 1.3 million in France and I think we're close to 1.5 million tickets in Spain, which seems to be the country where we're doing best, outside Sweden and Denmark. We've almost finished negotiating a US release, and the film has recently been sold to Japan, the UK and Australia. So far, *The Girl with the Dragon Tattoo* has sold a total of more than 6.5 million tickets in the twelve countries where it's being distributed. In Denmark alone we've sold 985,000 tickets. It's absolutely crazy.

Jørholt: And now you've moved to the United States.

Arden Oplev: Yes, I had two reasons for moving. My wife is American, and I thought she deserved a chance to get on with her life. She's a political scientist but has never been able to use her education in Denmark, even though she speaks Danish fluently. We've been talking about moving to the US for years, but we have four kids, so we felt we needed to have a certain sense of economic security before making the move. The second reason is that I have a number of professional opportunities in the US right now, because of the success of *The Girl with the Dragon Tattoo*. I just signed with two top-level American agents who are sending me projects so big that I can't help but think: 'Shit. Will they really allow me to make *that*?' The projects are mostly action films, though, and that genre doesn't interest me that much. What I'd really like to do is make films like Steven Soderbergh's *Erin Brockovich* (2000) or Clint Eastwood's *Changeling* (2008), that is, films with stories based on real life, perhaps even with a political angle. My agents have now sent me a project that looks like the right kind of thing. It's incredibly exciting!

Jørholt: How did you get into film?

Arden Oplev: A friend of mine opened the first video shop in Hobro, and we wanted to make a feature film together about the biker community in Jutland. I wrote a script that I thought was fantastic, but actually it really sucked. We were *really* amateurs and knew absolutely nothing about anything. But I got on my motorbike and drove to Copenhagen where I met with the producer Just Betzer at Panorama Film. He allowed us to use his name, and he said that if we did, all doors would open for us. So, we called the Danish Film Institute and referred to him, and it bloody well worked! Abracadabra, and all of a sudden we had a consultant, Mogens Kløvedal from Nordisk Film. And when I first met Mogens, he was repairing a car with one of his Hell's Angels pals. It was all completely absurd.

I started to rewrite my inept script, over and over again. I'm sure nothing would have come of it, had it not been for my mother, who's from a family of rich Djursland farmers (my father's side of the family is very different; they're all sensitive peasants from Himmerland). I remember how my mother fed me Niels Jensen's *Filmkunst* [*The Art of Film*] along with my oatmeal, and told me that if I wanted to be a filmmaker instead of a lawyer or an engineer or whatever it was she'd planned for her son, I'd have to go and live where I'd actually stand a chance of becoming a filmmaker. Basically, she threw me out. But she was right, because all I did was sit there and dream my life away. And when I wasn't writing I was partying. In any event, I moved to Copenhagen, where I was admitted to Film Studies at the University of Copenhagen in 1984. At the time, studying Film was considered extremely fashionable. Equipped with my Suzuki leather jacket and all my filmmaking ambitions, I kind of stood out from the rest of the students. Besides, I liked the kind of films that nobody else thought much of at the time, films like Coppola's *Rumble Fish* (1983) and the Coen brothers' *Blood Simple* (1984), which were shown in some of the third-rate cinemas.

At the university I met Steen Bille who taught a dramaturgy class, and Steen took over as my consultant on the biker script after I'd more or less worn out Mogens Kløvedal. The same week I was admitted to the Film School, the Film Institute actually selected our project for script support. It was a pretty wild week. Steen was my personal consultant throughout my years at the Film School, and we continued to work together after I graduated. He was a consultant on my early films and co-wrote the script for *We Shall Overcome* and *Worlds Apart*.

Jørholt: What's the most important thing you learnt in film school?

Arden Oplev: I was simply awestruck when I got into the Film School. All the students who were from Copenhagen would show up around 11am with a cup of coffee and a sandwich, and say something like 'What's up?' I, on other hand, was there at fucking 9am every morning. Even though I worked nights in a post office in order to be able to support myself, and Florence, who'd come over from America, I don't think I ever called in sick during my four years at the school. My attitude towards things was very different. I came from a completely different place, compared with the rest of the students in the director's stream. I'd joke about being the one Indian or one African American who had to be admitted so the school could meet its minority quota. I didn't come from a family that was part of the Copenhagen cultural scene, so I couldn't refer to my cultured family members. My father was not the manager of Gyldendal or the cultural editor at *Politiken*. I was just someone who'd come in from the heath, so I was very different. But I also think there's strength to be found in that background. At the very least, there are lots of good stories there. I probably found the courage to make *Portland* somewhere in the clash between my own provincial stories and the culture of the capital city, which I made mine during my film school years.

To me, one of the most important things about the Film School was the opportunity to work with actors. When I started at the school, I knew absolutely nothing about acting, and the first film I made was a disaster. It had Anders Hove wandering around Benzinøen [an artificial island with huge oil tanks off the coast of Copenhagen] with a dead Christmas tree, screaming Arab proverbs. It could hardly have been worse. It was depressing. I felt that I wasn't capable of doing anything right. But after the first year,

I saw Tarkovsky's *Offret* (*The Sacrifice*, 1986) during the summer holidays. And I realized that I'd need to spend fifteen to twenty years learning this thing called filmmaking. When I returned to the school, we were given a so-called 'penneprøve' assignment, and one of the constraints was that the shooting had to be done in one day. I decided to concentrate on the acting and to pay no attention to anything else. What I produced didn't have to be beautiful or fancy; it just had to be credible! And then I shot a scene from the script I'd been working on for two years. I asked Jens Jørn Spottag and Benedikte Hansen to play a biker and his girlfriend, and told them the only thing they needed to think about was the goddamned credibility of the scene! The result was a two-minute scene, an argument between the two of them. And when you saw it, you believed it. It was a real argument, real people arguing. I was pretty proud of that!

To me, Wojciech Maciejewski was the most important teacher at the school. If it hadn't been for Wojciech, I'd probably not have become who I am today. The first time I met him, he said, 'I hate your first film, but I love your second film. What happened in between, Neils?' (he never could pronounce my name). I explained to him that I'd been caught up in this idea of being as cool, cultured, expressionistic and artistic as possible, and that's why I'd produced a load of crap. And that I was now working with a different approach. That was the beginning of my friendship with Wojciech, and he told me how he too had been an outsider who'd come in from the Polish countryside to the film school in Łodz. Wojciech gave me the courage to do things. When Max von Sydow agreed to appear in my graduation film, I was told the film would be the equivalent of artistic suicide: if I made a good film, everybody would say that it was only because of Max, and if I made a bad film, they'd say that I couldn't even make a good film with Max von Sydow. I ended up having doubts about the project myself, but Wojciech settled the matter: 'Of course you should work with him. What you'll learn from Max matters more than anything else.' If Wojciech hadn't said that, I don't know that I would have had the courage to use Max von Sydow.

In addition to Wojciech, there was, of course, Mogens Rukov, with his free-wheeling, almost fractal, dramaturgical ideas. And Pernille Grumme, who introduced me to acting. But if I were to single out just one of the teachers, it would be Wojciech.

Jørholt: How did you come up with the idea for *Portland*? That film was so unlike anything else in Danish cinema, thematically as well as aesthetically.

Arden Oplev: Like the rest of my films it's inspired by real life. For weeks, I walked around Aalborg with a couple of social workers who were in charge of a street patrol that they called 'Det sociale jægerkorps'. Targeting social problems, this 'special force' functioned as a kind of buffer between the police and the city's youth. And what I discovered was a Danish underclass that had fallen completely through the mesh of the social system. When these young people heard that I was going to make a film about them, they told me everything, the wildest stories about girlfriends, families, drug deals and how many times they'd been behind bars. They showed me stuff for which they would have been immediately busted, had I told the police. As far as they were concerned, it was simply fantastic to meet someone who actually took an interest in them.

At the same time, I realized that the people in this milieu had a huge need to feel numb. To be numb to the point where you can't feel anything at all is considered a really good thing. It's cool. And the violent tendencies I saw resembled what I'd seen in the biker milieu that I'd been part of in the late 1970s and early 1980s. We were based south of Aalborg but were embroiled in perpetual conflict with the guys from Aalborg. I've been in two knife fights in my life. I, unlike the other guy, was without a knife both times. Both of the guys were from Aalborg. In my mind, making *Portland* was also about investigating what had happened to that environment in the intervening thirteen to fourteen years. But it was a real shock to discover this whole world where you could be clean on entering prison for some minor offence, and a drug addict when you got out a year later. Was this America or fucking Aalborg?

The film's visual style is an attempt to show what it looks like inside the brain of a person who is as damaged as Anders Berthelsen's character is, someone who takes pills in order to keep everything at a distance. It's a way of showing that this world looks like ours; and doesn't look like ours at all. You could also say that the style involves a kind of 'aesthetics of the hideous', for there's something aesthetically beautiful about this 'factoryphilic' universe, as I like to call it. The cement factory Aalborg Portland is at the centre of a world in which everything is built of concrete.

But what people didn't get back in 1996, was the thin thread of irony that underlies the film and punctures the film milieu's own fascination with violence. All young filmmakers want to shock people, and I was no exception. But I think I did this with a certain psychological insight and irony, and thus signalled that the violence wasn't to be taken at face value. My documentary *Headbang on the Mainland* was like this too. It was about these heavy metal guys who were fascinated by death, and I showed how their stage personas were constantly being punctured by their real I's. For example, they'd go home to their mothers with 100 pairs of tennis socks that needed laundering. All through *Portland* you have a surface reality consisting of the community's rules and the roles the characters adopt, but

Ulrich Thomsen as a young misfit in the provincial town of Aalborg (*Portland*). Frame grab.

underneath it all there are private human beings. Take Anders Berthelsen's character as an example. He becomes completely square and ends up with a church wedding and a drawing-room picture in bad taste. The film sides with these people and shows both their good and their bad sides.

Jørholt: *Portland* was one of the first films of the New Danish Cinema, maybe even the very first, depending on whether or not you include Ole Bornedal's *Nattevagten* (*Nightwatch*) from 1994. Did you feel you were taking Danish cinema in a new direction?

Arden Oplev: What was new about *Nightwatch* was that it was a genre film, but I don't think it belongs in the same category as my own first feature film, and Thomas Vinterberg's, and Nicolas Winding Refn's, all of which were released in 1996. *Portland* was the first film that Zentropa produced, and it was actually finished in the autumn of 1995, but no distributor had the courage to release it. In the end, it was released in three to four copies by Buena Vista, Disney's company – Bambi and *Portland*, nice!

My aim was to make a film that would smash the neatness of Danish cinema to pieces. In fact, I've referred to *Portland* as 'a military boot in the face of neatness'. But when the film was released, it provoked a howl of indignation, and I was called everything from psychopath to genius. At the Berlin Film Festival somebody threatened me and yelled that I was crazy. I was actually quite shocked, but tried to be cool and made the V-sign because I didn't know what else to do. It was my first real film festival, and I thought the Berlin festival would really rock, given that it had had the courage to take my film. But what I experienced was something that was as conservative as a convention for dentists. Some of the viewers really didn't like the film. There were almost tumultuous scenes in Zoo Palast, with people stumbling over each other as they headed for the exit. I was shocked at how culturally bourgeois the festival and its audiences were.

As far as I was concerned, I'd made a ground-breaking film, but a lot of people in the Danish film business reacted quite negatively to it: you clearly weren't allowed to portray Denmark in that way. Trier's *The Element of Crime* (1984) had created quite a stir, of course, but that film was culturally provocative without really questioning Danish society. *Portland*, on the other hand, raised a lot of questions. It's a film that's critical towards society. In a way it's a '68-style revolt in the 90s, a way of saying that there's something terribly wrong in this country, and that the things we think of as rosy aren't rosy at all.

One critic wrote that *Portland* was to the Danish cinema of the 90s what *The Element of Crime* had been to the 80s, and the entire film business simply went ballistic over this. Some of my colleagues, people I'd gone to film school with, even criticized the film in public. They simply couldn't bear to see my film compared with a sanctified masterpiece like *The Element of Crime*.

On the other hand, *Portland* also prompted an invitation from James Cameron's company, and in 1997 Steen Bille and I spent a couple of months in Los Angeles, working on a script for a European sci-fi thriller for Cameron's development department. But things dragged on, probably because I wasn't sufficiently known at the time, so we ended up going back home. In many respects, Alfonso Cuarón's *Children of Men* from 2006 resembles our project, which we haven't definitively abandoned. There's a lot of cool stuff in it.

Jørholt: What was new about *Portland* was also its parade of young actors, all of them practically unknown at the time: Anders W. Berthelsen, Iben Hjejle, Ulrich Thomsen, Jens Albinus and Bjarne Henriksen.

Arden Oplev: I'd discovered Anders Berthelsen when he was at the Theatre School in Copenhagen, and I cast him during the summer of 1994. The plan was to shoot the film during the autumn, but Anders had signed a contract with a travelling theatre group. So I decided to postpone the shooting for three to four months. That's how sure I was of Anders' talent, even though he had very little experience at the time. As for Iben Hjejle, I'd made the short film *Naked* with her back in 1991. I'd seen her on some casting tapes for *Drengene fra Sankt Petri* (*The Boys from St Petri*; dir. Søren Kragh-Jacobsen, 1991) and thought she looked right for the part. And she turned out to be so damned good that I encouraged her to apply to one of the theatre schools if she was serious about acting. Ulrich Thomsen had had a very small part in *Nightwatch*, but that was it in terms of his screen acting experience, and it was Jens Albinus' very first film.

Jørholt: After *Portland* you did a fair bit of work for television. What has your TV work meant to you, career-wise?

Arden Oplev: After *Portland* Anders Berthelsen got his real breakthrough in the TV series *Taxi*, and he asked if I'd be interested in working with him in that context. So I visited the set and thought it looked extremely cool. It was also exciting to work within an established framework, because that takes some of the responsibility off your shoulders. There was already a super cast in place and scriptwriters who wrote the script for you, so the job involved simply doing your absolute best within the given framework. It was kind of liberating not to be responsible for everything, and to know that if something went wrong the director wouldn't automatically be blamed. But of course there's a world of difference between just directing episodes and being a 'concept director' which was the role I played later, for *Unit One*, *Defense* and *The Eagle*. As a concept director you are indeed responsible for the cast, the visual look and so on. It's almost like making a feature film.

I guess I've directed about 20 to 25 hours of television drama. The good thing about this is that it trains you to function as the boss of a large team. To a very young director, that may be quite a fearful experience, but in television everything has to be done so quickly, and there are so many decisions to be made that you somehow overcome the fear. You find a more instinctive way of working instead of all this nervewracking nonsense, where you ponder everything 117 times more than you should before making a decision. Prior to the launch of these new TV series, one of the problems in Danish cinema was that filmmakers never became routinized in this way until they were so old as to be virtually incontinent! The Danish Broadcasting Corporation's TV Drama department has simply functioned as a kind of boot camp for many of the younger directors, myself included. That institution has provided us with the opportunity to prove that we can work in a properly professional manner, instead of just making strange and depressing little short films that only other directors would ever want to see.

Working for television may, however, also be dangerous, in the sense that you have to be careful not to become lazy. When everything has to be done so quickly, it's tempting to choose the easy solution because it's worked before. It's extremely important to make sure that you retain your curiosity vis-à-vis the material, and your willingness to be challenged by doubt. But if you can avoid becoming lazy, television is a fantastic medium to work with. I also believe that we filmmakers have helped to professionalize the TV medium, and have moved it closer to the feature film, whereas I don't really think that the TV series have had the effect of pushing the feature films in a particular visual direction.

Jørholt: Your feature films are quite different from each other, but it's nonetheless possible to discern a kind of anti-authoritarian red thread running through all of them.

Arden Oplev: I guess that's true, even though I see each new film as an opportunity to try and do something I haven't done before. But reality is always my most important source of inspiration. Basically, I don't think of reality as being particularly well ordered. Our humanistic mind-set, and the attitudes towards life that go with it, are something we've acquired along the way, which doesn't make them any the less valuable. On the contrary. They're like plants that need nurturing and protection. And just beneath the civility, there are lots of uncontrollable, law of the jungle-style feelings that surface when people are under pressure. Just think of the way many people react in heavy traffic. I see reality in a 3D sort of way. I see double: on the one hand, I see goodness, authenticity and the aesthetic sides of life; and on the other, I see the grotesque and absurd. At the same time, I like the diversity that exists within our small country: if you're playing death metal in a basement in Ribe, dancing ballet and living in the suburbs north of Copenhagen will seem like another planet. We always tend to think of Denmark as a unified whole, but in my view there's actually room here for a lot of diversity. And I've tried to get at that diversity, and in a way that involves solidarity, in my films about social misfits: *Portland*, *Headbang on the Mainland* and *Chop Chop*.

But after *Chop Chop*, one of the managers at the National Broadcasting Corporation asked me, 'When are you going to make a film with real emotions, Arden?' He was right. When was I going to do that? That question was put to me at a time when I was dealing with my father's death. He died while I was shooting *Chop Chop*. And so I started to write *We Shall Overcome*, which is dedicated to him and is an homage to his way of seeing things. My father was a pensive, intelligent farmer with a pantheistic view of life, a heart of gold and also a mind that encompassed both sensitivity and weakness. My first real film was *Hugo from Himmerland*, which is a portrait of my father, and he's also the character Peder in *We Shall Overcome*, although I've, of course, created a certain distance between Peder and my father through fiction.

We Shall Overcome is once again a film that criticizes society, a film about rebellion and the price of rebellion. I went to that school myself, and there's not a single emotion in the film that I'm not 100 per cent familiar with. Almost all the characters in the film have been pieced together from people I knew, including the headmaster Lindom-Svendsen. I didn't invent him, nor did I invent his lines. He died in 1974, and I recall that day the same way older people remember the jubilations in the Townhall Square in Copenhagen on 4 May 1945. His death meant as much to us, as kids, as the liberation at the end of World War Two did to our parents' generation.

The reactions to *We Shall Overcome* were completely overwhelming. But in the wake of a film that successful, you're actually a bit at a loss. In that sense, tailwind can be quite terrible. It's much easier to be the injured party who's struggling against the wind. But I started to look for material that could provide the basis for a contemporary drama with the same kind of emotional power. I was juggling three or four ideas when I came across the story of Tabitha in a newspaper. Tabitha was a young girl who'd broken out of the Jehovah's Witnesses environment in which she'd been raised, and suddenly that idea was more compelling than all the others. I guess it takes a certain amount of north Jutlandic foolhardiness to believe that anyone will be interested in watching a film about Jehovah's Witnesses. But people did take an interest in the story, perhaps because *Worlds Apart* is also about a family that is blown to smithereens, and about a father who must face the fact that the dreams he had for his children won't come true. I think that's an issue many people can relate to, young as well as old. And again, there's an autobiographical element, because I grew up with a father who thought I would become a farmer and eventually take over the farm. At some point, I had to tell him that that wasn't going to happen. It was a terrible emotional burden, because it wasn't clear what would happen to our farm if I didn't become a farmer myself. You don't just sell a farm. It's the soil, you know, the soil that sticks under your fingernails. It was almost unbearable.

And finally *The Girl with the Dragon Tattoo*. Even though *Portland* is a small art-house film and *The Girl with the Dragon Tattoo* is a big entertainment film, there's a straight line connecting the two. I see a direct parallel between Janus, the character played by Anders Berthelsen in *Portland*, and Lisbeth Salander in *The Girl with the Dragon Tattoo*. Both are damaged young people, sociopaths to a certain degree, violent, ticking bombs, filled with hatred and anger because of a bad childhood and a rotten adolescence. To me, *The Girl with the Dragon Tattoo* involved a circular movement back to a place where I'd been before; back to the evil room where you let the demons in.

Jørholt: Did you consciously target a larger audience with *We Shall Overcome* and *Worlds Apart*? They are reported to have sold more tickets outside Copenhagen than most other Danish films.

Arden Oplev: Both films have actually done quite well in Copenhagen as well, but yes, with both films I was quite consciously addressing myself to a larger audience. I could, for instance, have chosen to shoot *We Shall Overcome* in the autumn season. And I could have shown the landscape, with all the ploughed brown fields, dripping with rain. That would, however, have made for a rather depressing look, albeit perhaps a more 'artistic' one. But I wanted the corn fields to be dripping with yellow colour, and the sky to be blue. I wanted so much beauty that it would be almost painful. And then, all of a sudden the cruelty would be there. The intention was to strike when my emotional grip on the audience was at its strongest. I wanted to make a film that would prompt the most intense form of viewer identification and have the greatest possible impact, because I was convinced this story both could and should reach a large audience. I'm very faithful to the essence of my stories. That goes for *The Girl with the Dragon Tattoo* as well. It would be completely ridiculous to turn a book that's sold 10 million copies into a small and obscure art film. *The Girl with the Dragon Tatoo* had to be a Scandinavian *Silence of the Lambs* (dir. Jonathan Demme, 1991), a Scandinavian *Nikita* (dir. Luc Besson, 1990). It had to be a really huge and entertaining film, made for a large audience.

Human beings need entertainment, especially entertainment that invites them to think. And I think that both *We Shall Overcome* and *Worlds Apart* do precisely that, as does *The Girl with the Dragon Tattoo*. That's something I'm immensely proud of.

Jørholt: All your Danish films are set on the margins of Denmark, or in the provinces, and now you've made a Swedish film and decided to move to the US. What does the concept of the national, also as it applies to Danish cinema, mean to you?

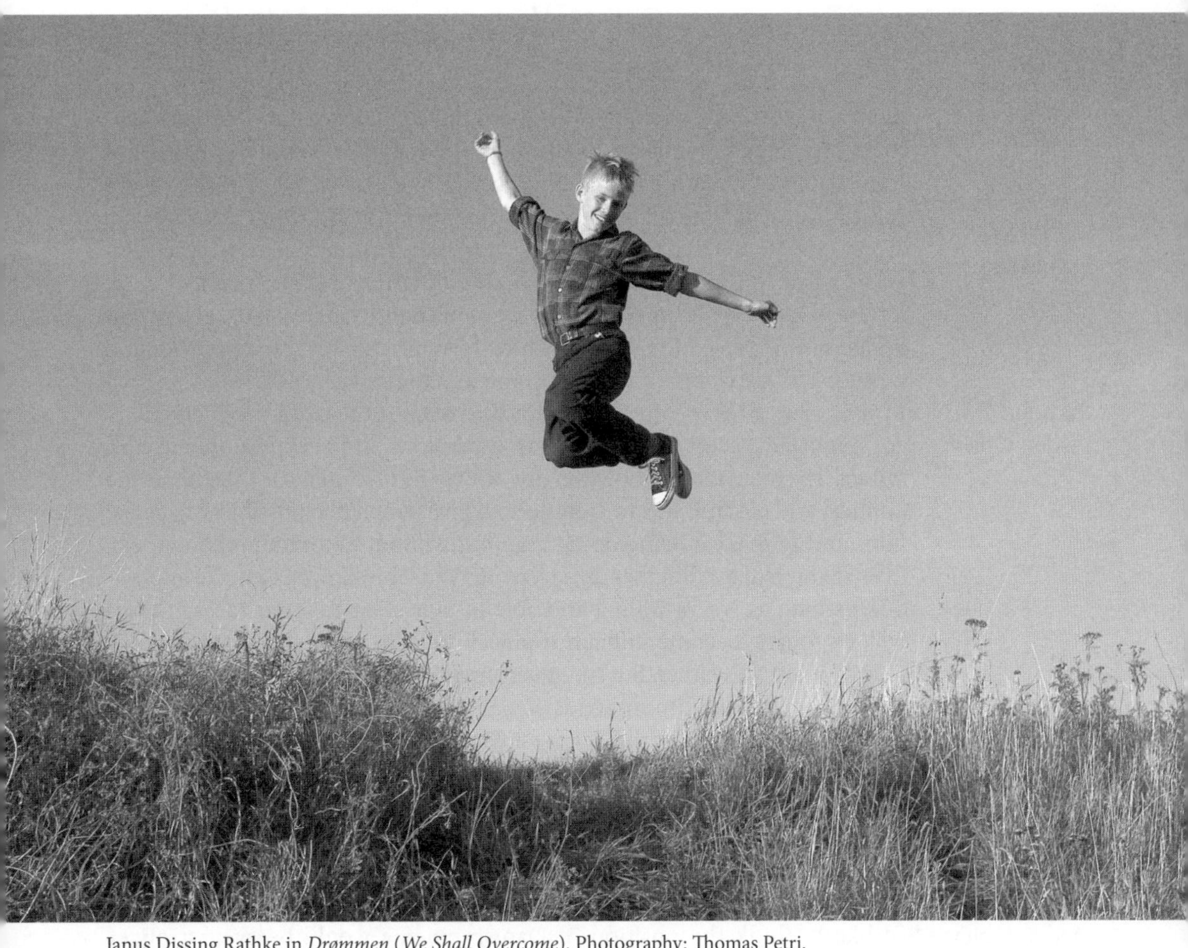

Janus Dissing Rathke in *Drømmen* (*We Shall Overcome*). Photography: Thomas Petri.

Arden Oplev: That's a pretty tough question to answer. I do feel connected to Denmark, and to my own culture and the stories that it contains. But I can't say I have a special relationship to Danish cinema, even though the first film that really meant something to me from a cultural point of view was Carl Th. Dreyer's *Ordet* (*The Word*, 1955). I saw that with my father, and it was an amazing experience. But I don't relate to Danish cinema as a specifically national phenomenon. I think it's fantastic that we've broadened the scope of Danish cinema to the extent that we are now capable of making anything from drama to vampire movies and westerns. It's all happened within just thirteen to fourteen years.

Jørholt: In your view, what are the reasons for the recent success of Danish cinema?

Arden Oplev: An important factor is that we have a fabulous and very resourceful film school. The main reason, however, for our fertile film milieu is that there's the political and cultural will in Denmark to give people the possibility to make films and to make a living doing this (but without becoming millionaires). Even if you make a film that doesn't work, you'll be allowed to make another one, as long as you're willing and able to fight a bit for your ideas. Things will, of course, become difficult if you don't sell tickets and don't win any awards at festivals either. But the government puts a lot of money into Danish cinema, and so the film milieu is actually quite privileged. And this breeds new talent. People know that it's possible to make films, and so they go ahead and give filmmaking a go. The result is a film milieu that's simply buzzing with creativity. By way of comparison, I know a lot of young filmmakers in the UK and the US, and the difficulties they face are almost grotesque. It could well take decades before they're allowed to make their first film.

Jørholt: Where do you think Danish cinema will be ten years from now?

Arden Oplev: I'd like to think the position of Danish cinema would be even stronger by then, with national and international films in Danish and English, respectively. I do believe that Danish film has the capacity to continue to spearhead cinematic creativity, and that it can function, as a result, as a brand for Denmark internationally. But this will only happen if there's the political will to continue to stimulate the film industry, and to maintain the Film School's strong creative milieu.

Jørholt: And where will Niels Arden Oplev be ten years from now?

Arden Oplev: Hmmm, he'll probably be working on a film about one of the first stave churches in Himmerland. Or maybe on some other film that lies dormant inside this elongated Himmerland skull of mine, some film that can't be pursued right now because other things need to be done first. I'll probably always be a part of Danish cinema; there are simply so many good stories, and so many good actors, out there in the Danish landscape, and I just wouldn't want to turn my back on them. But I've always felt at ease in more than one world at a time, so I don't think I'll have any problems working both in and outside Denmark. That's always been my dream, and now I'm making it come true.

Chapter 13

Lone Scherfig

Lone Scherfig. Photography: Robin Holland.

Born 1959. Lone Scherfig graduated as a director from the National Film School of Denmark in 1984. Her graduation film, *Den onde cirkel* (*The Vicious Circle*, 1984) is considered one of the finest in the school's history. Whereas this black and white short film is a highly stylized work with enigmatic characters and relationships, Scherfig's first feature, *Kajs fødselsdag* (*The Birthday Trip*, 1990), draws on various realist traditions to explore the basic humanity of an overweight lower-class man, Kaj (Steen Svare), who is taken on a surprise birthday trip to Poland, for the purposes of what is essentially sexual tourism. The children's film *Når mor kommer hjem* (*On Our Own*, 1998) is an adaptation of Martha Christensen's novel by the same title. Focusing on how three young children are left to cope on their own when their irresponsible mother is jailed for shoplifting, *On Our Own* is a fine example of Denmark's strength in the area of films for children and young people. While generally comic in its tone, the film successfully raises such serious issues as divorce, parental neglect, criminality, bullying and the failure of various state-run institutions adequately to assess and provide for the needs of children. Lone Scherfig achieved her international breakthrough with the Dogma film *Italiensk for begyndere* (*Italian for Beginners*, 2000). At once serious and comic, this ensemble film, about damaged souls who find the strength to move on in life, won the Silver Bear at the Berlin International Film Festival. Seen by almost 1 million Danes during the year of its release, this low-budget Dogma film was sold to more than 60 countries, including Pakistan, Turkmenia, Tadjikistan, Uruguay, South Africa, Taiwan, Ethiopia, Morocco, Tunisia, Peru, Panama, Libya, Ethiopia and Israel, and is one of the bestselling Scandinavian films ever. Set and shot in Glasgow, the Scottish–Danish co-production *Wilbur Wants to Kill Himself* (2002) helped to establish a productive alliance between Glasgow-based Sigma Films and Zentropa. Scherfig wrote the script for *Wilbur Wants to Kill Himself* with Anders Thomas Jensen, one of Denmark's most prolific scriptwriters and a director in his own right. While less successful than *Italian for Beginners*, *Wilbur Wants to Kill Himself* became the impetus for the Dogma-derived Scottish project known as 'Advance Party'. Scherfig and Jensen provided the character descriptions for this three-film project with rules developed by Lars von Trier. *Hjemve* (*Just like Home*, 2007) built on working methods developed by Scherfig in connection with her contribution to the net-based film initiative called *Avistid* ('Newspaper Time'), and was an attempt to take some of the principles of Dogma further, and in new directions. With a script by Nick Hornby, Scherfig's second English-language film, *An Education*, is a period film based on British journalist Lynn Barber's account of her life-changing involvement, as a young schoolgirl, with a married mythomaniac. The generosity that is a trademark feature of Scherfig's films has also characterized her role in the Danish film milieu. That directors now regularly work with actors during their years at the National Film School of Denmark is very much the result of Lone Scherfig's efforts as a committed teacher at the school, and it is clear that many a younger director thinks of her as a supportive mentor figure. Scherfig is closely associated with Lars von Trier's Film Town and with Zentropa, and she directed thirteen episodes of the company's TV series *Morten Korch* (1999). She has either written or been involved in the writing of most of the films she has directed, and has established a strong collaborative relationship with Anders Thomas Jensen. Lone Scherfig is related, through her father, to the canonized left-wing writer Hans Scherfig.

Feature films

2008	*An Education*
2007	*Hjemve (Just like Home)*
2002	*Wilbur Wants to Kill Himself*
2000	*Italiensk for begyndere (Italian for Beginners)*
1998	*Når mor kommer hjem (On Our Own)*
1990	*Kajs fødselsdag (The Birthday Trip)*

Short films

2006	*Jeg er bare den logerende (I'm Just the Lodger)*
1984	*Den onde cirkel (The Vicious Circle*, graduation film)

Television

2005	*Krøniken (Better Times*, one episode)
1999	*Morten Korch: Ved stillebækken (Still Brook)*
1997–1998	*Taxa (Taxi*, two episodes)
1994	*Flemming og Berit (Flemming and Berit)*
1993	*Den gode lykke (Luck and Happiness)*
1984	*Margrethes elsker (Margrethe's Lover)*

Hjort: We've talked at great length about your earlier work, in connection with my book on *Italian for Beginners*, published by University of Washington Press (2010). So I'd like to focus quite intensely on the film that didn't get discussed in that book, *An Education*. How did you end up directing that film?

Scherfig: The film's script is by Nick Hornby, and he based his script on a story by the journalist Lynn Barber. Hornby and I have the same agent, and I'd told her I was interested. So at a certain point I was called in for a whole series of meetings with the producers who wanted me to talk to them about what I liked about the script, and what I'd like to do with it. I told them I liked the tone of the script and that I'd read Hornby's books and have always liked the compassion he manages to convey for his characters. In the case of *An Education*, I particularly liked the character David, who as you know is a real person, someone who's still alive. I liked the idea of making a film with a male character who has enormous drive and who isn't entirely sympathetic. As a character David is a lot more dubious than the male characters in my earlier work, with rare exceptions. Peter Gantzler's role in *The Birthday Trip* has a bit of what I'm talking about.

Hjort: You've usually been involved in the scriptwriting process yourself. What was it like to work with a script by someone else, and by an established writer?

Scherfig: My position from the start was that it was Hornby's script, and that I didn't have any intention of somehow making it mine. I do think the producers had the idea that by bringing in a Danish director, as opposed to a British one, they might be able to give the film a certain edge. I don't know whether I managed to do that. It's not a film where I wanted to be really visible as a director. The film is very much about the characters, so it's important to be able to pull back as a director. It's not the director the audience should be noticing, but the characters, especially Jenny. If people leave the cinema and remember her, then we've achieved our goal.

Hjort: You've made two feature films outside Denmark. *Wilbur Wants to Kill Himself* is set and shot in Glasgow, and *An Education* is set and shot in London. What's it like as a filmmaker to work in a language and culture that's not your own?

Scherfig: In the case of *An Education* I was very conscientious about the film's look, in relation to the time in which it's set. I worked a lot harder on this film than on any of my earlier films, precisely because it's about English culture, and because I know there are things I can't take for granted when I'm working in a foreign language and in a foreign country. I did things I would never have dreamt of doing, had it been a Danish film. It was also a matter of living up to that concept of excellence that is so noticeable in a British context, where absolutely everyone seems always to be doing their best. I was met with a thoroughness and self-discipline unlike anything I've seen before. And that works well with this kind of film, but the challenge then becomes to ensure that the film also has lots of narrative energy, and some real levity. I felt that an important part of my job was to ensure that the film didn't get crushed in the production machine, because it's a film that really depends on fine details.

Hjort: The crew credits list none of the names from your earlier films. Why?

Scherfig: The entire crew was new, at least to me, and I was the only Dane. The producers had stipulated as a budgetary condition that I couldn't bring along any of the people I normally work with in Denmark. Fortunately I was very pleased with the crew I got. It would have been quite nice to have been able to include someone I'd already worked with and trusted, but there are definite gains to be had from working with new people.

Hjort: The film has original music by Paul Englishby and some tracks. What were you looking for in the way of music?

Scherfig: I'd heard Paul Englishby's music on several occasions and had wanted to work with him before. I knew Paul was able to compose symphonic music with the tranquility and sensitivity that the film needed. We knew all along that the film's lighter moments couldn't be backed up by a musical score. To give the film the energy it needed, we had to find tracks from the right period. I think we heard something like 2000 tracks before settling on the ones we used in the film. Kle Savidge, who is Canadian, was incredibly persistent. The editor, Barney Pilling, is also a DJ and very musical. And Nick Hornby was also an incredible resource. He'd only comment on things when we asked him to, and we did ask him for input about the music, because he knows a lot about music and loves music. We were looking for very English music that would really convey the flavour of London at the time. We also wanted tracks that would create the right atmosphere, and tracks with lyrics that were right in terms of the accompanying image sequence.

Hjort: How did you end up working with Barney Pilling, the editor?

Scherfig: I was supposed to have met quite a number of editors, but Barney was the first person I was to meet, and when I did I knew there was no point looking further. I knew I'd be quite happy sitting in a dark room with him over a period of twelve weeks. I could tell that he had the self-confidence needed to speak his mind and to make decisions.

I really enjoyed working with him. Barney is extremely fast and I love that because it means you have the opportunity actually to *see* far more possible edits. The emphasis is on just doing it, and showing the results, and not on describing, discussing and explaining. I like it when people have the courage to try something that might not work. Barney hasn't actually done that much, so we were taking a bit of a risk. I hope the film will help him to establish himself as an editor. I'm very grateful to him.

Hjort: How did you and John de Boorman approach the cinematography in *An Education*?

Scherfig: John de Boorman is half French and loves the French New Wave. We saw *An Education* as having a clear connection with *la nouvelle vague*, because Jenny loves those films. And then there was my Dogma background, which also provides a connection to that particular moment in film history. We talked a lot about the innocence those films have. You can't simply reproduce that innocence, clearly. But you can believe that if you really care about the whole process – the characters, the story, the details – and don't betray them, then the film will have a certain authenticity. We were looking for that same sense of curiosity and enthusiasm that characterizes the French films. Innocence became a kind of guiding thread for us, which is why it's not a very showy film. There's not a lot of technical bravura in it. Whenever the production design became a bit flamboyant, we were quick to tone things down. You visited the set at the Twickenham Studios, so you saw that house and know how minimalistic it was compared to what that house would actually have looked like. Normally you'd have had many more props. There would have been knick knacks, and cushions, and flowers, and rugs, and throws all over the place. But I didn't want this sort of material culture to compete with the characters, and I wanted the images to be calm. I didn't want the images to be busy, and I'm also always terrified of suddenly discovering a bright red umbrella, or its equivalent, in the frame. Something everyone ends up looking at instead of the characters. So innocence and simplicity, these were concepts that John and I emphasized throughout.

Hjort: What were some of the key considerations during the process of casting for the film?

Scherfig: In the case of Jenny, we knew we needed to find a young woman who really could carry this leading role, and thus the film. She had to be a credible sixteen/seventeen year old – in reality Carey Mulligan is much older – and she had to be able, in the course of just six months of story time, to mature quite considerably. Jenny goes from being just a schoolgirl to being a mature, responsible and also somewhat damaged woman. The lead also had to be able to handle enormous pressure because Jenny is in every single scene. The problem is that you can't get an actress with a lot of experience when you're looking for someone who fits the role's age requirements. Carey had hardly done anything, a little TV, and she'd had a minor role in *Pride and Prejudice* (dir. Joe Wright, 2005). As the days went by the risks diminished. Carey would show up on time, she was prepared, she didn't create scenes, she enjoyed the whole filmmaking process and she was able to keep track of the psychological process, even though we were shooting scenes out of order. I started to think, 'I don't just want her to be good. I want her to be really outstanding in this role.' So I told her that I was going to try to get her to explore more facets of her character, so that we'd end up with someone who was really fully developed, and not just partly so. In terms of working tools, I gave her a little pocket agenda from 1961, so she could chart the entire story chronologically. So she was able, for example, to say, 'OK, it's April 16. That means that it's my birthday tomorrow and that I have yet to meet so and so and that I still haven't been to Paris.' And I would be able to say things like 'You don't need to show you are nervous in this scene, because you can do that in the scene immediately preceding it, which, incidentally, we will be shooting *after* this one.' She'd never had to play such a major part before, and I'd never had to direct anyone in such an important role, so I felt I needed to come up with something. And this very concrete and pragmatic approach worked quite well.

Hjort: Were there any particularly difficult scenes in the case of Jenny?

Scherfig: The most difficult scenes were the ones where she just admires what's going on. In these scenes she's got an enormous appetite for life, but no real pragmatic drive. Also, there are no external dramatic obstacles to overcome in these scenes and that makes them hard to pull off. The things that Jenny finds really extraordinary aren't necessarily extraordinary from the audience's perspective. We have to show Jenny's response to seeing a sexy singer on stage for the first time in her life, but the audience has seen this sort of thing in hundreds of films. It was hard work making sure viewers would see the scene with Jenny's eyes. But Carey really pulled it off. In the beginning I think Nick Hornby and I both felt that we were doing her a favour, and now it's very much the other way around. We're both proud to have been there when Carey Mulligan played her first major role!

Hjort: Did you enjoy working with actors from a very different background?

Scherfig: I enjoy working with British actors. Britain has an extraordinary dramatic tradition to draw on, and it shows. I noticed this already with *Wilbur*. British actors are much less inclined to introduce textual changes than Danish actors are, and they are incredibly disciplined. I like the fact that they tend to be very technical in their approach to acting. They think of acting as a discipline, one that requires you to enter into a certain kind of psychological process. They expect the feelings that process involves to lie in the images, in the film itself. They don't expect the feelings to be there on the set, between the actor and director. I'm not the kind of director who's on the phone with actors all night long. And the British actors I worked with are to a very large extent self-directed. I really didn't need to direct them that much.

I found working with Peter Sarsgaard, who plays David in *An Education*, very interesting. The role is incredibly challenging because it's very hard to keep track of when the audience is supposed to know what, and what David is supposed to feel when, and when he really is in love as opposed to having his head in a quite different place. It's hard to keep track of all his secrets and to make sure that when they're finally revealed, the revelations seem logical but not at all predictable. And David had to be played in such a way that it was possible to defend and even like the character, although there was no real basis for approving of him. It's that 'love your villains' idea. Peter said that he didn't have a problem with that idea at all, because he liked David right from the start. And I felt the same way. David is a bit of a small-time crook, and there's something quite moving about this character

Carey Mulligan and Peter Sarsgaard in *An Education*. Photography: Kerry Brown.

who so desperately wants to live the kind of life he could have lived if he'd had 'an education'. But Peter is extraordinary. As a person, he's very charitable and generous, deeply ethical. As an actor, I'd find him coming up with things that were much more true or authentic than what I'd had in mind. I've never experienced that with any other actor. Not to that degree. I also loved working with Alfred Molina. He's a very warm and lovely person, and I was actually quite sorry that his time on the set was so limited. I'd very much like to work with him again.

Hjort: What about Cara Seymour who plays Jenny's mother?

Scherfig: I'd seen Cara Seymour, who plays Jenny's mother, in Lars von Trier's *Dancer in the Dark* (2000) and in Spike Jonze's *Adaptation* (2002). She was Charlie Kaufman's girlfriend in that. She's got something very sweet and delicate about her, which was what I wanted, because I didn't want Jenny's mother to fit the cinematic stereotype of the English housewife. I wanted someone who could convey a certain sense of boredom. She's in that house, and it doesn't take that long to clean it, and so she's sort of on hold, waiting. There's an incredible emptiness there. And that's what explains why it's so easy for her to accept David into their lives. There's a bit of the 'mother's little helper' to her characterization too. She's somewhat out of touch. I didn't want her to have her feet too firmly planted on the ground, because the sins she commits are sins of omission. What happens is made possible by the mother's neglect. There had to be a sense of a mismatch between the mother and both the father and Jenny. You could almost say that the family dynamic is one where it's the father and Jenny who are married, or, rather, who have an adult relationship. The mother has opted *not* to be intelligent. And that's very different from the real-life story on which the fiction is based. Lynn Barber's mother is not that way.

Hjort: Could you say more about the film's relation to Lynn Barber's story?

Scherfig: The film is much lighter than Lynn Barber's story. Barber's story is about how she lost her faith in people, and about why she as a journalist always knew that it's necessary to dig well below the surface of what people say. As you know she's much feared as a journalist, although people are always very flattered if she wants to talk to them. I have to say that I've only known her to be sweet and smiling, and very cheerful. But there was a conscious decision throughout to make sure the film's tone was different from that of Lynn's story. I remember having countless conversations with the producers about how we needed to make sure that people wouldn't leave the cinemas with a strong sense of having seen a film with a sad ending. So we kept talking about the extent to which the film is and isn't about a young woman who falls into the hands of a psychopath. The film we ended up making is more a love story than it's a story about a young woman and a psychopath. But it's supposed to balance right at the edge of that other story. What Lynn Barber experienced was something far more diffuse, lasting and fateful. I don't think I'd want to make that film.

Hjort: You've played an important role at the National Film School of Denmark, and quite a number of people in the Danish film industry see you as a gifted teacher and a valuable mentor. How would you describe the role you've played at the National Film School?

Scherfig: Some students hate that school while they're there, but afterwards they love it, and keep going back. There's a strong sense of affinity among people who've gone to the School, a sense of somehow speaking the same language. Even in Denmark I feel there's a clear difference between working with someone, a cinematographer say, who went to the School, as compared to someone who didn't. As former students, we all have this strong sense of gratitude, and as a result a lot of us keep going back, but as teachers now. When the School calls us and asks us to do something, we show up. If we're available, that is. The School really depends on this kind of support, which helps to sustain it. I taught a director's cohort for two or three years, when my daughter was very young. So I was back at the School on a permanent basis for a few years, but otherwise I've been in and out. I'm always very happy to be there. One thing I did do while I was teaching there was I got the Danish Actors Association to pay for a set-up that allowed the students in the director's stream to work with far more professional actors than ever before. It's not the only reason why the acting in contemporary Danish film is better today than ever before, but it is part of the explanation. Directors who graduate from the National Film School just aren't afraid of actors anymore. They've learnt to work with actors by actually doing it. I'm also on the School's Advisory Board, and that's because I think it's important to continue to fight to ensure that the School remains under the auspices of the Ministry of Cultural Affairs, rather than the Ministry of Education.

Hjort: You're very much part of the Zentropa family. How would you describe your involvement with Zentropa?

Scherfig: When I first came to the Film Town in Avedøre the place had this pioneering spirit, and that was something I'd been looking for from a very young age.

I'd always wanted to help get something meaningful off the ground. We walked around in mud, and there was old military furniture all over the place, and mice, and it was freezing cold in the editing rooms. And it was fantastic, because we were creating something new and worthwhile. The hard thing has been to preserve that enthusiasm, especially in the wake of Zentropa's success. Slowly but surely people started quietly to paint their offices, to bring in a flower or two. It's been hard to sustain the idea that film is everything and that we don't care about what we look like, or what our working environment looks like. Lars von Trier and Peter Aalbæk are still very unconcerned about externalities. Except food!

The Film Town doesn't draw me in quite the same way that it once did. At one point I rented a house out there, together with ten writers. It was a former officers' building and had also at some point been used for surveillance purposes.

So there were 10,000 telephone sockets, or that's what it felt like at the time. We set up a common room, where we could meet, also with actors, and then we had our individual offices. But I eventually moved out, and moved over into what's known as the 'hut town', where I have my own hut. I work at home a lot, and I travel a lot, so I don't use it that much. But I refuse to give up my 'office', because I still want my pigeon hole, and a hug from time to time, and some kind of connection to the place. But I don't have shares in Zentropa, although many people think I do. I've always worked freelance for them. My relationship to Zentropa is about friendship, and artistic trust and freedom.

Hjort: Your Dogma film, *Italian for Beginners*, is one of Danish cinema's biggest successes, ever. Does Dogma continue to inform your filmmaking?

Scherfig: When I was making *An Education* people said they could tell I'd been influenced by Dogma. When you've made a Dogma film, you can't help but try to turn obstacles into opportunities. For example, if someone tells me that something just isn't working, location-wise, I'm more likely now to say 'Well, let's try to rethink the script, so that *it* fits the reality that's on offer, instead of trying to force the real world to match the requirements of the script.' That's really become my method.

For example, if a dress is ten centimetres too long, and we know it will look terrible if we hem it, then I might say, 'Well, yes, a hem will look really ugly. And there *is* an ugly hem in the dress *precisely* because the mother can't sew, or she was quite out of it the day she hemmed the dress.' There are also plenty of examples of unorthodox editing in *An Education*, and that's because of Dogma. Dogma's rule requiring synchronicity between image and sound taught us that it was quite possible to do things that the 'film police' don't allow. So I'd say, 'Look, just do it.' Not because I lacked an understanding of cinematic norms, but because I knew that from an aesthetic point of view it was quite possible to violate those norms. This sort of thing requires a lot of courage, especially on the part of the producers. They have to buy into that idea, which is so central to Dogma, that it is good to be somewhat less in control, to relinquish a bit of professionalism and to let reality control things a bit more. I have to say that my experience with *An Education* was that that aspect of Dogma fit very poorly with the work ethos of the Brits.

Hjort: You were involved in the development of the Scottish 'Advance Party' project, which draws heavily on Dogma. What was this all about?

Scherfig: 'Advance Party' was motivated by a desire to help some young directors make their first feature film. It is extremely difficult in Scotland to make the transition from shorts to features; much harder than it is in Denmark. It all started with von Trier's *Breaking the Waves* (1996), which was a pre-Dogma film. The reason *Breaking the Waves* was shot in the Hebrides was that Scotland offered some very attractive financial incentives at the time. So Zentropa set up a company in Scotland, and

Adrian Rawlins and Jamie Sives as the two brothers in *Wilbur Wants to Kill Himself*. Photography: Per Arnesen.

began collaborating with the Scottish producer Gillian Berrie. Zentropa co-produced David MacKenzie's *The Last Great Wilderness* (2002), for example. And Zentropa also got involved in the creation of Film City Glasgow, which is modelled on the Film Town in Avedøre and located in the old Govan town hall in Glasgow. Gillian's Sigma Films co-produced *Wilbur Wants to Kill Himself*, and that's how I ended up becoming aware of some of the difficulties faced by aspiring young directors in Scotland. We – Sisse Graum Jørgensen, Gillian and I – decided to ask Lars von Trier whether he could come up with an idea that would do for Scotland what Dogma had done for Denmark. And he came up with 'Advance Party'. Dogma had taught us to think of restrictions and constraints as opportunities, and the rules governing 'Advance Party' were supposed to work in the same way. The rules specified that the three 'Advance Party' films were to feature the same characters and were to make use of the same cast. Anders Thomas Jensen and I had written the script for *Wilbur*, and so we ended up writing up the profiles for the 'Advance Party' characters. Anders and I wrote short descriptions, no more than a page, for each character, and our intent was to be as concrete as possible. So in the case of Alfred, for example, we know that he lies. Jackie is burdened by enormous grief. A third character owns a shoe shop. We also tried to make sure that the character profiles could work in the context of very different genres. It had to be possible to use them in a more tragic film, as well as in a comedy, for example.

The 'Advance Party' set-up was basically inspired by the kind of collaborative culture that characterizes the National Film School of Denmark. People really do help each other a lot at that school. You might ask someone to read your script, to help you identify the problems it has and, just as importantly, to identify a solution to those problems. We wanted 'Advance Party' to have that collaborative spirit, which was also very much the spirit of Dogma. It's interesting, because Zentropa is now trying to do something similar in Ireland. I know that Sisse and Peter Aalbæk Jensen have had some young Irish directors over to the Film Town. Working together, helping each other get going, helping each other sort problems out, these are all things that are part of Danish culture. And they're things we feel we can, and would like to export. It really does work this way in the Danish film world. People really do wish each other well, if only for selfish reasons. Every time a Danish film succeeds, things become that much easier for everyone else.

Hjort: Women play a prominent role in Danish film. How do you explain that?

Scherfig: Our language, which is spoken by such a small number of people, is a factor. We have to work with very small budgets, and women are very good at being flexible, and at finding solutions to budgetary constraints. They're good at telling stories that are about just a few people and that take place in a modest location. At least that's what you notice when you look at what the women are putting out there. Very little of what they do is technology-intensive.

There are also a lot of women in leadership positions in the Danish film industry, and at the Danish Film Institute, at least at the level of middle management. It also makes a real difference that both Lars von Trier and Peter Aalbæk really like women, and surround themselves with women, both as producers and directors. Look at Trust Film, which used to be Zentropa's sales company (they've now merged with Nordisk). People used to think that Peter Aalbæk had hired everyone at Trust Film on the basis of their looks. Every time he showed up with his sales team, six tall, glamorous blondes would walk through the door. But these women are all tough as nails and formidable negotiators, so he'd definitely not hired them on the basis of their looks. But they made quite an impression!

I have to say that, as a woman, I have absolutely no complaints. I can't begin to count the number of times I've brought my daughter to work. And my bosses would welcome her with open arms. Lars von Trier taught her to drive his golf buggy! I feel that the only way I can really thank people for all the kindness I was shown is to make sure that I somehow reciprocate, indirectly and in relation to the next generation of film practitioners. Anyone working for me knows that his or her children are always welcome in our various workspaces.

Hjort: What are your plans for the future?

Scherfig: It's very encouraging that *An Education* has been well received. This means that there's a much greater likelihood of my being able to make the kinds of films I'd like to make. I'd like to do something different, something much more serious, something darker, more plot driven and more visually distinctive. At the moment I'm reading a book or a script a day. I come across a lot of scripts where I think, 'That could be a good film, but I'm not the right person to direct it.' Either because I feel I wouldn't really be able to do anything with the script, or because I just don't want to put years of my life into precisely that film. I'm quite marked by an experience that I've had twice, uncannily. My father died while I was shooting *Italian for Beginners* and my mother died while I was shooting *An Education*. When I watch these films I can't help but ask myself whether they were worth it. When you start to look at the whole filmmaking process with those eyes, then there are really a lot of scripts that life is simply too short for. And maybe life is also too short for repetition. I've told various producers, and also my agent, the one from *An Education*, that I'm interested in doing something different.

Chapter 14

Omar Shargawi

Omar Shargawi. Photography: Abu M.

Born 1974. Few people in the Danish film business had heard of Omar Shargawi when he suddenly won the Tiger Award at the Rotterdam Film Festival and the international film critics' award in Gothenburg for the gangster drama *Ma Salama Jamil*. Shargawi is an autodidact director who worked as a photographer and actor before taking up filmmaking. *Ma Salama Jamil* grew out of a short film made in the context of the Film Workshop in Copenhagen. The opportunity to develop this short into a feature film arose after the director presented a promising trailer to Zentropa producer Peter Aalbæk Jensen in Cannes. The rough, big-city drama takes place in Copenhagen, but is played out almost exclusively in Arabic and in immigrant milieus that could in principle be anywhere. In the film everyday life is dominated by religion and the age-old conflict between Sunni and Shia Muslims. The story focuses on Jamil (Dar Salim), who saw his mother being murdered when he was a little boy in Lebanon. Jamil escaped to Copenhagen with his father, and when Jamil happens to discover that his mother's murderer is in Copenhagen, he decides to settle the score. This starts a chain reaction of death and misery, which is contrasted with the teachings of the Koran. Thus, for example, the film leaves the viewer with the following quote: 'For he who kills a person it will be as if he had killed all mankind.' Shargawi's film was well received by the Danish press, with critics comparing his hard-hitting debut with, among other films, Nicolas Winding Refn's *Pusher* (1996).

Feature film

2008 *Gå med fred Jamil* (*Ma Salama Jamil*)

Documentary

2010 *Fra Haifa til Nørrebro* (*My Father from Haifa*)

Redvall: In 2008 you came out of nowhere and established yourself as a promising new name in Danish film with the award-winning feature *Ma Salama Jamil.* How did you get into film?

Shargawi: I've always been interested in film. It probably started when I was five or six years old. My father bought a video player early on, and many a weekend at his place was spent watching eight or nine videos that we'd rent from a local Pakistani video rental outfit. My father, my brothers and I could spend the entire weekend watching Charles Bronson, Bruce Lee or Clint Eastwood films. We saw the films over and over again, and my father also took us to the cinema to see Superman films or Bud Spencer and Terence Hill films. That's where the magic started, the magic you felt when you settled into your seat in the cinema and the lights went down. I still feel this magic even today when I go to see a film. That feeling has stayed with me but it wasn't like I had some dream of becoming a film director when I grew up.

I've worked as a still photographer and I've had some small acting parts, and when people ask me what I do today I still have a hard time telling them that I'm a film director. I usually say something about how I'm trying to make a film. And I'd been trying for years before I finally made *Ma Salama Jamil.* I'd applied to the Film Workshop and to Short Fiction Film Denmark several times. I also applied for support from the consultant scheme once, and was actually called in for a meeting, but I never showed up. I've probably always been in a bit of a hurry, and if people didn't immediately see how brilliant my ideas were, then I stopped caring. I had this very youthful need to have everything happen here and now, otherwise I'd quickly move on.

Redvall: Did you ever consider applying to the National Film School of Denmark?

Shargawi: No, I didn't have the patience for that whole process either. I couldn't see myself attending the school and having to leap through a lot of hoops and do things for the sake of other people. I didn't want to spend years of my life doing assignments. I had so much I wanted to tell and I just wanted to get started. I probably felt that I'd simply have to come in from the margins, that I'd have to challenge the establishment somehow.

Redvall: *Ma Salama Jamil* did to a high degree come from the margins of Danish film. It's a film with a unique atmosphere and a very dramatic story that plays out primarily in Arabic, amongst Arabs in Copenhagen. Where did that story come from?

Shargawi: I wanted to tell a universal story and in this case my story found a starting point in the age-old conflict between Sunni and Shia Muslims. Basically the story is about revenge and about human traits and feelings. The main character can choose between revenge and reconciliation. Even though the characters in the film are Arabs, I perceive the story as being about much more than their conflict. Their conflict was just the starting point for a story with universal dimensions. At the same time the story is based on a sense of puzzlement: how is it possible for people to believe in a number of really beautiful ideas, all of them purveyed by religion, and for them then to live in a way that is completely contrary to those ideas? So the film springs from some very basic questions about why the characters live and act the way they do.

Redvall: The feature film grew out of a short film for which you were given funding by the Film Workshop in 2003. How did the short film become a feature film?

Shargawi: I applied to the Film Workshop with an idea for a short film and I was given 10,000 DKK and some equipment. At the time the Film Workshop was promoting the idea of shooting everything on video, but I'd made a firm decision to shoot on 16 mm. I was still a photographer at the time and I refused to shoot digitally. It had to be film. I've never liked the digital look. I've never been a fan of Dogma films. Those films might tell powerful stories, but I've never enjoyed them as cinematic experiences. It was a huge fight to get to shoot on 16 mm, but I got my way. Originally, the film was only supposed to be fifteen minutes long, but we shot a version that was half an hour long because the story developed as we were filming. Along the way we got more money out of the Film Workshop and we also got some additional money from some sponsors. Wanting to film more was a problem, but we pressured people into accepting what we wanted to do. I think that both my photographer Aske [Foss] and I brought a fierce energy to the project. People were almost afraid to get in our way because we were just so incredibly motivated.

Redvall: How did you get in contact with Aske Foss who also filmed the feature film version? Often the challenge of making films without being able to draw on established networks, such as the ones the Film School creates, seems to be that of putting together a production team.

Shargawi: I met Aske at the early stages of making the short film through someone who'd worked with him on some commercials. Aske and I just clicked right away. We saw things in the same way and were inspired by the same things. That was important to me, since finding a shared vision was something that had been very difficult in some of my earlier attempts to work with others. Aske and I gradually started working on the film together and developing it visually, and as it turns out I was lucky. He had as much to prove as I did. He'd applied to the Film School and hadn't been accepted, and the film became his baby as much as it was mine. The process of moving the film from the short film stage to its feature-length development was simply something we did together, as a team.

Redvall: The story about how the short film was turned into a feature film is quite unique in the context of Danish film. You showed up at Cannes with a three-minute trailer comprising material from the short film and won over Peter Aalbæk Jensen from Zentropa?

Shargawi: A week before Cannes I was trying to finish editing the short, but I wasn't happy with it. I had lots of cool scenes, lots of nice images and plenty of good acting to draw on, but I just wasn't happy with it all, as a film. Somehow the story I was trying to tell just wasn't there. I wanted to shoot extra material and to re-shoot certain scenes. I wanted to shoot all the material that would be needed for a feature film, which is what I'd dreamed of making all along. That evening I was playing a game of poker, and one of the guys said: 'Why don't you go to Cannes and try to show it to some key people?' When I woke up the next morning, I thought: 'That's what I'll do!' I contacted my editor and during that week we produced a three-minute edit, and we colour graded it and produced the sound. A friend and I then left for France, and found a shoddy hotel twenty kilometres outside Cannes. We knocked on doors and jumped across fences and threw the DVD at all the people we could get near. We became fixtures at the Scandinavian stand, and that's where we got hold of Peter Aalbæk. We just asked him whether he had three minutes. He did, and when he'd seen the trailer he said he thought it was amazing and that we should make the film.

Redvall: You often hear stories about producers saying yes to a lot of projects, but not having much follow through. How quickly were you able to move forward in this instance?

Shargawi: What happened was that there was actually a lot of interest in our project. Not just from him. Suddenly three or four production companies were interested, so I was in the privileged situation of being able to choose. When I got home from Cannes, Peter set me up with a producer, but that producer was making his own feature film on the side, as a director. And I really felt that I needed more attention. One day I saw Meta Louise Foldager on TV where she was being interviewed about her role as Lars von Trier's new producer. Afterwards I called Peter Aalbæk and said that I'd like to have her be my producer. He didn't really know whether it was a good idea, but I called her on Christmas Eve anyway and we agreed to meet on the first of January. And after that meeting I was completely convinced that she was the perfect producer for my film. It had to be a young woman like that, who really knows what she wants.

Redvall: Given the choices that you had, why did you choose to make the film with Zentropa, and how would you describe the partnership that emerged?

Shargawi: To me Zentropa's strength is that if you have international aspirations as a filmmaker then they can really help you. I want my films to get beyond the borders of Denmark, and to reach people in all kinds of other countries around the world. I don't want to make films that target only Danes and are intended primarily for distribution inside Denmark. If you have your eyes set on international audiences, then Zentropa is clearly the best place to be, because they have a very structured approach to all the relevant issues. At a smaller production company things might be easier on a day-to-day basis, but that probably doesn't make the film any the better. Zentropa is definitely not the easy choice, because you can end up disappearing into the crowd. At

Dar Salim in *Ma Salama Jamil*. Photography: Christian Geisnæs.

Zentropa you constantly have to work at drawing attention to yourself and to your project, but that isn't necessarily a bad thing. It means that you can't be lazy and comfortable.

Redvall: Given Zentropa's level of interest in your film, after Cannes, how would you describe the process of getting support from New Danish Screen? Did the Danish Film Institute also express interest from the beginning?

Shargawi: I think it made a big difference that I was no longer applying for funding as a solitary director. I applied to New Danish Screen with Zentropa backing me. That also meant that someone was almost running the show for me. It wasn't any longer quite so disastrous if I didn't immediately manage to get someone to put 5 million DKK on the table. I still wanted everything to move very quickly, but it was a lot easier being patient with Zentropa on my side. And it was probably also an advantage that Vinca Wiedemann, who was in charge of New Danish Screen at the time, knew who I was. I'd met her in Cannes. We hadn't actually talked about the project, but the fact that I'd just recently met her made a difference. So there's no doubt that the decision simply to go to Cannes was the right one. I don't think it would have worked if I'd tried to reach Peter Aalbæk in Denmark.

Redvall: How did the people who read the script along the way react to the project? What did people think about your wanting to make a Danish film with mainly Arabic-speaking characters?

Shargawi: I was in quite a unique situation, because the people I met – both those who assessed the project and those who were going to be part of it – told me that they didn't really know what to say. They could see that the project had a certain quality, but they couldn't really comment on it in any detail because I'd brought them something they'd never seen before. In principle I could have told them anything, really, about Islam, or Arabs, or the language in the milieu. That's not to say that the process was quick or smooth, but people just didn't question the conflict I wanted to explore, or the environment that I was trying to describe. They didn't know anything about all that, so what were they supposed to say? It was an advantage to be putting something new out there, but there were also clear risks. Unfortunately there are many examples of films being made about Islam or Arabs, where it's clear that the filmmakers have absolutely no idea what they're talking about. And yet they've been given a green light. People have just clapped their hands because they didn't know how to set standards in relation to the material in question. In that way I felt that I was carrying a huge responsibility since I didn't want to do a disservice to the communities I was depicting.

Redvall: Could you clarify your thoughts about that sense of responsibility you just mentioned? Your film doesn't provide a politically correct portrayal of the milieu, but rather a dramatic image of a parallel reality in Denmark, one dominated by crime, historical strife and religious conflict. How is the immigrant milieu in Denmark served by this kind of portrayal?

Shargawi: Suddenly I had the opportunity to make this film, and I went from having an immense desire to just make it to suddenly being a bit anxious because the subject I'd chosen to explore was potentially explosive. The story was certainly one I wanted to tell, but the challenge was to tell the story in the right way. I felt a huge sense of responsibility because I didn't want to fan the flames of conflict, or to expose people who are already exposed enough. I had to be able to face my own family and walk in the streets afterwards! So suddenly there were many issues to think about, but then I was introduced to Mogens Rukov, whom I'd only heard of up until then.

Redvall: As Head of the National Film School of Denmark's Scriptwriting Programme, Mogens Rukov has collaborated with a number of former students at the school. How did you meet?

Shargawi: I met Mogens through Aske. His wife is Mogens' personal assistant, and she suggested that we meet. When I told people that I was meeting Mogens their reactions were quite mixed. Some people thought it was really exciting. Others said he was anti-Arab, that he hated Muslims and that I really shouldn't agree to meet with him. 'He'll ruin your film', they said. But that's not at all how I felt about him. From the start the chemistry between us was good, and that initial feeling developed into real friendship. I didn't think that everything Mogens said had to be an epiphany, just because he was Mogens Rukov. And perhaps that attitude helped.

I'd thought I'd write the story on my own, but I soon discovered just how intelligent Mogens is. On more than one occasion he really helped me to stay in control of the writing process. He kept insisting that I tell a story about people. Initially I didn't give much thought to the issue of prejudice. The idea of being careful was one that I couldn't be bothered with. I just wanted to tell the story in as explosive, open and honest a way as possible. Mogens was good at making me remember that we were making a film that could be seen by a lot of people, and that I had to think about the question of how much violence I wanted to show. That is, I had to focus on the film's being about people. Mogens will also be involved in the next film I make, and in exactly the same capacity. I write a number of scenes and send them off to him, and then we talk about them. And then I re-write them.

Redvall: If you didn't know in advance that *Ma Salama Jamil* is a Danish film, you could easily think of the story as being set in any number of places. Foreign critics have pointed out that viewers could be well into the film before realizing that the story doesn't take place in the Middle East. Was it important for you to make a film that didn't have a clear geographic anchoring in Denmark?

Shargawi: Yes, it was. I live in Denmark and I make films in Denmark, and that's the starting point for the film. But the story could have played out anywhere. That's one of the reasons why Denmark is cut out visually. I'm not trying to hide that it's Denmark, and the characters do sometimes speak Danish, but I'm trying to capture what it feels like to live in those communities, how people who are part of them see the world. I think those immigrant environments are very similar across Europe. They're small, closed societies.

But I've taken some liberties in the description of the milieu. As far as I'm concerned films have to look cool. Films have to be film. They have to seduce. First and foremost, I myself need to be seduced by my film. That's the reason why the clothes they wear in the film are quite unrealistic, given how that generation actually dresses. I modified the clothes because I wanted a particular stylistic image that matched the overall expressive form and visual style. Many things in the film are only there for the sake of the film, but hopefully viewers choose to accept them for that very reason. People simply dress too poorly in Denmark for me to be able to depict that aspect of their lives realistically on film! I'd have fewer problems drawing on reality if I lived in Italy. In Denmark people are simply not stylish enough to look good on film.

Redvall: The film achieves a high degree of authenticity on account of the many unknown actors who seem at home in the depicted milieu, and who seem to know what they're talking about. For example, when they discuss why they won't eat a sausage or how to behave in a mosque. Where did you find the many new faces in the film?

Shargawi: I knew many of the actors before I embarked on the film. Several were personal friends, and then there was my father, and my daughter also played a small part. I got to know the guy who plays Jamil through the short film, and this was true of many of the others. It was very much a process of somebody knowing somebody who knew somebody. People in the Arab milieu all know each other, so even if I didn't know of a particular person, then my father no doubt did. In fact my father might even have looked after him when he was little. But a lot of time was spent on casting and it's not as though people got the parts just because I knew them. The people who became part of the project were super-professional because they really got into their parts, and they were all cast because they had traits that really suited their roles. The demands made on the performers were very high, because the process was almost unreasonably concentrated and intense. Many of the people who acted in the film didn't do so because they dreamt of becoming actors. They really had to make up their minds as to whether they'd be able to stand by the film, because it was such an explosive subject. So everyone had really thought about whether they'd feel comfortable playing the roles they'd been asked to play. Thinking these things through carefully helped to establish a very serious framework for the film's

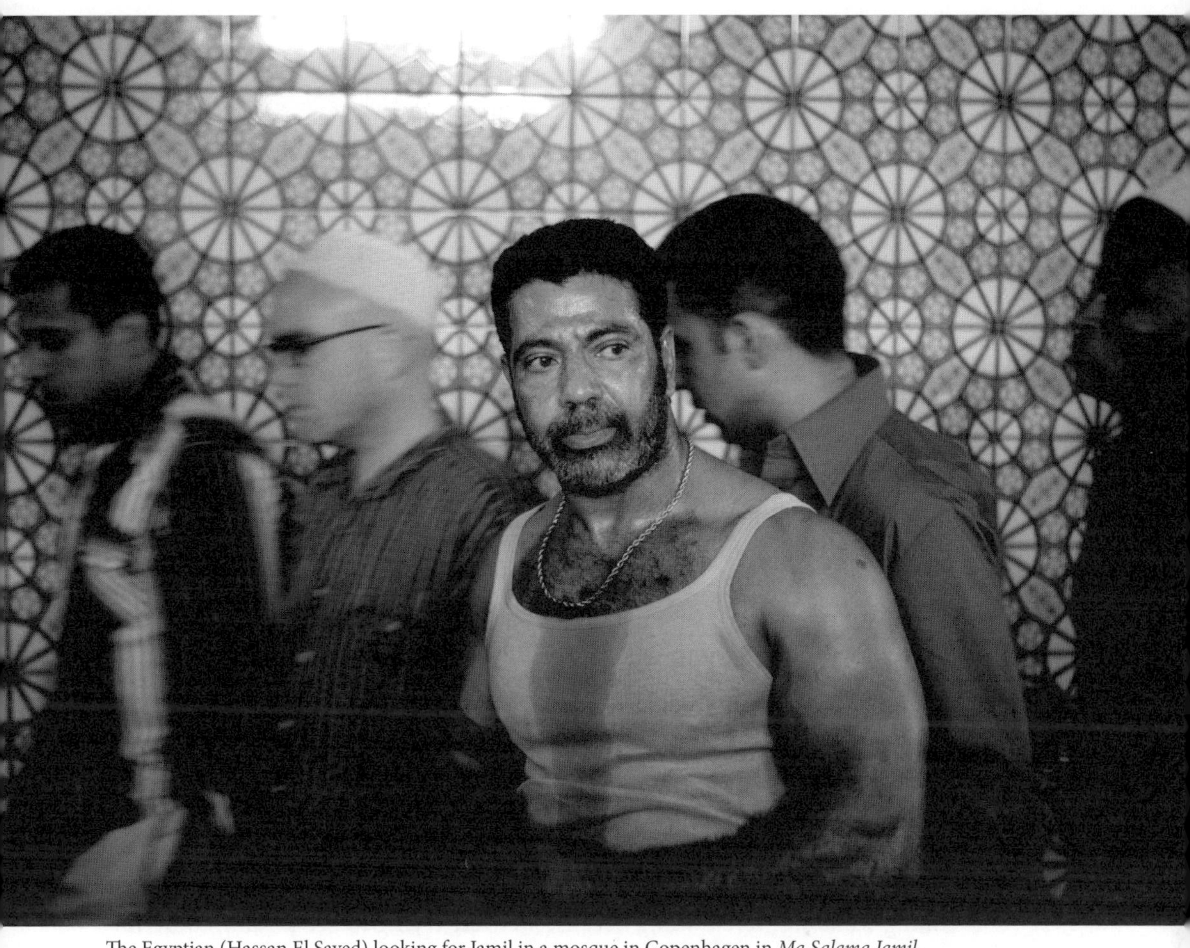

The Egyptian (Hassan El Sayed) looking for Jamil in a mosque in Copenhagen in *Ma Salama Jamil*.
Photography: Christian Geisnæs.

production, which was helpful. We were all very aware that we weren't making some light comedy. But we were plagued by accidents, especially once we started shooting. It was quite chaotic and conflictual.

Redvall: Why?

Shargawi: Everything went wrong. I also think that most of the Danish members of the film crew had a hard time keeping up much of the time because the action being shot was so strange and different, at least from their point of view. So it was quite hard to involve them 100 per cent. They didn't really understand the story, and I just didn't have time to spend 30 minutes every day explaining each individual scene. Both Aske and I had the attitude that people simply had to keep up, and if someone did fall behind, we'd deal with it. I think that Meta, my producer, who was extremely supportive, sometimes found this way of working a bit challenging. But that was also how we'd made the short film and maybe there have to be conflicts when the story itself is about conflict.

Redvall: You had some minor parts as an actor before you started directing. Were you able to draw on that experience as a director?

Shargawi: My experiences on various sets have mostly given me an understanding of how I don't want to do things myself. For instance, I've never understood why the director stands half a kilometre away from the actors, looking at a monitor. When I'm filming, Aske often has to shout that I'm in the frame again. I just have to be as close as possible.

Redvall: There were three editors on the film, among them the experienced Anders Refn. Was it difficult to make the material come together?

Shargawi: Yes. We started with two editors, Per Sandholt and Henrik Thiesen. They started editing while we were filming because we were trying to get the film to Berlin. This quickly turned out to be unrealistic because I really needed to be in the editing room. Even though there was a simultaneous interpretation track on everything it was hard for them to edit the material. So we only really started editing when we'd finished shooting. We edited a lot of good scenes but the story that I wanted wasn't there. We had almost four hours of edited material, but couldn't find the story. I knew it was there, somewhere; the diamond was in there, we just had to find it. But you can't spend two years looking for your story in the edited material, and that's why Anders Refn was brought in. I hadn't met him before, but my view was that any editor who was to be brought in should be a sensible older man, skilled and with authority, and able to put me in my place. Anders came by and we saw a cut together. Afterwards he said to me: 'I have to say, Omar, you speak Danish really well.' And then I said; 'Yes, I'm half Danish. My mother is Danish and I was born and raised here.' 'Yes, but still', he said. And then we worked from there!

It was amazing having him on the film. He was to the editing process what Mogens had been to the scriptwriting process. I needed to work with someone whom I really respected and who'd be willing to contradict me. I found that in Anders. I think that together we found the core of the story quite quickly. He'll also be editing my next film. Now that I understand the process, it will be about including everything that works the next time around. Also, I now know that I need to bring Anders in with his medical kit.

Redvall: What was it like to experience the way in which production realities can constrain what's possible in a film?

Shargawi: It was my first film and I wasn't always able to understand that things had to be done to a budget and within a given timeframe. I felt that everything was possible. Things happen when they happen and you just have to work at it. That was my assumption, and I think I probably still have some trouble understanding the constraints that come with filmmaking. I don't really understand budgets, the idea that there's money for this and not for that. I'll probably get better at that side of things eventually, but I don't really want to get involved with budgets. They take my focus off the most important things, and when that happens I start thinking about the story in terms of what's possible and what's impossible, budget-wise. I start thinking about ticket sales, and so on. I'm convinced you just have to hold onto your story. Sometimes you almost feel that you have to be at odds with the entire world just to get one little thing through, but you have to hold on to what moves you.

Redvall: *Ma Salama Jamil* won the Tiger Award at Rotterdam and has been to lots of other film festivals. How important are film festivals for a film like yours?

Shargawi: The festivals are incredibly important as a means of getting the film seen internationally. But on a personal level I have to say that the festivals bring out the worst in you. When you're standing in the middle of it all and think you just might win, then you start really *wanting* to win that prize. But that's not the bloody reason you made the film. When you're nominated and don't win you're upset and then suddenly everything is reduced to winning an award. I've learnt a lot in the past year. I've been on the festival circuit a lot. I should only have gone to a few festivals because suddenly you find yourself saying things that start to feel empty because you're repeating yourself. The words start to seem meaningless, and your whole point of departure, which was to challenge a certain sense of normalcy, starts to seem rather distant. Suddenly you're part of the reality you were trying to contest. Of course I'm happy with the awards I've won, but next time I'll do my best to focus less on the awards. I'll try not to get quite so caught up in the festival scene, because it shouldn't be the reason for making a film. It's about having something to say and a message, not about winning or not winning an award. You can lose your way very quickly if you start to think along those lines.

Redvall: How have you experienced audiences' responses to the film at festivals? Do people react in the same way?

Shargawi: In more or less the same way. The message usually gets through clearly. In that sense I feel the film is a success because people have actually understood it the way I wanted them to understand it. There was a strange episode at the Cairo Film Festival, however. The journalists went completely crazy at the press conference and started proclaiming that the film was part of the Danish conspiracy with the Muhammed cartoons and I don't know what else. There was actually a fight in front of the cinema. The young students who loved the film and defended it got into a fight with the journalists, who hated it. This initial conflict developed into a huge fight, which the police had to stop, and we ended up being escorted away from there. I see the journalists down there as representing a dictatorship that's made possible by exactly the same type of people who support the Danish People's Party in Denmark. When something doesn't work in Denmark, these people blame the 'foreign' elements. The journalists' response was quite predictable, really, when you think about it. But ordinary Egyptians generally responded to the film in the same positive ways that I've encountered in the rest of the world.

Redvall: Speaking of the Muhammed cartoons, one of the reviews published in connection with the Rotterdam Film Festival criticized *Ma Salama Jamil* for not even mentioning the Muhammed cartoons. What do you make of that?

Shargawi: I read that too. But, first of all, I started writing the story long before the Muhammed cartoon crisis. Secondly, I think it smacks of racism when my film gets criticized for not discussing integration, or for not mentioning the cartoon crisis. To me it's pure prejudice to assume that a film about Arabs has to talk about the cartoon crisis, and in a certain way too. Some Danish reviewers also spent half their reviews talking about how I should have made the film differently, so as not to fan the flames. I wonder whether those same reviewers also dislike *The Godfather* (dir. Francis Ford Coppola, 1972). If you apply their logic to other films, then *The Godfather* is criticizable because it represents Italians in a certain way. I can only shake my head at this line of reasoning, and at those well-meaning critics who think immigrants shouldn't be represented in a certain way. You can only please those people if you make a nice film about a well-integrated Pakistani family where the father votes for the Social Democrats and the daughter is studying to be a dentist. But who wants to see a film like that? My view is that if you don't offend some people, then you've probably made a bad film. At the very least, you can't assume that your film is bad just because it gives offense.

Redvall: Do you have the impression that directors with ethnic backgrounds other than Danish have a hard time getting their stories told in Denmark?

Shargawi: There are others like me, with a background that isn't purely Danish. But there isn't a well-defined underground that brings together people with other backgrounds. I almost wish there was. Not because I think revolt is needed, but because that kind of milieu would really sustain those who are trying to tell stories that are different, and that audiences here in Denmark and Europe more generally aren't used to. I'd like to see more such stories. At the moment it's very rare for someone with another ethnic background to make a film, but there's plenty of talent out there. I don't think people should get together just because they have the same skin colour. But those of us who share an interest in film do get to know each other and we do sometimes meet each other. And whether we like it or not, we do have something in common by virtue of our other ethnicities. That said, I'm quite hostile to the idea of being classified as some immigrant director. I'm a Danish director.

It's definitely the case that there's a need for people with another skin colour to be taken seriously in Danish film, because at the moment that's just not happening. When you see a Danish film, foreigners or the Other always have some very precise function in the narrative. They're never just there as characters who can drive the story forward. They have a function as a foreigner; as a *perker*, as a terrorist, as a well-integrated immigrant or refugee. They're not treated the way Danish actors or characters are. For that reason alone I'd like to see some new faces and hear some new voices. I'd like to see the platform being shared a bit more. And film practitioners with non-Danish backgrounds do need to talk about these things. We do need to ask what can be done to change the stereotypes that persist in Denmark. When it comes to alterity, Denmark is light years behind the rest of Europe – not least the Swedes – and the US. Well, behind most other places, I'd say.

Chapter 15

Simon Staho

Simon Stabo. Photography: Henrik Stenberg

Born 1972. Simon Staho has made most of his films in Sweden, with Swedish actors. His debut was the Danish feature film *Vildspor* (*Wildside*, 1998), with Mads Mikkelsen and Nicolai Coster Waldau as two friends who are reunited in Iceland, under dramatic circumstances. The short film *Nu* (*Now*, 2003) also features Mads Mikkelsen in a leading role, as a man who leaves his wife and child for his male lover (played by the Swedish star Mikael Persbrandt). *Now* was to become the first of a whole series of feature films that Staho would direct in Sweden, and it was the beginning of his collaboration with Persbrandt. The work with Persbrandt continued in *Dag och natt* (*Day and Night*, 2003), *Bang Bang Orangutang* (2005) and *Himlens hjärta* (*Heaven's Heart*, 2008). In *Day and Night* Persbrandt plays a divorced family man who goes on a trip to say goodbye to family and friends before his planned suicide. In this film the camera never leaves the car, and in *Bang Bang Orangutang* a car is also pivotal. In the 2005 film, Persbrandt plays a successful businessman who is driving around looking for love after having accidentally run over his young son with his car. *Daisy Diamond* (2007) was shot in Denmark, but with Swedish Noomi Rapace in the leading role. Rapace won both a Bodil and a Robert award as best actress for her performance as the single mother and aspiring actress Anna, who commits a gruesome act when it turns out to be difficult to achieve professional success with a young daughter in tow. In *Heaven's Heart*, 2008 and *Kärlekens krigare* (*Warriors of Love*, 2009) it's not easy being human either, although both films are about love. In *Heaven's Heart* two otherwise happy couples end up in a crisis caused by infidelity; in the black and white film, *Warriors of Love*, two young women choose life over death on account of their love for each other.

Feature films

2009	*Kärlekens krigare* (*Warriors of love*)
2008	*Himlens hjärta* (*Heaven's Heart*)
2007	*Daisy Diamond*
2005	*Bang Bang Orangutang*
2003	*Dag och natt* (*Day and Night*)
1998	*Vildspor* (*Wildside*)

Short films

2003	*Nu* (*Now*)

Redvall: You've described the director's job as a search for purity. What kind of purity do you try to achieve in your films?

Staho: Film can show an emotion in its pure state. You have to choose every image with precision, because in every image there's potentially a lot of impurity. I work hard to avoid that element of impurity. What is crucial to me is finding a way to portray the real or true emotion, the essence of a given feeling. Equally important to me is the idea of making films out of a sense of necessity.

In my latest film, *Warriors of Love*, I want to portray an extraordinarily strong love, a love so strong that the characters can't even begin to question their willingness to sacrifice everything, including their own life and that of others, for it. The love in question is like a volcanic force, so it's important to focus on its sheer strength, but I also wanted to depict this love as wonderfully *pure*. Many people think that ten violins equal great passion, and that 100 violins equal even greater passion. But that's emotional pollution. To me that sort of thing has nothing to do with the emotional intensity and purity that might motivate me to kill myself or others.

Redvall: What kind of necessity do you have in mind when you say that films should be based on a sense of necessity?

Staho: You have to be a servant of the story. The director's ego shouldn't dictate the nature of the film. Everybody should subjugate him- or herself to the point of the story. The way I see it making a film is not a matter of choice, at least not in some deep sense. There's no sensible reason why you'd expose yourself to the filmmaking process unless you felt that you absolutely had to, and not just for pragmatic reasons.

Nowadays there's a kind of sick way of looking at film, this view that you can somehow put all the ingredients together as you wish. But making films isn't an all-you-can-eat buffet. It's either or. Directors are being told they can do anything, but this is all part of an attempt to limit their power. Many people think they know as much as the director does about his or her film, but that's rather scary, because the director really *should* know best. Ultimately he or she is the only person with the magic formula.

Redvall: How are people trying to limit the power of the director?

Staho: This happens when the director is told that a film can be put together in many different ways. If you make it in this way, you'll get a lot of money, and if you make it in this way instead, you won't get as much, and perhaps even nothing at all. There are a lot of people who think they know how to make a film, and that it's possible simply to send the director into the field to get the images, and then to leave it to all sorts of other people to put the film together afterwards. There's this concept of the director as just a messenger boy who's sent out to shoot the images, and to do the hard work that no one else wants to do.

Nowadays the director is subdued, battered and reprimanded, because most people don't like the thought of the director having a secret that only the director knows. There's this fear of actually putting the film in the hands of the director, because then there's a loss of control. But that's exactly what used to happen, back in the earliest days of film's history, which is when masterpieces were made.

Redvall: You've previously said that most directors are forced to censor themselves, consciously or unconsciously, and that making films is a creative process that is influenced and even sullied by many different mechanisms. What do you have in mind when you speak about the filmmaking process in this way?

Staho: You're always being hit on the head with various possible consequences. If you do this, then this is how we'll punish you. Sometimes the threat of punishment is subtle, but it can also be very direct and brutal. I've actually been told things like 'If that's how you opt to make the film, we won't distribute it.'

To me test screenings are completely alien. They simply encourage the director to relinquish responsibility for the film. If you asked a painter to remove some brush strokes, or to change the colours in a painting, and all of this in response to art viewers' reactions, you'd be told that this was the craziest request ever. Should there be a little more red here? Is the theme actually wrong? Should viewers hear music here while looking at the picture? As far as I'm concerned that approach to filmmaking is contrary to everything that makes filmmaking meaningful. You don't stop a birth halfway and say: 'Let's just get a test audience in here. How should we turn this baby?'

Test screenings are a way of depriving the director of control. But the director has secret and exclusive knowledge of his film. Making a film is magical, because the director has a secret to which nobody else is privy. To me making films is a dictatorship. It's a beautiful dictatorship. It's the only remaining legitimate dictatorship. And it *has* to be a dictatorship.

Redvall: It sounds like you're an advocate of a robust auteurism. What do you think of the European auteur tradition and its place in Danish film today?

Staho: In the decades when the auteur idea had support, there was no doubt as to who controlled the filmmaking process. The *director* did. This was also the period when filmmaking produced directors who merit the term 'true masters'. If you look at the films of the past many years, no one has been proclaimed a master. Is that a coincidence? Or could this be connected to the fact that directors – much like singers who are not allowed to sing with their own voices – are being diminished, diminished and diminished yet again? At the moment it's hard to tell who's directed what, because films are supposed to look alike.

Films were once supposed to be a stone in your shoe. It was legitimate for there to be an element of resistance; or for a given director or film to be a bit like a stick of dynamite; or for the film to be in opposition to something; for the director to be an anarchist or a rebel; for people to throw things at the screen, or to boo the film, or simply to storm out of the cinema. When was the last time you saw spectators attack the screen or rip the cinema seats to pieces? Or get up and leave? Or hit the director? Spectators don't do that sort of thing anymore and the people involved in producing films would be scared stiff if they did. The immediate assumption would be that the film was bad, as evidenced by the audience's powerful response. Some time ago such reactions on the part of spectators would have prompted a quite different thought: 'Ah ha, the film must be really interesting since…!' The lack of civil courage that I'm drawing attention to affects the entire filmmaking process. Nowadays everybody is terrified of being hit in the face and of being told something to the effect of 'That was the worst bloody film I've ever seen.' But if you're not willing to run that risk, then you can't make a good film.

Redvall: The story in *Day and Night* takes place exclusively in and around the car that Mikael Persbrandt's character uses as a means of saying a last goodbye to his friends and family before commiting suicide. Your other films are similarly characterized by very few locations, and by storyworlds in which the main characters, and especially their faces, are central. Are we seeing evidence here of purely artistic choices relative to specific stories? Or is this style also the result of efforts to create a financially manageable production framework?

Staho: I can't say that it's not a conscious process. Hopefully what you're seeing is a happy confluence between what's financially possible and what's best for the story, in terms of narration. But I'm afraid I think too much in terms of budgets, because I've been brainwashed by all those people who are always shouting at me about the financial realities of filmmaking. However, I am sceptical of big budgets. When there's more money, you end up watering things down. To me making cheap films is a way of maintaining control over what I'm doing. That's why I try to find a way of telling the story that doesn't require me to beg for money from people who

Mikael Persbrandt and Maria Bonnevie in *Dag och natt* (*Day and Night*). Photography: Peter Widing.

will ask for my soul in return. In that sense the features you refer to are part of a conscious strategy aimed at retaining control.

After *Heaven's Heart* there was a sense that I should make a more expensive film next. But my own feeling was that I needed to do exactly the opposite; the most dangerous thing you can do is lean back, relax and repeat everything you've just done, but at far greater cost, with more glamour, greater ease and probably poorer results. It was important to avoid the trap of thinking that bigger is better, and to create serious obstacles for ourselves instead. We needed to opt for what was most difficult and painful, with regard both to the financing of the film and our own private finances. That's why I decided, on the very night *Heaven's Heart* opened, that the next film should be the cheapest yet. So I said to my producers and team that we had to test ourselves. We had to set ourselves the task of making a film that was entirely consistent with our conception of filmmaking, the most radical and pure film possible. *Warriors of Love* is the cheapest film we've ever made, and I've yet to be paid for making it. The same is true of my producer, scriptwriter and editor.

Redvall: Do you have to work with small budgets in order to achieve the purity that you're after?

Staho: Everything has a price. Why do things get more and more expensive? No one has ever come to me and said: 'I'm going to give you some money, and you then have to make sure you make the most real, most genuine and most uncompromising film.' That's the sort of thing that happens when you talk to a carpenter. You say: 'I want that chair to last for many years. I want you to put real craftsmanship into the making of this chair, and to think carefully about every piece of it.' No one says anything like that in the world of film. On the contrary. In the film world they say the equivalent of 'Get the cheapest plastic from China, and if the chair breaks it doesn't matter as long as people sit on it.'

More money always has a price. That price comes in many forms: having to use specific actors in the film, being required to refashion the film's ending, having to settle for a certain kind of music, having to make the film in colour or in black and white. And at the end of the day, all these compromises leave you thinking thoughts like: 'I hate myself and I want to die. I've sold out and I've contributed absolutely nothing to humanity because all I've done is produce something that 10,000 other people have made before me.' There's a pact with the devil in the world of film, and you enter into that pact the minute you want more money. I want to postpone the day, for as long as I possibly can, when I have to look at myself in the mirror and acknowledge that I've sold out.

Redvall: The purity that you talk about must be said to have a hard time in a society of visual abundance. Back in the days of the great auteurs, film had a unique status as an audio-visual media. Today we're bombarded with images and stories in many different media. Do you think it's harder to hold onto your own vision as a director nowadays?

Staho: You have to think carefully about what makes for an honest, true and genuinely narrative image. Which images tell a story? What is honest and what is dishonest about an image? You have to relate to these issues every single second of the filmmaking process. What does this camera movement add to the film? What's gained by having no camera movement? Every image in a film means something. Every image expresses a choice, and you can't leave that choice to others. You have to have a stance on everything that's within the frame. Everything!

Redvall: Where do you look for visual inspiration?

Staho: As far as I'm concerned it's about making myself less and less clever, less knowledgeable, so that I'm able to discard all the gear that envelopes me. It's a question of freeing myself from things I've allowed myself to be shaped by, as well as from things that have been stuffed down my throat, or that influence me at an almost unconscious level. I try to achieve a mode of expression that is genuinely my own. At some point you have to lay bare who you are. That's why I try to peel away everything that I've absorbed. I have to embrace myself in all my self-loathing and tell myself that things will neither get better nor worse than this. This is me. What's there may be infinitesimally small and insignificant, but it is, after all, me.

To me the capacity to expose yourself 100 per cent, like pure alcohol, is itself a great strength. As far as I'm concerned, it's the greatest gift a director can give to others. Whether a film is a good or a bad film doesn't interest me that much. I want to see a human being, a human being who exposes him- or herself by making a film. So what I'm trying to do is to become more and more stupid. I'm in the process of cleansing my inner self, of constantly cleansing this inner space. Life is a process in which you're served an enormous amount of garbage, so when I make a film I have to find a way of moving in the opposite direction, of discarding the rubbish.

Redvall: Your films often break with what is considered to be classical, invisible film style, by having characters peer straight into the camera, for example, or by violating the 180 degree rule. What's your attitude towards so-called classical film language?

Staho: You're always told you have to adhere to certain rules regarding what's good and bad, what you're allowed to do and what you aren't allowed to do. You're supposed to accept these rules, and then at some point you're supposed to say: 'Now I know how to make a film.' But you haven't asked yourself the relevant questions: what do *I* think the process should be like? Is it necessary to stick to the rules? Or are the rules limiting? You have to keep asking yourself those questions, and to dig out some kind of purity through that questioning process, a purity that no one else can give you. And then you have to hold on to that purity with all that you've got. There are no rules other than the ones you make yourself.

In *Warriors of Love* I jump over the line of action many times. Actually, up until just before we started shooting I was working with the idea of having a school class of fourteen year olds shoot the film, because I was looking for new images. We all know what a 'good' image looks like. I was curious to see what kind of images you'd end up with if you put someone behind the camera who hadn't been brainwashed with conventional film aesthetics. The result could no doubt have been good or bad, exciting or numbingly uninteresting, but just getting some new images would have been a victory.

So I wanted to knock down the wall of so-called good taste, which you're constantly up against and which the film crew can't escape from. Sometimes people just go ahead and adjust the light, or they do something they think you want, because they're thinking about the standard practices, and, after all, that's how you get a 'good' image. They make these adjustments without ever asking themselves questions like: does this really look good, or do I like it because we've all seen it before? Have we seen this before because this is what sells? It's important to work hard to get through that wall of good taste, because it's the most dangerous thing there is. What you think is good, and what you're constantly told is good are nothing more than accepted 'good' taste. But the style or image that's considered the worst might actually be the very best.

Redvall: Does this business of good taste also come into play in connection with story content and the nature of the characters, or is it mostly an issue that arises with reference to the images? Your films have dealt with suicide, incest and the murder of a young child, none of them obvious subjects if what viewers are looking for is the equivalent of sweets, as you once claimed.

Staho: My experience is that there's a bourgeois conception of what life should be like, and that conception doesn't exactly harmonize with the way life actually is for many people. By labelling people or stories or subject matter as 'dark' and 'hard' you make them safe, by containing them in a box, where they can be effectively hidden away. My films will of course be perceived as hard to watch if you have this idea that films should be a beacon of light in the darkness, or something you can relax with after a hard day at work. But I think that films should reflect the variety, richness, beauty and complexity that many people fortunately have within them.

With reference to a film like *Daisy Diamond* it was shocking to experience just how puritanical a lot of viewers are. I simply had no idea! I was shocked to discover the extent to which events that are actually part of a lot of people's lives still prompt this Victorian fearfulness, or narrowminded Puritanism. And that Puritanism functions as a convenient shield that protects the viewer from having to relate to the film as a film. But a film that is challenging is not some disease that needs to be cured, or from which the viewer requires protection.

Redvall: In Denmark there's sometimes talk about how Swedish films have a more serious tone than Danish films, not least on account of Ingmar Bergman and his influence. Do you think it's possible to talk about Swedish and Danish film in terms of film traditions?

Staho: There's nothing particularly Danish or Swedish about the films being made in this part of the world, as far as I'm concerned. Most of the films made in Denmark and Sweden are really American films.

Redvall: I'd like to get you to talk about your place within the Danish film scene. You've made most of your films in Sweden and you weren't trained at the National Film School of Denmark, where most feature film directors have learnt how to make films. What's it been like making films without the approval of the Film School or an established network of film practitioners?

Staho: I'm rather suspicious of the establishment. The establishment does everything to maintain power, and does this, among other things, by telling the surrounding world that you can only make films if you manage to get through the eye of a needle. That kind of talk simply instills fear in the aspiring filmmaker: if you don't get through the eye of the needle, you won't be able to be creative and make your films. That discourse is a way of removing the fearlessness that's needed to make an interesting film; a way of making the director afraid. Essentially what it says is: 'You alone are not enough. You don't have enough secret knowledge within you. You need something else.' Well, no, you don't! You just need yourself, and you'll only ever be able to rely on yourself. No one is really interested in your films. Basically nobody cares whether I make another film or not, so it makes no sense for me to think of myself as dependent on others.

The kind of keyhole tyranny I've described is a way of taming a director's wildness. There's a real fear these days of all that's unruly. Unruliness is no longer a quality, and you're constantly being called into the principal's office, where you're told that if you offend again you won't be allowed to make another film. But you make films to contest something, and as a form of opposition, not to confirm an existing state of affairs. It's always dangerous when somebody tells you that being a director is anything but a very, very lonely job. As a director you're completely on your own and you always will be. You're an outsider relative to the establishment, and there's no outsider community to be part of. It's easier to accept this if you're aware that filmmaking starts and ends with loneliness.

Redvall: Can you alleviate that loneliness through established collaborations? You've consistently worked together with scriptwriter Peter Asmussen, the producers Anne Katrine Andersen and Jonas Frederiksen and also the editor Janus Billeskov Jansen. What have those working relationships meant to you?

Staho: In each and every film, everyone who's involved should have a burning desire to make precisely that film. I have no sentimental attachment to other film practitioners just because they worked with me previously, and I think their relation to me is similar. I don't have any illusions about my being of particular interest to them. I'm very happy if they want to work on a new film I'm making, because they're interested in the *film*.

Redvall: What's the basis for your preference for working with Swedish actors?

Staho: Working with an actor is most interesting when the actor acts out of a sense of necessity; when the actor feels that being an actor is all important, a kind of calling requiring sacrifices of both a practical and emotional nature. Without that sense of necessity, which may manifest itself as a lack of balance, a kind of madness or an obsession, the process of working with an actor becomes less honest than it should be. That process is reduced to mere work, to an exercise, to emotional accounting, and this in turn reduces the film itself to something that is governed by common sense and petty bourgeois reasonableness. The actors I've been drawn to, and thus have chosen to work with, have had that element of madness, a mad willingness to make sacrifices. They've all had that unreasonable obsession with trying to find truth in their acting, whatever the cost. These actors want to expose themselves, to bare themselves, emotionally speaking, and all the way to the bone, if necessary. They're willing to strip away their defences, to act without vanity. Actors' beautiful madness draws me like a magnet, whereas vain, career-oriented actors reduce film to a soul-less industry. These are the reasons why I've worked with the actors I've worked with, and why the films have been shot in Sweden. Is it a coincidence that the actors have been Swedish? I have no personal connections to Sweden, so my choice of actors has been based on my sense of who, at a given moment in time, would be willing to go all the way, and to sacrifice more for the film than just blood, sweat and tears.

Redvall: You were part of an internet Christmas calendar project to which various directors contributed a film clip. Your contribution consisted of ten seconds of solid black, with the following accompanying statement: 'Film is beautiful, but it's got a disease called image and sound.' Would you like to describe that disease more fully?

Staho: Every choice you make when making a film destroys the beauty that's in the film at the outset. The perfect purity of the film as an idea is destroyed as soon as you start making it. Every image or sound that you produce tarnishes the original purity. When you're in the process of making a film it's all about protecting the film from unnecessary impurity. That's why you need to be aware of every choice you make. As an idea the film starts as a form of perfect, untarnished purity, and then it degenerates into something that's less than pure in the process of its realization. My task is to figure out how to add as little as possible to the black screen. The damned problem is that you have to add image and sound!

Four Swedish actors in *Himlens hjärta* (*Heaven's Heart*). On the left: Jakob Eklund and Lena Endre. On the right: Maria Lundqvist and Mikael Persbrandt. Photography: Bilduppdraget/Bo Håkansson.

Chapter 16

Paprika Steen

Paprika Steen. Photography: Jan Buus.

Born 1964. Paprika Steen graduated from the Odense Theatre Drama School in 1992. As a performer, she was initially associated with satire and comedy through her appearances in TV 2's popular *Lex & Klatten* (1997), a series that she also wrote, together with fellow performers Martin Brygmann, Peter Frödin and Hella Joof. Steen's theatre performances include roles at Dr Dante's Aveny Theatre and the Royal Danish Theatre. As a screen actress, Steen won international recognition for her role as Helene in the first Dogma 95 film, Thomas Vinterberg's *Festen* (*The Celebration*, 1998). She had smaller parts in two of the other Dogma brethren's films, Lars von Trier's *Idioterne* (*The Idiots*, 1998) and Søren Kragh-Jacobsen's *Mifunes sidste sang* (*Mifune*, 1999). In 2002 Steen won a Robert award and a Bodil as best supporting actress for her performance as the likeable mother and wife, Marie, in Susanne Bier's Dogma film, *Elsker dig for evigt* (*Open Hearts*, 2002), and a Robert award and a Bodil as best actress for her role as the controlling social worker, Nete, in Jesper W. Nielsen's *Okay* (2002). In 2007 she appeared as the alien teacher, Ulla Harms, in Ole Bornedal's family drama, *Vikaren* (*The Substitute*). Steen's status as one of Scandinavia's finest actresses was definitively established by her performance as the alcoholic actress Thea Barfoed in Martin Zandvliet's award-winning *Applaus* (*Applause*, 2009).

Paprika Steen has directed two feature films to date. *Lad de små born* (*Aftermath*, 2004) is a hard-hitting drama about a couple who struggle to cope with the loss of their daughter due to a drink-driving accident. In *Til døden os skiller* (*With Your Permission*, 2007) Steen combined grandiloquence and humour in a story about a man who is beaten by his wife. Paprika Steen is the daughter of the jazz musician Niels Jørgen Steen and the American-born Danish actress Avi Sagild. She lives together with producer Mikael Rieks, whose company Koncern Film produced *Applause*. Her son, Otto Leonardo Steen Rieks, played the role of one of Thea's sons in *Applause*.

Feature films

2007 *Til døden os skiller* (*With Your Permission*)
2004 *Lad de små børn* (*Aftermath*)

Hjort: One sometimes gets the feeling that people who have opted very clearly to be 'just' directors aren't that keen to see actors make the transition to directing. How did the directors you know respond to your decision to direct films?

Steen: The response was mixed. Some people thought that it made perfect sense for me to direct my own film. Thomas Vinterberg said 'Of course you should direct your own film.' But I have to admit that I found it really, really hard to tell all my director friends about my plans. In some ways I found my decision to become a director really embarrassing. I suppose it's because I have such enormous respect for them. But I think it's wrong to assume that there aren't enough resources to go around, and that actors who also direct are somehow diverting resources away from those people who are committed only to directing films. If you have a good script and you are a sufficiently interesting human being, you will be allowed to direct your film. That's the way it is in Denmark. And you'll never have to wait more than two years to be given a green light, unless you're very new or an unknown name in the business.

Hjort: What prompted you to make the shift?

Steen: People had been encouraging me to direct for years. Thomas Heinesen at Nordisk was one of several people who'd encouraged me along these lines. When I won all those prizes in 2002 – two Bodil awards and two Robert awards, as best actress and best supporting actress – I thought, 'Ok, now what?' Awards are both a curse and a blessing. The awards meant I suddenly had a lot of visibility, but I also felt that I'd hit a ceiling. So it seemed like a good time to contact Thomas about directing a film. I've known Thomas since I was sixteen. Not that we've been really close, but we've been part of the same network of friends. I knew he had a lot of experience, and I just knew he'd be a great producer for my first film.

Hjort: I gather that it wasn't that easy to get funding for *Aftermath*.

Steen: Yes and no. Vinca Wiedemann who was the first consultant I talked to felt that I needed to learn the craft of directing first, by making some commercials and such. I insisted that this really wasn't necessary, given the amount of experience I'd had in front of the camera. And since we weren't able to agree on this point, I went to the other consultant at the DFI, Morten Grunwald. I do think time has proven me right. *Aftermath* didn't become the kind of box-office success that someone like Susanne Bier is able to deliver, but then it also deals with some really heavy issues. *Berlingske Tidende*, *Jyllands-Posten* and *B.T.* gave *Aftermath* five stars, whereas *Politiken* and *Ekstra Bladet* gave it three. I think the film's reception shows that I was in that area where the people around me didn't really know if it was a serious choice, or just luck. I do love it, though, that the critics didn't agree; they don't either when it comes to the movies I love.

Hjort: *Aftermath* has a script by one of Denmark's most productive scriptwriters, Kim Fupz Aakeson. How did you end up collaborating with Fupz?

Steen: I got to know Fupz quite well through the reading rehearsals we did for *Okay* (dir. Jesper W. Nielsen, 2002), and I'd asked him whether he'd like to collaborate on a film at some point. When I talked to him about making a film, I emphasized that I wanted to make a darker film that resembled me more, rather than a film with somewhat lighter material. He then sent me a synopsis, about a page and a half. And that was basically the *Aftermath* story. I immediately said, 'That's exactly the film I want to make.' The idea was to make a film about loss, and about the fear of loss, and to touch spectators where they are most vulnerable in this regard. Loss can be so many things: missed opportunities, a loss of direction, confusion, a loss of perspective. We spent about a year talking about different aspects of the story, while Fupz developed the script. Some of what's in the script is mine, but most of it is his. I felt the script he wrote was so well developed that there was absolutely no reason to insist on a lot of changes. But Fupz does a lot of research as part of the scriptwriting process, so there tends to be a lot of factual material in his scripts. And that really bores me, which makes him laugh. But we did end up removing some of that kind of material. I also brought some intuitions I had as an actress to the scriptwriting process. Good actors don't need a lot of words, unless they're supposed to be very loquacious. So my contribution mainly consisted of excisions.

Hjort: Your remarks about research are interesting. There are several directors in Denmark these days who emphasize research as a crucial part of the filmmaking process.

Steen: I'm the exact opposite. I see myself as, or I insist on being, an artist who interprets. Like a painter interprets the sunrise or death. I look for a kind of abstractionism that doesn't come from a lot of research. Unless, of course, it's technical or something like that. My emphasis is on how I see things, because I'm the person telling the story. My job as a director is to convey my understanding of things. I think that research easily can kill a project and turn it into something that really belongs on TV and not in the cinema. I don't think it's important to go out and find people who can help you experience the pain you want to describe in your film. The pain that's in my films is not something I have to go out and find. It comes from me. I think you create a lot of distance between yourself and your art by emphasizing information and facts.

Hjort: What kinds of considerations guided your choice of cinematographer and editor when you started putting your crew together for *Aftermath*?

Steen: I knew Erik Zappon, the cinematographer, from my role as Nete in *Okay*. Actually, I've known him for ages, and have always really admired him. He's very calm, and his approach to lighting is really brilliant. And we worked well together, as actress and cinematographer. We ended up disagreeing quite a bit, though, when we started shooting. I wanted a fixed camera on a dolly, and he wanted to use a steadicam. We finally had one of those cathartic disputes, where we found a middle ground. Actually, to be honest, I got what I wanted. I think he did a fantastic job. We were shooting with 16 mm film and we had very little money. But he still managed to produce a film that has a lot of really fine aesthetic qualities.

As far as my editor is concerned, the original idea was to work with Susanne Bier's editor, Pernille Bech Christensen. But she wasn't really able to commit to my film because of other things. So suddenly I found myself without an editor. People were always talking to me about Anne Østerud, who is Jang's [Nicolas Winding Refn] editor. I was really nervous about meeting her, because I think she's a truly amazing editor, one of the best in northern Europe. As people we're very different, but she said yes, and she also did the editing for my second film, *With Your Permission*. She has an extraordinary ability to understand what the director is trying to do, whether she's working with me, with Jang or with someone else. She's also a classically trained musician, a really gifted person. Her contribution to both films has been huge.

Hjort: You do a really brilliant job of defining the two central characters, Britt (Sofie Gråbøl) and Claes (Mikael Birkkjær) really early in the film, especially the self-absorption that their grief produces. There's that scene in the car, just after they've left the support group. They're both chewing gum, and then Sofie Gråbøl sticks her gum up behind the mirror.

Steen: I'm glad you liked that. The gum was something that happened quite by accident. Sofie was chewing nicotine gum during one of our reading rehearsals, and she had to deliver some lines, so she just took out her gum and stuck it on the table. And I really liked the way she did it, because it gave her the kind of toughness that I was after. I wanted her to be less warm, less accommodating and slower to smile than she usually is. I suppose I wanted her to be more like me! Actually, that's what she told me at one point: 'You just want me to be you!' But that gesture helped to establish the matter-of-fact aspect of her character. By the way, do you notice that I do the same thing with chewing gum in *Applause*? That's a little gift to Sofie. I think she's a truly brilliant actress.

Hjort: Your first film is dedicated to your mother, the US-born Danish actress Avi Sagild, who died in 1995. You've sometimes talked about making a film about her. What would you focus on if you did?

Steen: Yes, I'd like to make a film about her, or to write a book about her. There are things about myself that I also see in her. She had enormous energy, but there was also a deep sadness there. I would focus on fate. At her funeral we couldn't help but ask ourselves whether she'd lived the life she wanted to live. There was so much potential that didn't get realized, in spite of all that drive, because there were so many things she hadn't worked through. As someone who's been very close to all the problems she had, it's clear that it's that tension between capacity and psychological obstacles that interests me. I realize that had I had a happy-go-lucky mother I probably wouldn't be the person I am. I'm sure the films I would have made would have been very different. There's an element of melancholy in many of the artistic projects I undertake. My mother's strange, complicated, almost secret inner life had a huge impact on me, of that I'm sure. I'm not Bergman, though, and I do have

Sofie Gråbøl as Britt, and Mikael Birkkjær as Claes in *Lad de små børn* (*Aftermath*). Photography: Erik Aavatsmark.

a certain distance from it all at this point. But I do think that all great artists have issues with other people, typically a mother or a father, and that these issues fuel the artistic work they do. I'm now talking about myself as though I were a great artist, without knowing whether I am. That's something you'll have to decide. But artists are often loners and eccentrics, people who've had all kinds of strange thoughts and eventually find a way of expressing them, because if they don't they'll simply go mad.

Hjort: Your mother's life was marked by long periods when she was unable to find work as an actress.

Steen: Yes, and she was in a state of deep depression for the last fifteen years of her life as a result.

Hjort: It's not hard to find parallels between your mother's life and Sidse Babett Knudsen's role as Bente in *With Your Permission*. Is that film in fact already a film about your mother?

Steen: Bente is my mother, quite simply; without the violence, though. Anders Thomas Jensen had shown me an initial script – and it was very much a script with his trademark traits, including humour – about a man who is being beaten by his wife. And then we spent two years developing the script. The original script was fine, had Thomas himself wanted to direct it, but I couldn't work with it the way it was. I had a lot of questions I wanted to see answered. Questions like: 'Why is Jan so bloody annoying?'; 'Why does Jan allow himself to get beaten?'; 'Why does Bente hit him?'; 'How did things end up going so wrong for these two people?' This is very much a story about self-deception, about a Salieri/Mozart-style rivalry within a marriage, about the strange lives of artists.

The home I grew up in didn't have some of the things that characterize Jan and Bente's life together, but it was equally strange. My mother would invite workers up for a chat, as Bente does in the film. So when we came home from school there'd be some workers sitting on the couch, and my mother would want us to get to know them. She was a communist. But she was also the biggest snob imaginable, and would feel very distinguished about any offers I got from the Royal Danish Theatre. She loved the idea of being in the spotlight. What I'm describing here is just one part of her, and very much the person she became towards the end of her life. Because we've all heard the stories about how wonderful she once was. She came to Denmark as an eighteen year old, learnt Danish and got accepted into the Royal Danish Theatre's Drama School. I still have a letter from Poul Reumert, in which he talks about how beautiful her Danish was.

My mother is basically the person who got political theatre off the ground in Denmark. And her decision to do so pretty much wrecked her career. For years I was ashamed of all the dark and complicated things in her life, but at a certain point I decided to focus on just how much she's actually inspired me. She was extraordinary, and I wanted to look at all that complexity, without hatred and

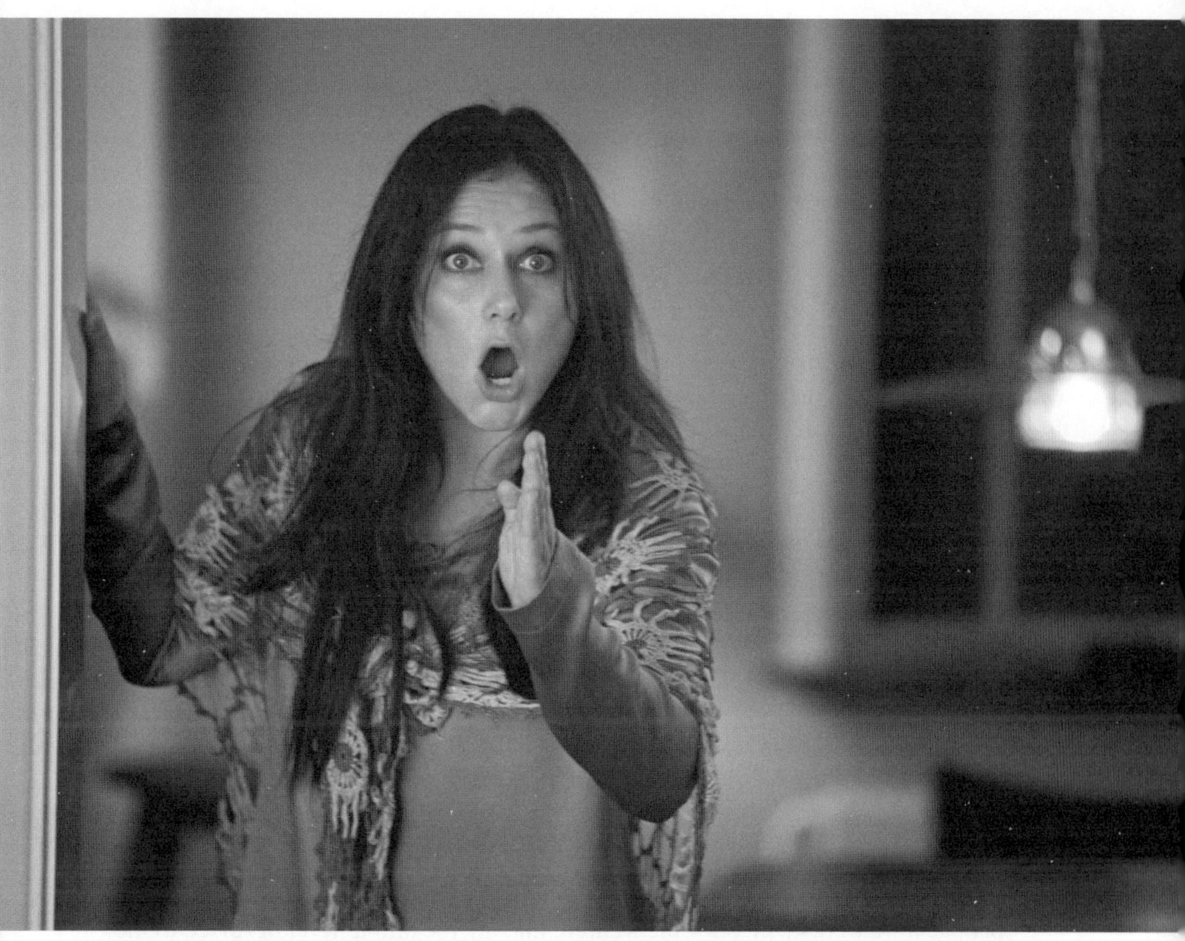

Sidse Babett Knudsen as Bente in *Til døden os skiller* (*With Your Permission*). Photography: Erik Aavatsmark.

contempt, but equally without excessive love. My mother was really high much of the time, because she took loads of prescription drugs. Every now and again she'd sort of wake up and be lucid and then she'd start to tell stories. And Paprika was the person she'd tell the stories to. It was all very dramatic and then afterwards she'd collapse on the sofa. It was a strange experience trying to create a character who resembled her in so many ways. As I said, my mother was American. And although her Danish was really excellent, she'd come up with these extraordinary phrases, by inverting words and such. In the film Bente says all kinds of strange things. Suddenly, out of the blue, she says 'Black is the colour of fantasy.' I don't recall my mother ever actually saying that, but it's the kind of thing she easily could have said. She was a funny, vivid, strong woman, who fell into the hole of her own weaknesses and the mediocracy of our society. I believe that story is worth telling again and again.

Hjort: You played Helene in Thomas Vinterberg's award-winning Dogma film, *Festen* (*The Celebration*, 1998), and you had small parts in von Trier's *Idioterne* (*The Idiots*, 1998) and Søren Kragh-Jacobsen's *Mifunes sidste sang* (*Mifune*, 1999). Has your experience of Dogma, as a screen actress, influenced how you work as a director?

Steen: I was a bit like a small child who's only ever tasted vegetables and knows nothing about all the foods that are bad for you. The Dogma films were my first real attempt at screen acting. So I just assumed that the way we were doing things was pretty much how one made films. Of course I knew that there was a set of rules, but I didn't really give them that much thought or think they were that important. You have to remember that when we were shooting *The Celebration* we didn't for a second think that we'd end up at Cannes with it. We thought the film would be seen by about five people, if we were lucky. So while we were making the film it never occurred to me that the day would come when I'd be asked a whole lot of questions about Dogma. At some level I was probably a bit sceptical. All I knew was that I wanted to do something new. I was tired of doing satirical and comic work as a live performer, and I wanted to do something more dramatic. The Dogma films made that shift possible. I did learn from working with Thomas, Lars and Søren. Of course I did. I watched them, and absorbed the things I felt they were especially good at. And then I've brought a lot of myself to the director's role as well. But I wouldn't say that my work as a director is influenced by Dogma. Not really.

Hjort: What did you learn from the directors you've worked with?

Steen: I think that being matter of fact and down to earth is important, also as an actor. I learnt very early on that a lot of acting for the camera ends up on the floor, not in the film. You can stand there and feel all kinds of things, but that doesn't mean the take will end up in the film. Thomas and Lars have certain things in common as directors, although they're very different as people. They both tell the actors when they think the take really sucks, and they manage somehow to do this in a really loving and witty way. I loved their honesty. I've always been very frank about when I thought something was good and when it was rubbish, but I'd always been made to feel that this was a flaw. So I've spent an enormous amount of energy on learning how to keep my mouth shut. And suddenly I was working with these directors who were extremely sensitive and very human, but also very direct and honest. I've also learnt a lot about directing from Susanne Bier. She's very good at getting actors to let go of things. She might say, 'Try doing the scene without smoking', or without swearing, without doing the things that have become habitual. And then of course I learnt all kinds of things from life itself, and I also bring all of that to the director's role, and a lot of personal traits. I can't lie. I can conceal things, or keep a secret, but I can't lie. I can't say that somebody performed brilliantly if I thought the acting was really bad. I just can't. So actors either feel very, very safe with me, or they feel really anxious about me. And that's the way it is with all my colleagues. It's either/or. The actors in my first film called me Leni Riefenstahl while we were shooting. It was just for fun, but the joke got going because everyone agreed that my directing style was really controlling. I wasn't quite that way with *With Your Permission*, but to be honest I think that, as a director, my inclination is probably to be quite controlling.

Hjort: When you do the casting for your films, do you find yourself drawing on your background as an actress?

Steen: Absolutely not. I find Denmark a really small country when it comes to casting. I really don't think there's that much talent. I know I'm not supposed to say that and that there are people who say the contrary, but that's how I feel. I think Danes tend to think that there are a whole lot of people like Sofie Gråbøl, but there aren't. There are three or four people in Denmark who are at her level. I find the casting process insanely difficult, but also very interesting. In the case of *Aftermath* I test screened everybody, including Sofie. No, that's not quite true. I didn't test screen Søren Pilmark. I didn't quite dare do that. Nor did I test screen Lena Endre or Lars Brygmann. I'd done so many things with Lars, and besides, in *Aftermath* I only needed him for four days, and he knew exactly what he was supposed to do. But the people for all of the big parts – Mikael Birkkjær and Laura Christensen and Karen-Lise Mynster – I test screened them all. Some of them are far more experienced than I am, so it was really quite a transgressive thing to do. But it actually worked very nicely. In the case of *With Your Permission* I test screened some of the actors for the smaller parts, and worked with a professional caster. I hadn't done that with *Aftermath*. I spent a lot of time talking to people about how they saw the script. I'd read once that Sidney Lumet had said that if an actor has too many objections to a script, he or she shouldn't be given the part. And I think that's absolutely right. But I knew from the beginning that I wanted Lars Brygmann to play Jan in *With Your Permission*. I think he's simply fantastic.

Hjort: If we look at your career as an actress, you've played the following key roles as a screen actress: Helene in *The Celebration*, Nete in *Okay*, Ulla Harms in Ole Bornedal's *Vikaren* (*The Substitute*, 2007) and now Thea in *Applause* (dir. Martin

Zandvliet, 2009). You've received praise for your performances in all of these roles, but I'd like to focus on Nete. Matter of fact, efficient and domineering, Nete took you in a new direction, and clearly established your range as an actress.

Steen: There's no doubt that that role was a milestone in my career. It was really the first time a director acknowledged my temperament and decided he could make good dramatic use of it, instead of feeling uneasy about it. Instead of being the sourpuss in a minor role, I was now the lead, for the first time. *Okay* was a film that was both serious and funny, and it was the first of what would become a whole slew of kitchen-sink style films. Without wanting to sound arrogant I have to say that when I look back at my career, I've been involved in a lot of things that were milestones in one way or another, and that ended up inspiring others. But that's a good thing I think, when I look back.

Hjort: Could you be more specific?

Steen: The satirical theatre group *Lex & Klatten* is a good example. That was the first attempt, at least in Denmark, at a completely absurdist form of humour. We had four people against a white backdrop, doing the most absurd things. Søs and Kirsten [Søs Egelind and Kirsten Lehfeldt] had done some things that pointed in that absurdist direction, but their work was still quite character-based, unlike ours. And when I started doing theatre, the way Danish was spoken on the stage really started to shift. Line Knutzon, an enormously talented contemporary playwright, played a really important role in all of this, because she used language in a new and different way, and helped to facilitate a different sense of what was humorous. Knutzon contributed the plays that helped to define new Danish theatre, and I contributed a new way of acting. It was a very expressive style of acting, and in the beginning it was almost caricatural or cartoon-like. I liked the idea of doing things that were extremely Danish, while acting in a way that was far more American, and then involving the Danish language and specific Danish terms in that cultural mix. I developed a particular style of acting that others then imitated. I know that many of the applicants to the theatre schools ended up performing bits of various roles that I'd performed, partly because Line had written such great texts, but also because I'd played the parts convincingly enough to make them dare to do the same thing. People who saw me perform felt that they were watching a real human being, and not some theatrical construction. And on those few occasions when I've been given roles in classic plays, my performances were seen as offering a new take on those classic roles. I see myself as a rebel, and for a long time I saw myself as an outsider. I've always wanted to do things differently. This is also true of my work as a director. When I started directing films, the idea was to do something new and different. *With Your Permission* is a good example. Sure, it's a film with a script by Anders Thomas Jensen. And, sure, there are some actors in it whom we've seen before. But it's still something really different, because that film is a mixture of all kinds of things, melodrama and humour, subtle comedy and opera, among other things. I actually wanted to make a kind of modern Chaplin film, a contemporary *Modern Times* (1936) or a contemporary *Great Dictator* (1940), or *Limelight* (1953). I wanted to tell an impossible love story about two people who do actually end up together, and about a strange tramp-like person who ends up figuring things out, and all of this with lots of exaggerated emotions. I don't think anybody ever really realized what it was I was trying to do, but that was the idea. Maybe it didn't succeed perfectly, but at least I tried not to do 'the right thing'.

Hjort: You've received a lot of recognition internationally for your remarkable performance as Thea in *Applause*. The film was produced by your husband Mikael Rieks, so I take it you were quite involved in the entire production process, including the early phases when Mikael was developing the project together with director Martin Zandvliet and scriptwriter Anders Frithiof August.

Steen: It was Mikael who found Martin and Anders and decided he really wanted to do something together with them. Mikael is a really talented producer. He's been producing documentaries for years, but *Applause* is his first feature film, produced through his new company, Koncern Film, which he created in 2008. Mikael, Martin and Anders had been working on *Applause* for about a year by the time they really started to involve me. But then again, I'd sort of been involved throughout, because so many of their discussions took place in my kitchen, which is where they developed a lot of their ideas.

Hjort: The film received support from New Danish Screen, a subsidy scheme that emphasizes the idea of creative teams and an understanding of the consultant as a sparring partner who is genuinely involved in various phases of the filmmaking process.

Steen: When Mikael, Martin and Anders first approached New Danish Screen, the idea was to produce a one-hour film. But they soon discovered that their story required a much longer film. I knew early on that that was the case, but didn't say anything. I wasn't really involved in the discussions with Jakob Høgel at New Danish Screen, but my impression is that he was very supportive and helpful. For example, when Mikael first suggested the idea of producing the film as a full-length feature film, Jakob expressed some legitimate concerns. He felt that, as a first-time director, and one who hadn't gone through years of training at the National Film School, Martin might end up feeling really weighed down by it all. But Jakob allowed himself to be persuaded. So I think his input was really thoughtful and constructive, and that he was a good listener.

Hjort: *Applause* includes some really remarkable footage of you in a live theatre performance of Edward Albee's *Who's Afraid of Virginia Woolf?*

Steen: Yes, I was playing Martha in *Who's Afraid of Virginia Woolf?* at Østre Gasværk in the early part of 2008 and we were going to start shooting in September. We decided it might actually be quite nice to see the lead character 'in action', given that she was an actress. So they filmed me for two days, with two cameras. That way Martin would have the material to work with. Initially the idea wasn't really to include sequences with me saying a lot of lines. But then they started the editing process, and they could see how good it would be to include more footage of the live performance. We didn't have a clue whether Albee would let us use the material, and getting the rights cleared was a long and arduous process. In that sense my husband really took quite a risk.

Hjort: Your son, Otto Leonardo Steen Rieks, plays the elder son in *Applause*. With your husband producing, and your son in a central role, *Applause* was very much a family endeavour. What was it like to work with your son in a professional capacity?

Steen: There's a Cassavetes connection here. The way we worked, our insistence on the local, on scenes shot indoors, all of this was very much inspired by Cassavetes. And it was what Martin wanted. One of my best friends is Xan Cassavetes, the daughter of John Cassavetes and Gena Rowlands. She's told me a lot of stories about what it was like to be included in their films as a child. Otto had to compete against about 40 other children, in a casting process. So in that sense he didn't have an edge. But he's really, really good. And he certainly thought it was a lot of fun. There was one day that was a bit rough, and where there was some mother/son stuff going on. But I'm pretty sure he'll end up pursuing acting, or something related, when he's older. I won't push him though.

For God's sake 'No!'

Hjort: What are your plans for the future? Do you see yourself as collaborating further with your husband? Will you be pursuing acting or directing next?

Steen: Definitely. If he has roles to offer me that suit me. That won't always be the case, of course. Right now what's on the agenda is a lot of festival appearances in connection with *Applause*. And I have to say that after my role as Thea in *Applause* I feel that I want to do more acting in the near future. But I'd like to direct again, if I come across a script I really like. I've been talking to Kim Fupz Aakeson and to Anders August about doing something together, and we're just beginning to explore some ideas. I'm also in the process of developing a TV series. I'm represented in the United States and in Sweden, both as an actor and as a director. But it's not as though I'm being inundated with offers. This year I've worked exactly one month. I've become too much of an institution or something. People think I'm involved in any number of things and that I'm always working, but that's just because the films I've been in have done quite well. Much of my working life takes place outside Denmark. I'm very much an established figure in a film festival context, where I seem to have some kind of iconic status and represent a certain concept of Scandinavian quality; or so they tell me when I'm at the festivals. But work is important for me, very much so. It's easy to become apathetic if you're not working, and it's also hard to pay the bills! But everything comes in waves, like love, peace and great movies.

Chapter 17

Jacob Thuesen

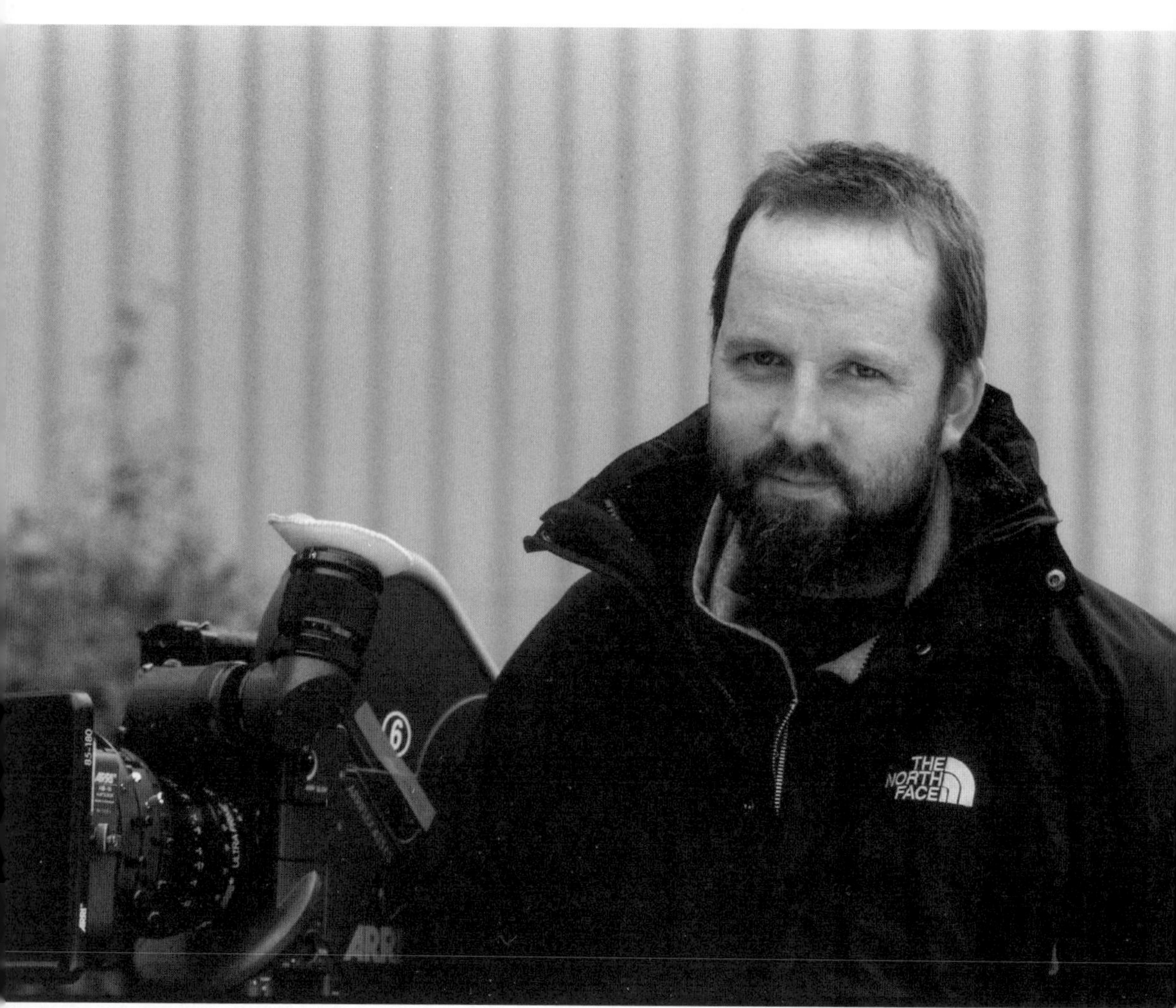

Jacob Thuesen. Photography: Ole Kragh-Jacobsen.

Born 1962. Jacob Thuesen graduated as an editor from the National Film School of Denmark in 1991. He worked as an editor on numerous films – among them Lars von Trier's *Riget* (*The Kingdom*, 1994) – before directing his first film, *Under New York*, in 1997. The award-winning film is a documentary about a police officer and a homeless man in New York's subway. Thuesen has also directed the documentaries *FCK – Sidste chance* (*Last Chance*, 1998), about the football club FC Copenhagen, and *Freeway* (2005), which paints a mosaic-like portrait of life, on and alongside the freeways around Los Angeles. His first fiction film, *Livsforsikringen* (*The Life Insurance*, 2003), is an absurdly grotesque and stylistically vivid comedy, about a man who dies while taking out a life insurance policy. This film was followed by *Anklaget* (*Accused*, 2005) which experiments with point-of-view narration as it tells a story about a man who is accused of having abused his daughter. *Accused* has won a number of international awards, among them European Discovery of the Year. In 2007, Jacob Thuesen directed *De unge år: Erik Nietzsche sagaen del 1* (*The Early Years: Erik Nietzsche Part 1*), based on Lars von Trier's script about his time at the National Film School of Denmark.

Feature films

2007 *De unge år: Erik Nietzsche sagaen del 1* (The *Early Years: Erik Nietzsche Part 1*)
2005 *Anklaget* (*Accused*)

Medium-length films

2003 *Livsforsikringen* (*The Life Insurance*)

Documentaries

2005 *Freeway*
1998 *FCK – Sidste chance* (*Last Chance*)
1997 *Under New York*

Television

2009 *Blekingegade* (TV series, five episodes)

Work as editor (selective list)

2008 *Lille soldat* (*Little Soldier*; dir. Annette K. Olesen)
2008 *Gaven* (*The Gift*; dir. Niels Gråbøl)
2003 *It's All About Love* (dir. Thomas Vinterberg, additional editor)
2001 *P.O.V.* (dir. Tómas Gislason)
2000 *Den højeste straf* (*Maximum Penalty*; dir. Tómas Gislason)
1997 *Sekten* (*Credo*; dir. Susanne Bier)
1996 *Haïti. Uden titel* (*Haiti. Untitled*; dir. Jørgen Leth)
1994 *Riget* (*The Kingdom*; dir. Lars von Trier)
1994 *Fra hjertet til hånden* (*Heart and Soul*; dir. Tómas Gislason)

Thuesen has also edited about 2000 commercials and trailers.

Jørholt: After you graduated from the National Film School of Denmark, you soon came to be known in the business as 'Mr Fast Edit'. Why is that?

Thuesen: When I started out as an editor, film language was different. There'd been the Russian montage school in the 1920s, of course, but in Denmark, the montage concept as such didn't emerge until the 1980s when a small group associated with Tómas Gislason, Trier's old editor, started to think about editing in more dynamic terms. I edited Tómas' portrait of Jørgen Leth, *Heart and Soul*, and that gave me the reputation of being an editor who made films that were more dynamic than was the norm in Danish cinema at the time.

Jørholt: You also edited the first four episodes of Lars von Trier's *The Kingdom* which is renowned for its very distinctive and unconventional editing style. How much influence did you have on the editing style of *The Kingdom*?

Thuesen: Quite a lot. I guess Godard and the directors associated with the French New Wave were the first to experiment with jump cuts, but later on, this way of editing was taken up by American television, in the series *Homicide*, for example. Because of *Homicide* and Tómas' film about Jørgen Leth, that way of editing was not unfamiliar to me. The first scene I edited for *The Kingdom* was a kind of morning meeting involving a lot of people inside a room – and after that, I had a very clear sense of how the material could be edited. I was hired in a way that generated quite a bit of tension between Trier and myself, but the moment you decide that it's OK to cut in time within each scene, as a director you simply have to let go. Which he did. But not without conflict. I did actually have a free hand. He didn't look over my shoulder all the time, while I was editing.

Jørholt: You once said that prior to Trier, *Pelle Erobreren* (*Pelle the Conqueror*; dir. Bille August, 1987) and Henning Camre, Danish film was nothing. Can you elaborate on that?

Thuesen: By the start of the 1980s, it had been almost twenty years since Dreyer made his last film, and then, suddenly, Bille August drew international attention to Danish film with *Pelle the Conqueror* which won both an Academy Award and the Golden Palm at Cannes. *Pelle the Conqueror* is quite a traditional film, but it's also a film that takes itself seriously.

At the same time, Henning Camre was appointed Head of the Film School, and he also took both himself and film seriously. That kind of attitude was really rare in the Danish cinema milieu back then. And he did things in a very determined, almost dictatorial way, the result being that politicians who wouldn't normally have touched art with a ten-foot pole lowered their defences and allocated a lot of money to Danish film. Camre essentially succeeded in creating a school where film is seen as a form of art, and as being just as important as the other arts.

It was in that context that Lars made his graduation film, *Befrielsesbilleder* (*Images of a Relief*, 1982) which won numerous awards. *Images of a Relief* may in many ways be a rip-off of Tarkovsky but in a Danish context, it was absolutely unique and ended up challenging the entire Danish film milieu: 'Take that! See if you can beat that!'

Jørholt: The impression you give here of the Film School seems rather at odds with the one that is conveyed through *The Early Years: Erik Nietzsche Part 1*, which is Lars von Trier's take on his time at the School.

Thuesen: The Erik Nietzsche film is fiction. It's entertainment and is only partly related to reality. The fact that Lars was able to make the best graduation film ever to come out of the National Film School of Denmark is the best proof that he had an absolutely free hand. But it's difficult to make a film in which a film student encounters resistance but also gets everything he wants, so Lars and I consciously chose to focus on the obstacles.

Speaking of the revival of Danish cinema, it's important not to forget Ole Bornedal's *Nattevagten* (*Nightwatch*, 1994). Whereas Lars' film was in English and Bille August left Denmark soon after his international success with *Pelle*, *Nightwatch* made Danish viewers realize that something was happening in Danish cinema. That film was unlike any other Danish film, and it introduced Danish viewers to a new generation of young actors. Bornedal took emerging Danish acting talent seriously and he was also very deliberate about his use of genre formulae. One of the big problems in Danish cinema up until that point was that many directors were unclear about the nature of the genre they were working with on a given production.

And then there was Dogma 95, which was visionary and a stroke of genius. Dogma stimulated the directors' previously dormant energies, and it forced them to express themselves in a way that was easy to understand and didn't cost a fortune. These are all things that can help a film industry to flourish. Eventually, Dogma got watered down, and at this point the tendency is to return to more traditional kinds of film. But compared to earlier, the quality is really significantly improved, and we've seen the emergence of a lot of new and pretty confident directors, people like Christoffer Boe, Simon Staho and Henrik Ruben Genz.

Jørholt: You made your directorial debut in 1997, with the documentary *Under New York*. What made you take the step from editing to directing?

Thuesen: The main reason is probably that *The Kingdom* was such a tough experience. Partly because of all the personal conflicts, but also because the entire process with the Danish Broadcasting Corporation was pretty trying. Right from the beginning they weren't exactly happy with the series. And after having edited Tómas Gislason's portrait of Jørgen Leth, I thought that I'd investigated pretty much all the nooks and crannies of film editing. I felt there was no more fun to be had in an editing room. I felt empty, exhausted. And at that point, Nikolaj Scherfig said something like 'Why don't we just go to the United States and make a film?'

At the time, the New York subway system was fascinating because there were still so many homeless people making use of it, for shelter. So if you took the subway you'd meet lots of different kinds of people. So the film was motivated by a mixture of things, our desire to make a tourist film and a certain amount of social concern. The question of social concern was not, however, what

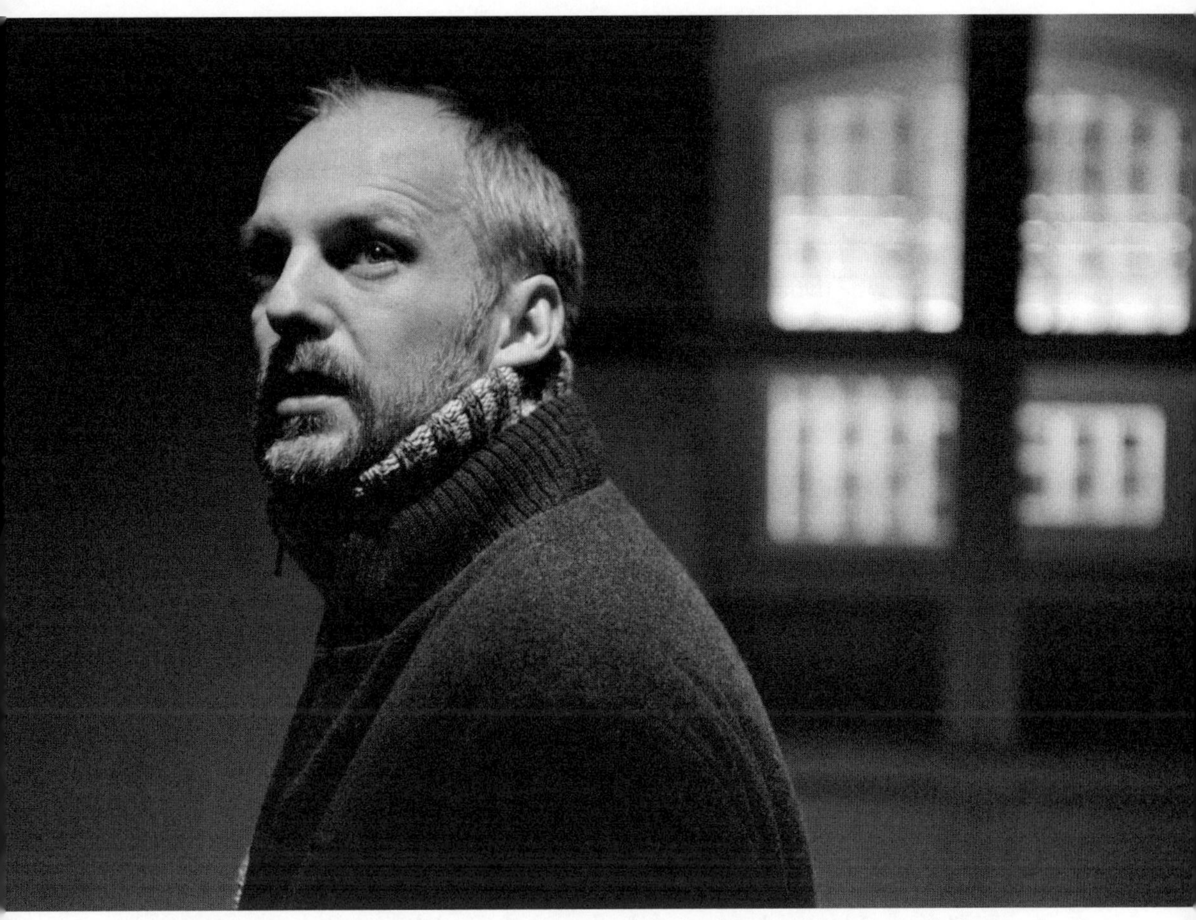

Troels Lyby plays the father who is accused of having abused his daughter in *Anklaget* (*Accused*). Photography: Ole Kragh-Jacobsen.

mattered most to me, and here and there the film gives way to pure observation in an almost Jørgen Leth-like manner. There's that fascination with simply just watching another human being.

I see *Under New York* as an extension of the work I'd done on Tómas Gislason's *Maximum Penalty*, *P.O.V.* and on the Jørgen Leth film, in the sense that it explores the dynamic dimensions of film as a medium. No one in Danish film is as interested in those dimensions as Tómas Gislason. Danish documentaries tend to show a real lack of understanding when it comes to this aspect of film – I'm not criticizing their subject matter, just their less than dynamic quality – but in a way, the same can be said about the feature films.

Jørholt: One could see *Freeway* as a sort of companion piece to *Under New York*, but at the same time the films are very different from each other.

Thuesen: Yes, they are. Even though social issues are not the main point of *Under New York*, the film does raise them. *Freeway*, on the other hand, is an experiment with the spectator who is invited simply to sit back and float along with the images. If you want to, you can also find an element of social critique in *Freeway* though, a critique of the never-ending and utterly meaningless construction of freeways.

Jørholt: Your first venture into the realm of fiction was the medium-length film *The Life Insurance* which can perhaps be described as Beckett meets Kafka in a hyper-expressive universe. How did you experience the step from documentary to fiction film, and especially the new task of directing actors?

Thuesen: I found myself really groping in the dark. After having looked at monitors for twenty years or so, I had absolutely no idea about directing. It was like learning Chinese. I had to begin completely from scratch. The only redeeming factor about that project was that I was able to control what happened in front of the camera. As an editor I'd had to work with the available material, and when you're making documentaries, you often spend a lot of time just waiting for the protagonists to do something. But now I could say, 'What if you entered from here instead of from there?' or 'What if we lowered the camera to the floor?' That was a fantastic experience for me.

When I was given the opportunity to make *The Life Insurance*, I didn't really feel like making a fiction film. I was very blasé about it, and thought of fiction as a petty bourgeois thing that really didn't interest me that much. At the time, I was very into the ultimately rather boring theory that since documentaries can be fictionalized, there's no need to make fiction films.

Jørholt: You've claimed that your approach to fiction filmmaking involves a kind of investigative stance. Does that mean that there are certain similarities in the way you work with fiction and documentary films?

Thuesen: Investigation is a very neutral word, but what I mean is that I just don't see the point of making a film if the result is known beforehand. The very process of

Jonatan Spang as the young Erik Nietzsche/Lars von Trier in *De unge år: Erik Nietzsche sagaen del 1* (*The Early Years: Erik Nietzsche Part 1*). Photography: Per Arnesen.

making the film can make you wiser. The best fiction films have always been tentative about their own subject matter. A film has to some extent to be an exploratory process, and if it isn't, people will soon notice that it's not. Even in a James Bond film, the audience will be able to tell whether the filmmakers made the film because they had to, or whether their approach to the material was somehow exploratory.

Jørholt: One does indeed sense an investigative attitude in *Accused*. What were your reasons for making a film about incest?

Thuesen: I don't know anybody who's been abused, so the investigation was primarily about trying to understand a subject that I knew next to nothing about. Of course, incest is awful, but that wasn't what triggered me. Kim Fupz Aakeson, the scriptwriter, and I had decided to tell the story exclusively from one of the characters' point of view, and I found this approach really exciting. We ended up opting for the father's POV, and the challenge was to think through the various scenarios you'd experience if you – I myself, for instance – were accused of something like that. How would you react? At the outset, we didn't know whether the father would turn out to be guilty or not. I only decided that at the very last moment.

Jørholt: The audience certainly doesn't know whether or not he's done the things he's accused of until the very last moments of the film. But because the film aligns the viewers with the father and has us experience everything with and through him, we cannot believe that he could be guilty. You have, however, managed to keep a tiny element of doubt alive throughout the film, and this makes the viewer extremely attentive to details. The way you work with the narrational distribution of knowledge recalls Hitchcock.

Thuesen: Having paid 70 DKK for a ticket, most viewers expect to be able to think the best of the central protagonist. I tried to play with that basic assumption, which is also about trusting the director, by only letting viewers see what the father sees. In and of itself that choice is a kind of declaration of sympathy. In that sense, I have indeed stolen from Hitchcock. Think of *Psycho* (1960), where we stay with Anthony Perkins in the bathroom, and watch him clean the floor after he's stabbed Janet Leigh. That has to be the ultimate declaration of sympathy. We don't run away in terror but stay put there with the protagonist. And through him we experience what must be done in order to remove all traces of the crime.

Jørholt: The total humiliation of the protagonist at the end of the film also made me think of Pasolini, *Accatone* (1961), for example. In that film the complete degradation experienced by the protagonist has a certain pathos. Were you consciously inspired by Pasolini?

Thuesen: I thought a lot about Pasolini, whom I admire immensely. One of the fantastic things about Pasolini is that he was able to free himself entirely from good taste. He didn't have a problem merging a pitiful cinematic language with Bach, which is what he did in *Accatone* and *Il vangelo secondo Matteo* (*The Gospel According to St Matthew*, 1964). Actually, the music we use at the end of *Accused* is a sampled version of Bach that has been combined with something else. In those two films, Pasolini succeeds in turning something that looks quite ordinary into something huge and utterly universal. A certain cinematic naïveté is what makes this possible, and I find that absolutely fantastic. To me, that simplicity is a huge strength. It's what makes *The Gospel According to St Matthew* and Pontecorvo's *La battaglia di Algeri* (*The Battle of Algiers*, 1966) so great.

Jørholt: The Erik Nietzsche film tells Lars von Trier's story. Trier wrote the script, lends his voice to the voice over and we even see some of his earliest films. To what extent is this a Trier film, and to what extent is it your film?

Thuesen: It's a Trier script, but from the moment I got the script, it was my film. At the time, Lars was suffering from a nervous breakdown, which is probably why he kept away from the set. In any case, he didn't interfere at all, and I'm really grateful that he didn't, because I believe he intended the film to be more of a comedy along the lines of *Direktøren for det hele* (*The Boss of It All*, 2006), i.e. extremely dry and understated. That would probably have been fine had it been a Trier film, but I can't make a film the way I think he would have made it. So in the end it became a mixture of the subtle humour that I think characterizes *The Life Insurance* and then the intellectual dimension of the characters' lines. Also, I like to dwell on details that probably don't deserve as much attention as I give them. When Søren Malling explains a painting by Hieronymus Bosch, I just want to stay with him until the painting makes him start to cry. From a dramaturgical point of view, the scene is not important; it's just that I like to lose myself in it.

Jørholt: In 1997, you created the production company Tju Bang Film with Søren Fauli, Niels Gråbøl and Per K. Kirkegaard (who'd edited both *Accused* and the Erik Nietzsche film). Why did you create your own company? And why did you later sell it to SF Film, one of the biggest players in Danish cinema. Are small companies no longer viable?

Thuesen: Originally, all we wanted was a place where we could edit films without anyone interfering. For example, when you're producing a documentary film, it's simply impossible to do the editing in three months, even though that's what the producer wants. So, we wanted a place that would be available to us for, say, ten months. Subsequently we decided to establish a production company that would specialize in documentaries and would be managed by the creative people themselves instead of by producers. We wanted some space, quite literally a physical environment, where we'd be able to sit and simply talk about the films we were making. That's something that isn't sufficiently emphasized in the Danish filmmaking milieu.

And yes, small companies are no longer the solution they once were. Each and every little film production company has its own editing room. Why don't we have some large, central editing facilities? The entire Danish film scene is so small, and yet there's such an abundance of talent, so it's really time to create some structures that reflect all this. It would be infinitely better if all the small companies could be subsumed beneath a much larger umbrella structure, and if people could figure out how actually to talk to each other. When Nordisk Film bought Zentropa, I was naïve enough to believe that the two companies would come up with a new and exciting strategy. But that didn't happen. The whole thing was just some financial arrangement.

Jørholt: Don't you directors talk to each other? Do you never ask a colleague for advice if you're experiencing some kind of problem while making a film?

Thuesen: Personally, I have a habit of inviting some of my friends to watch my films at an early stage, and the same goes for Tómas Gislason and Thomas Vinterberg. Other than that, the communication among directors rarely goes beyond a certain level of politesse, although we all know each other through the Film School. I really don't understand the secrecy and competition that are so common in Danish cinema. There's a high degree of animosity which only creates deep divides, between the various film companies and internally in each company. We all walk around in our own little 'ego' bubble instead of meeting up and benefiting from each others' creativity.

Jørholt: Do you see any signs of crisis in Danish cinema at the moment?

Thuesen: No, but I think the way we make films is, in some respects, absolutely pitiful. When it comes to the technical aspects of telling a story through the cinematic medium, we're still in the stone age. Danish film tends to emphasize emotion rather than the technical aspects of cinematic storytelling. For example, I have a big problem with the fact that very few filmmakers understand the concept of POV. I probably feel this way because I still work as an editor. There's a failure to understand that it's often more interesting to film what the characters see instead of filming the characters. And, as I said, the editing in Danish films tends to be anything but dynamic, with the exception of films by Tómas Gislason and Lars. Especially in Lars' latest film, *Antichrist* (2009), there's a return to a certain kind of dynamic approach that I find very exciting. It has to do with the way he works with extremes.

Jørholt: What does Danish cinema mean to you?

Thuesen: Whether or not something is Danish is irrelevant as far as I'm concerned, so the national aspect of, say, a new wave in Danish cinema means absolutely nothing to me. I'm still crazy about Bergman's *Det sjunde inseglet* (*The Seventh Seal*, 1957) and Kieslowski's *Krótki film o zabijaniu* (*A Short Film About Killing*, 1988). There are 30,000 other films that I'm likely to think about before I start thinking about Danish cinema.

Jørholt: *Accused* is made within the framework of Nordisk Film's Director's Cut programme. The central idea here is that expensive films are a reflection of poor thinking and that there's an equivalence between economizing on the production side of things and narrative economy. Much as in the case of Dogma, the aim is to turn financial constraints into a creative force. What do you think of that line of reasoning?

Thuesen: In 99.9 per cent of the cases, it's true that the more expensive a film is, the less interesting it is. It has to do with the fact that if you don't have enough money, you have to start thinking in a more creative way. You become lazy when you have lots of money.

Jørholt: Some people think that Danish films have become far too neat and tidy, too cinematically proper. Is there not enough madness? Do we need more experimentation?

Thuesen: There are definitely far too few experiments! The Film Workshop is the only context that allows for experimentation, but it tends to produce bizarre sado-masochistic sex films. And however much I love Super16, that outfit resembles the Film School to a really significant extent. There's the same emphasis on that idea of going through an established, almost mechanical, process, one that starts when you enter the school and extends right up to the graduation films, which tend to be incredibly boring and mediocre. Some of the documentary projects still have a certain wildness, but even there a certain tidy correctness and certain populist attitudes are beginning to prevail. Danish cinema has become tremendously good at making two kinds of films: serious, well-made thrillers with an element of horror – *Frygtelig lykkelig* (*Terribly Happy*; dir. Henrik Ruben Genz, 2008), *Män som hatar kvinnor* (*The Girl with the Dragon Tattoo*; dir. Niels Arden Oplev, 2009) and some of Ole Bornedal's films – and contemporary popular comedies about dysfunctional families. We could do with a reminder that film can also be something else.

Glossary

Aakeson, Kim Fupz. Born in 1958, Aakeson graduated as a scriptwriter from the National Film School of Denmark in 1996. Before applying to the Film School he worked as an illustrator and as an author, publishing comic books, children's books, short stories and novels. One of Denmark's most productive scriptwriters, Aakeson has provided scripts for many of the films that make up the New Danish Cinema, and thus for many of the films that provide the focus for *The Danish Directors 2*.

Bodil. Danish award established in 1948 and named after the actors Bodil Kjer and Bodil Ipsen. The winners are identified by an association of Copenhagen-based journalists (Filmmedarbejderforeningen), and awards are distributed across a number of categories, including, for example, best Danish film, best actor, best actress and best cinematographer.

Consultant (Filmkonsulent). Danish Film Institute support for feature filmmaking was until 1989 allocated following an artistic assessment by one of three film consultants – two for films for grown-ups and one for children's films – each appointed for a period of up to five years. The consultant scheme is still effective, but the 1989 Film Act provides an alternative route to DFI funding in the form of the 50/50 (60/40) subsidy scheme (see below).

Danish Broadcasting Corporation (Danmarks Radio TV). Independent public institution providing public service television in a context of state monopoly from 1951 until 1988, and since then within a more liberal economy. Since the 1990s, the Danish Broadcasting Corporation's Drama Division has produced a number of award-winning TV series – such as *Taxa* (*Taxi*, 1997–1999), *Rejseholdet* (*Unit One*, 2000–2003) and *Ørnen* (*The Eagle*, 2004–2006) – in close collaboration with directors, scriptwriters, etc. from the film scene.

Danish Film Institute (Det Danske Filminstitut). Established in 1972 and since 1997 an umbrella institution embracing the previously autonomous National Film Board (Statens Filmcentral), the Danish Film Museum (Det Danske Filmmuseum) and the Danish Film Institute. The mandate of the Danish Film Institute is to support film art and culture in Denmark. Henning Camre (cinematographer, former Head of the National Film School of

Denmark, and former Director of the National Film and Television School in London) was the DFI's CEO from 1998–2007. He played a crucial role in forging the new Danish Film Institute, and in negotiating a significant increase in government monies for film. He was replaced by Henrik Bo Nielsen in 2007.

Dogma 95 (Dogme 95). 1) Film collective consisting of four Dogma brethren: Lars von Trier, Thomas Vinterberg, Søren Kragh-Jacobsen and Kristian Levring. 2) A manifesto-based, rule-governed film initiative underwriting the four Dogma films – *Idioterne* (*The Idiots*; dir. Lars von Trier, 1998), *Festen* (*The Celebration*; dir. Thomas Vinterberg, 1998), *Mifunes sidste sang* (*Mifune*; dir. Søren Kragh-Jacobsen, 1999), *The King is Alive* (dir. Kristian Levring, 2000) – made by the brethren. Dogma 95 went on to become a globalized phenomenon, and was officially brought to a close ten years after it was launched, in another flamboyant public statement by von Trier.

50/50; 60/40 scheme (50/50; 60/40-ordning). The Film Act of 1989 made provisions for a 50/50 subsidy scheme that was designed to stimulate cinematic productions with popular appeal. The 50/50 scheme enabled private investors to circumvent the authority of the consultants and to receive matching funds of up to 3 million DKK from the Danish Film Institute with relative ease and speed. The percentages were changed to 60/40 in 1998, with the larger figure representing the contribution of state monies, the maximum of which was raised to 5 million DKK. Since 2003, there is no set limit to the contribution from the Danish Film Institute.

Film Accord. Since 1999, the Danish parliament has laid down the financial framework and political objectives for Danish cinema in four-year Film Policy Accords stipulating, among other things, the financial support allocated to Danish film, and the co-production requirements for the two national public service television broadcasters: the Danish Broadcasting Corporation and TV 2.

FilmFyn. A regional film fund designed to attract film production to Southern Funen, FilmFyn has supported more than 35 feature films, documentaries and shorts, including such films as Hella Joof's *Se min kjole* (*Hush Little Baby*, 2009) and Niels Arden Oplev's *Drømmen* (*We Shall Overcome*, 2006), both of which are discussed at some length in *The Danish Directors 2*. FilmFyn offers production teams the use of a film studio, in addition to a network of contacts aimed at facilitating film production in Southern Funen. http://www.filmfyn.dk.

Film Studies at the University of Copenhagen. Established in 1967, the Film Studies programme (BA, MA and PhD level) focuses on the psychological, sociological, historical and analytical aspects of film. Although it does incorporate a practical element, the Film Studies programme is not a film school. Several of the directors interviewed in *The Danish Directors 2* started out as film students at the University of Copenhagen.

Film Town (Filmbyen). A Lars von Trier and Peter Aalbæk Jensen initiative, the Film Town is located in former army barracks in Avedøre, one of Copenhagen's southern and less privileged suburbs. Established in 2000, the Film Town is usually discussed in connection with the production companies Zentropa and Nimbus Film, but in fact houses many more film-related companies. The Film Town is known for its unique institutional culture, one defined, among other things, by a collectivist ethos, theatrics, a strong element of contrariness and a commitment to the production of art films. Some of Denmark's most accomplished producers work, or have worked, at the Film Town, including Peter Aalbæk Jensen, Vibeke Windeløv, Ib Tardini, Meta Louise Foldager and Sisse Graum Jørgensen. In addition to Lars von Trier, filmmakers such as Susanne Bier, Lone Scherfig, Pernille Fischer Christensen and Annette K. Olesen are closely associated with the former army barracks. The Film Town is home to Station Next, a training programme initiated by Zentropa, with the aim of stimulating young people's interest in the practices of filmmaking. http://www.filmbyen.dk/?reload.

Film Workshop (Filmværkstedet, DFI). Housed in the Film House in Gothersgade, Copenhagen, the Film Workshop provides aspiring filmmakers with access to equipment, and successful applicants with support of up to 20,000 DKK towards basic production costs.

Leth, Jørgen. Born in 1937, Jørgen Leth is one of Denmark's most accomplished and productive filmmakers, and one of its staunchest defenders of film as art. *The Jørgen Leth Collection*, released by the Danish Film Institute, provides insight into his cinematic oeuvre, and consists of five boxed DVD sets (*The Anthropological Films* (01–05); *Sports Films* (06–11); *Travel Films* (12–18); *Fiction Films* (19–21); and *Film Portraits* (22–29)). A close friend of former National Film School of Denmark Head Henning Camre, Leth has taught many of the filmmakers associated with the New Danish Cinema, including Lars von Trier, Thomas Vinterberg, Ole Christian Madsen, Annette K. Olesen and Per Fly, among many others. Leth introduced the concept of creativity under constraint to the school's curriculum, through the so-called 'penneprøver', and it was on this rule-governed approach to filmmaking that Lars von Trier and Thomas Vinterberg drew when they devised their Dogma 95 initiative. That same approach informs Trier and Leth's collaborative work, the award-winning festival hit entitled *De fem benspænd* (*The Five Obstructions*, 2003).

New Danish Screen. Established in 2003, New Danish Screen is a special Danish Film Institute support scheme for innovative low-budget fiction and documentary films, as well as digital games.

National Film School of Denmark (Den Danske Filmskole). Founded in 1966 and supported by the Danish Ministry of Cultural Affairs, the school offers programmes in the areas of Film, TV (and documentary), Scriptwriting and Animation Directing. Henning Camre was the school's Head from 1975 until 1992, a period that saw the development of a clearly structured curriculum and a more professional culture. Poul Nesgaard became the Head in 1992.

Nimbus Film. Founded in 1993 by Birgitte Hald and Bo Ehrhardt, Nimbus Film produced the first Dogma 95 film, *Festen* (*The Celebration*; dir. Thomas Vinterberg, 1998). The company has worked alongside Zentropa, first in Ryesgade in Copenhagen, and later at the Film Town in Avedøre. Currently owned by Hald, Ehrhardt and Vinterberg, Nimbus Film has produced over 30 feature films. Somewhat overshadowed by Zentropa, and with an institutional culture quite different from von Trier's company, Nimbus Film has not always received the recognition it deserves for its very significant contributions to the New Danish Cinema. Directors associated with the company, and interviewed in *The Danish Directors 2* are: Nikolaj Arcel, Pernille Fischer Christensen and Ole Christian Madsen.

Robert. Danish film award granted for the first time in 1983 by the then newly established Danish Film Academy. Prizes are awarded in a number of categories, including best Danish feature, best actor, best actress, best editing, best music and so on.

Rukov, Mogens. With a degree from the University of Copenhagen in Nordic Philology and Film, Rukov started teaching at the National Film School of Denmark in 1975. Together with then Principal Henning Camre, Rukov espoused the view that film school students should be taught by means of a structured curriculum, rather than self-taught through entirely subjective approaches to the medium. Referred to as the 'Dogma doctor' on account of his scriptwriting contributions to several of the Danish Dogma films, Rukov was for many years Founding Head of the Scriptwriting Department at the Film School. His emphasis on such concepts as 'the natural story' and creativity under constraint is widely regarded as having helped to make the emergence of the New Danish Cinema possible.

Tardini, Ib. One of Denmark's most prominent and productive producers, Tardini has produced a long list of feature films, as well as TV series, short films and commercials. He played a crucial role in the establishing of the local, Copenhagen-based TV station Kanal 2, which effectively broke the monopoly once enjoyed by the Danish Broadcasting Corporation, Danmarks Radio. Now closely associated with the Film Town and Zentropa, Tardini has developed a close working relationship with directors Annette K. Olesen and Per Fly, both of whom are interviewed in *The Danish Directors 2*. He also produced Lone Scherfig's Dogma film, *Italiensk for begyndere* (*Italian for Beginners*, 2000), one of Scandinavia's most successful films ever. In 2001 Tardini was awarded an honorary prize by the Bodil Awards Committee, along with fellow Zentropa producers Vibeke Windeløv and Peter Aalbæk Jensen. This prize was awarded in recognition of Tardini's outstanding contributions to the Danish film industry.

Trier, Lars von. One of Denmark's most significant filmmakers, von Trier's activities, both as a filmmaker and an institution builder, helped to create the conditions of possibility for the emergence of the New Danish Cinema. Von Trier graduated from the National Film School of Denmark in 1983. With fellow Film School graduate Peter Aalbæk Jensen, von Trier established the production company Zentropa in 1992, and the Film Town in Avedøre in 2000. Von Trier produced the rules for the manifesto-based film movement known as Dogma 95 with Thomas Vinterberg in 1995. Key films by von Trier include *Element of Crime* (1984), *Europa* (1991), *Breaking the Waves* (1996), *Idioterne* (*The Idiots*, 1998), *Dancer in the Dark* (2000), *De fem benspænd* (*The Five Obstructions*, 2003; with Jørgen Leth), *Dogville* (2003), *Direktøren for det hele* (*The Boss of It All*, 2006) and *Antichrist* (2009). His TV mini-series, *Riget* (*The Kingdom*, 1994) and *Riget II* (*The Kingdom II*, 1997) enjoyed considerable success, both nationally and internationally. Committed to film as art, and to an experimental and rule-governed approach to filmmaking, von Trier is known for his canny ability to take up the task of promoting his work and filmmaking persona in properly artistic ways. Rather than using his international success as a stepping stone to an international career, von Trier has opted to remain in Denmark, where he has significantly enhanced the opportunities enjoyed by Danish filmmakers, through various collectivist endeavours.

TV 2. National public service television broadcaster established in 1988 after the model of the British Channel 4. TV 2, which is based in Odense and has a strong regional profile, was originally funded by a mixture of advertising and a license fee, but is today almost exclusively funded by advertising. With its six national television channels, the still state-owned TV 2 is the most popular of the two national public service television stations in Denmark.

Video Workshop Haderslev (Det Danske Videoværksted, Haderslev). Founded in 1977 and an independent institution since 2003, the Video Workshop in Haderslev receives Danish Film Institute subsidies allowing it to support amateur and professional filmmakers with equipment and production funding.

Zentropa. Founded by director Lars von Trier and producer Peter Aalbæk Jensen in 1992, Zentropa went on to become one of the largest film production companies in Scandinavia. Developed in a flamboyant manner, and in a spirit of oppositionality, Zentropa joined forces with its former rival, Nordisk, in 2008. Nordisk now owns 50 per cent of Zentropa's shares. Zentropa is located in the Avedøre Film Town, which von Trier and Aalbæk Jensen also established.

Index

The Institutional Landscape and Central Topics

Titles and Names (of Persons)